# Top Federal Tax Issues for 2018 | CPE Course

Annette Nellen, CPA, CGMA, Esq.

Steven G. Siegel, J.D., LL.M. (Taxation)

James R. Hamill Ph.D., CPA

Jennifer Kowal, J.D.

Sidney Kess, Esq., CPA, J.D., LL.M.

Barbara Weltman J.D.

Robert J. Misey, Jr., J.D., LL.M.

Sara L. Rapkin, J.D.

D0711956

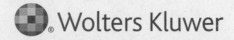

Wolters Kluwer

## Contributors

Contributing Editors . . . . . . . . . . . . . . . . . . . . . . . . . . . . . . . . Kelen Camehl, CPA

Technical Review . . . . . . . . . . . . . . . . . . Steven G. Siegel, J.D., LL.M. (Taxation);
Michael Todd Crowley, CPA, PLLC

Production Coordinator . . . . . . . . . . . . . Mariela de la Torre; Jennifer Schencker;
Vijayalakshmi Suresh

Production . . . . . . . . . . . . . . . . . . . . . . . . . . Lynn J. Brown; Anbarasu Anbumani

This publication is designed to provide accurate and authoritative information in regard to the subject matter covered. It is sold with the understanding that the publisher is not engaged in rendering legal, accounting, or other professional service. If legal advice or other expert assistance is required, the services of a competent professional person should be sought.

ISBN: 978-0-8080-4626-4

No claim is made to original government works; however, within this Product or Publication, the following are subject to CCH Incorporated's copyright: (1) the gathering, compilation, and arrangement of such government materials; (2) the magnetic translation and digital conversion of data, if applicable; (3) the historical, statutory and other notes and references; and (4) the commentary and other materials.

Printed in the United States of America

SUSTAINABLE FORESTRY INITIATIVE

Certified Sourcing

www.sfiprogram.org
SFI-01681

# Introduction

Each year, a handful of tax issues typically require special attention by tax practitioners. The reasons vary, from a particularly complicated new provision in the Internal Revenue Code, to a planning technique opened up by a new regulation or ruling, or the availability of a significant tax benefit with a short window of opportunity. Sometimes a developing business need creates a new set of tax problems, or pressure exerted by Congress or the Administration puts more heat on some taxpayers while giving others more slack. All these share in creating a unique mix that in turn creates special opportunities and pitfalls in the coming year and beyond. The past year has seen more than its share of these developing issues.

*Top Federal Tax Issues for 2018 CPE Course* identifies those recent events that have developed into the current "hot" issues of the day. These tax issues have been selected as particularly relevant to tax practice in 2018. They have been selected not only because of their impact on return preparation during the 2018 tax season but also because of the important role they play in developing effective tax strategies for 2018 and beyond.

This course is designed to help reassure the tax practitioner that he or she is not missing out on advising clients about a hot, new tax opportunity; or that a brewing controversy does not blindside their practice. In addition to issue identification, this course provides the basic information needed for the tax practitioner to implement a plan that addresses the particular opportunities and pitfalls presented by any one of those issues. Among the topics examined in the *Top Federal Tax Issues for 2018 CPE Course* are:

- Sale of a Principal Residence
- Income Taxation of Trusts and Estates
- When Your Client Dies: Final Form 1040, Post-Death Elections and More
- Proving Material Participation for the Passive Loss Rules
- Sharing Economy: Tax Issues for the Gig Economy
- Expense or Capitalize?
- S Corporation and Shareholder Tax Reporting
- Partnership Tax Filing Issues
- The Sourcing Rules: The Building Blocks of International Taxation
- Check-the-Box Entity Elections: U.S. and Foreign Tax Implications

**Study Questions.** Throughout the course you will find Study Questions to help you test your knowledge, and comments that are vital to understanding a particular strategy or idea. Answers to the Study Questions with feedback on both correct and incorrect responses are provided in a special section beginning at ¶ 10,100.

**Final Exam.** This course is divided into three Modules. Take your time and review all course Modules. When you feel confident that you thoroughly understand the material, turn to the Final Exam. Complete one, or all, Module Final Exams for continuing professional education credit.

Go to **cchcpelink.com/printcpe** to complete your Final Exam online for immediate results and no Express Grading Fee. My Dashboard provides convenient storage for your CPE course Certificates. Further information is provided in the CPE Final Exam instructions at ¶ 10,300.

**October 2017**

## PLEDGE TO QUALITY

Thank you for choosing this CCH® CPE Link product. We will continue to produce high quality products that challenge your intellect and give you the best option for your Continuing Education requirements. Should you have a concern about this or any other Wolters Kluwer product, please call our Customer Service Department at 1-800-248-3248.

## COURSE OBJECTIVES

This course was prepared to provide the participant with an overview of specific tax issues that impact 2017 tax return preparation and tax planning in 2018. Each impacts a significant number of taxpayers in significant ways.

Upon course completion, you will be able to:

- Identify and apply the gain exclusion rule of Code Section 121
- Recognize how to compute taxable and non-taxable gain on the sale of a principal residence
- Identify special definitions and rules
- Differentiate planning possibilities
- Recognize how to avoid issues and mistakes
- Identify recent developments and how they apply
- Differentiate policy considerations and legislative proposals
- Obtain a comprehensive basic understanding of how estate and trust income is taxed
- Determine how estate and trust income is defined, calculated and reported
- Gain awareness of key compliance and planning issues as well as concerns related to fiduciary income taxation
- Describe the tax reporting requirements for a decedent client's final Form 1040
- Discuss the key unique post-death elections and decisions that should be considered for a decedent client
- Accurately answer client questions regarding tax issues for a decedent
- Describe the seven tests for material participation
- Determine how to best defend your clients against a material participation challenge
- Describe where to report income and expenses earned in the gig economy
- Explain self-employment tax on gig economy earnings
- List the limitations on deducting rental losses
- Explain general rules determining when expenses should be capitalized
- Identify rules that require capitalization of transaction costs into basis of acquired assets
- Differentiate how section 263A requires capitalization of expenses into cost of goods sold
- Recognize how new "repair regulations" apply in common scenarios
- Describe essential reporting issues and obligations in S corporation taxation
- Identify planning opportunities with S corporation tax returns
- Apply best practices for preparing S corporation returns

- Describe essential reporting issues and obligations in partnership taxation
- Identify planning opportunities with partnership tax returns
- Apply best practices for preparing partnership returns
- Identify and apply a fundamental understanding of tax issues, consequences, and opportunities
- involved with the sourcing of income
- Differentiate the U.S. rules of allocating and apportioning expenses
- Recognize and apply how to properly advise clients so they can minimize their U.S. taxes
- Identify situations where double taxation may still occur
- Recognize scenarios where U.S. tax withholdings on income paid to a foreign person would apply
- Identify exceptions to the U.S. sourcing rules for interest income
- Understand the tax law, requirements and procedures for making check-the-box elections
- Identify opportunities where making a check-the-box election will save taxes

---

One **complimentary copy** of this course is provided with certain copies of Wolters Kluwer publications. Additional copies of this course may be downloaded from **cchcpelink.com/printcpe** or ordered by calling 1-800-344-3734 (ask for product 10024491-0005).

---

# Contents

## 8 Partnership Tax Filing Issues

## MODULE 3: INTERNATIONAL TAXATION

## 9 The Sourcing Rules: The Building Blocks of International Taxation

## 10 Check-the-Box Entity Elections: U.S. and Foreign Tax Implications

# MODULE 1: INDIVIDUAL TAXATION—
# Chapter 1: Sale of a Principal Residence

## ¶ 101 WELCOME

This chapter covers recent developments and longstanding rules relating to the treatment of capital gains upon the sale of taxpayers' principal residence. Advance planning with a tax preparer or financial planner is key to helping home sellers to take advantage of exclusions of gains under Code Section 121 and prevent negative tax effects when a home's sale price greatly exceeds its purchase price.

## ¶ 102 LEARNING OBJECTIVES

Upon completion of this chapter, you will be able to:

- Recognize how to apply the gain exclusion rule of Section 121;
- Identify recent developments for the principal residence gain rules; and
- Identify policy considerations and IRS guidance for the rules.

## ¶ 103 INTRODUCTION

The current gain exclusion rules of Code Section 121 were created in 1997 by the *Taxpayer Relief Act of 1997* (P.L. 105-34). That act made numerous changes to the capital gain rules, some of which introduced additional complexity to the tax code. Basically, the changes state:

- Section 121(a) Gross income shall not include gain from the sale or exchange of property if, during the 5-year period ending on the date of the sale or exchange, such property has been owned and used by the taxpayer as the taxpayer's principal residence for periods aggregating 2 years or more; and
- Reg. 1.121-2(a)(1) A taxpayer may exclude from gross income up to $250,000 of gain from the sale or exchange of the taxpayer's principal residence. A taxpayer is eligible for only one maximum exclusion per principal residence.

This chapter explores what qualifies as a principal residence, the use requirements for such a residence, the relevance of marital status on exclusion of gains, the special rules applied to such sales, how to calculate realized and recognized gain, and the election not to use the exclusion (Section 121(f)).

Here are some situations to consider at the outset. Somebody owns a home probably for the standard five to eight years. (Data about how long people own homes reveals it actually tends to be more than five years.) They owner sells it at a gain. The gain is less than the exclusion amount, and they can claim the exclusion on that year's tax return. But there is a lot more in Section 121 for the less common transactions, but they do still apply:

- Maybe somebody sold a home at a gain, but hadn't owned it for two years;
- Maybe the owner sold it because his or her employer relocated a spouse. Can the couple still use the provision?
- Maybe there was a divorce;
- Maybe the gain is more than the total gain exclusion allows;

- Maybe a couple marries or remarries when each spouse owns a home; or
- Maybe a couple is converting rental properties into homes that they live in for two years before they sell it.

So there are many variations that affect the gain a seller of a principal residence receives. This chapter examines how the gain exclusion rules of Section 121 can become more complex for the tax professional to apply.

# ¶ 104 BACKGROUND OF THE EXCLUSION RULES

Prior to 1997 change, there were two rules on treatment of gain on sale of a principal residence:

- Section 121 election for one-time exclusion of up to $125,000 on sale of a principal residence if taxpayer age 55 or older and in prior 5 years, owned and used home for total of 3 years; and
- Section 1034 rollover of gain on the sale of a principal residence
  - To the extent the taxpayer timely reinvested (24 months) the sales proceeds in a new principal residence, gain could be deferred (with a basis adjustment to the replacement residence)
  - Gain would be recognized to the extent of the sales price of the old home that was not timely reinvested in the replacement residence.

Subsequently:

- Section 1034 was repealed in 1997; but
- Section 1034 is still relevant for at least two purposes
  - Definition of a principal residence: There are many rulings under Section 1034 and some may still be of value in defining a principal residence
  - Determining basis of a home for which a gain was rolled over under old Section 1034 is calculated under Section 1016(a)(7).

Code Section 1034 was enacted in 1951. It limited the hardship in which a taxpayer buys a home and sell it at gain, but if the seller has to pay tax on the gain, that then limits how much money he or she has to reinvest in a new home—in essence, replacing one home with maybe a bigger home or moving because the owner got relocated or something. That seems like a hardship, so that's what the deferral was there to help.

Then Section 121 was added in 1964, primarily to deal with the thought that someone retires. They've got a big home. They're selling it to downsize. This provision offered retirees relief: Owners could exclude up to $125,000 if they were age 55 or older. But that was a one-time exclusion. Sellers only use that once in their lives, whereas under Section 121, sellers can use it as many times, as long as the provision is still there.

This current version of Section 121 was created in 1997 under the *Taxpayer Relief Act of 1997,* which also lowered capital gains rates. And there have been a few modifications since 1997, primarily because either Congress saw there was an injustice. For example, the rule used to literally be if a married couple owned the home and one spouse dies during the year. If the surviving spouse didn't sell the home by end of the year where they're still going to file married filing joint, then sold it next year when she was single, then she was down to $250,000 exclusion. The former rule could force a person to sell a home as quickly as possible if he or she needed to take advantage of her $500,000.' So that got modified to $500,000 per couple (without specific reasoning for the amount), and other modifications have been enacted since.

## Additional Modifications

And then there were other areas that Congress considered, such as abuse of the rules (nonqualified use). Congress does pay attention to inequities or possible unplanned tax sheltering. But before this change, we actually had two code sections dealing with the tax treatment of sale of a principal residence. The one was Section 121 in which one had a one-time lifetime exclusion of up to $125,000 on sale of a principal residence if the taxpayer was age 55 or older and in the prior five years owned and used the home for a total of five years.

An additional consideration is the tainted spouse rule. A person age 60 sells their home and then marries somebody who had never used the exclusion. That person wouldn't be able to use the exclusion—a tainted spouse.

Owners also had the rollover rule under Section 1034. So it wasn't a permanent exclusion. If an owner sells one home and reinvests all those proceeds into a new home within 24 months of the sale, then the seller can exclude the gain. Well, in that sense the seller is deferring the gain by adjusting the basis of the new property. So if the seller bought a more expensive property and was deferring a $50,000 gain, the seller would take the cost of the new property, reduce it by the $50,000 gain being rolled over, and that rule still applies. And there are certainly still taxpayers out there for which their basis in their current home is measured by Section 1034.

If a tax preparer gets a new client, the preparer must get all the relevant asset information. The preparer asks the client to show him or her the last three years of tax returns. The preparer won't have this information because obviously if anybody used Section 1034 it was before 1997. But taxpayers certainly might still own a home where they did roll over the gain from a prior home. And so when the preparer asks them, "You just sold your home this year. What did you pay for it?" If they just tell the preparer what they paid for it, they say, "I paid $350,000," but they're actually rolling over a $150,000 gain from Section 1034, their basis is $200,000, not $350,000.' So it's one of those questions when a preparer does get a new client. If it's their first home and they bought it after 1997, there is no exclusion issue. But the preparer wants to figure out if they might actually have a lower basis because there would have been a Form 2119 attached to that return. But usually the preparer is not asking to see their returns from before 1997.

Eventually, Congress settled on a $250,000 lifetime gain exclusion for a single taxpayer, or $500,000 for a married couple.

So when Congress enacted or modified Section 121 to broaden it, remove the age requirement, remove the lifetime limitation and then add other special rules, obviously Section 121 is going to apply far more broadly. Then Congress wanted to tighten up the rules. But again, Section 1034 is still relevant when a home is being sold today that

- The seller bought before 1997;
- If it was acquired through the 1034 rollover provision; and
- The seller's basis is not equal to what the price paid for that home. It's going to be adjusted by whatever gain they rolled over when they bought it.

Section 1034 has been around for a long time, since 1951, and there's a lot of case law out there, revenue rulings that defined the term *principal residence*. The term has not changed. So if the planner and client get stuck declaring substantial capital gains and this is truly their principal residence, that old case law might be relevant.

Figure 1.1 shows the basic mechanics of how to calculate the capital gains under Section 121.

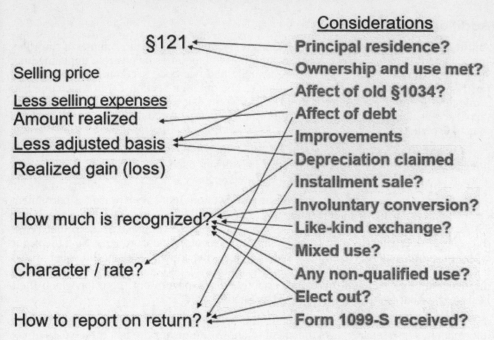

Figure 1.1. The Basic Mechanics of Calculating Capital Gains Under Section 121

This is how it works. The seller has selling expenses. He or she has an amount realized. The preparer calculates the wear-adjusted basis, goes to realized gain, and asks, "How much of that is recognized?" Well, the preparer has to ask, "Was that a principal residence? Did the seller use it for at least 24 months of the prior five years?"

If yes, did any other limitation apply, such as a period of nonqualified use? For example, at some point did the seller rent the property and claim depreciation on it? That depreciation will not fall under Section 121. That recapture will get taxed. What if the sale was negotiated using a like-kind exchange?

These are some of the different questions or rules that may come into effect in determining the tax treatment of the sale or exchange of a residence.

Here is the basic rule for Section121(a): The gross income does not include gains in the sale or exchange of property if during the five-year period ending on the date of the sale, such property was owned and used—and again, owned and used by the taxpayer—as their principal residence aggregating two years or more. So, for example all of 2014 the seller used it as a principal residence. All of 2016 the home was used as a principal residence, but in 2015 I lived elsewhere. As long as it had 24 total months—2 years in the prior 5 years—the home will fall into this mandatory gain exclusion. And then it's further defined in the regs, and the regs are quite helpful. They have some examples, and when all else fails we'll mention regs a few times in areas here.

## The *Hsu* Case

A court case is a good example of why we need to know these rules. The *Hsu* case is a PC summary opinion, which means the total liability was less than $50,000. It's kind of what they call the small claims division. And the taxpayer owned half of an interest in what was their principal residence, and they sold that in 2005 at a gain of $529,000. That was the total gain on sale of the home. This person only owned half of it, but did live in this principal residence. Her share of the gain was $264,000, and she figured, "Okay, I'm entitled to a $250,000 exclusion. I'm single, and so I'll pay tax on $14,000." She did that.

The revenue agent on her audit says, "Oh no, you only own half the home, so you only get half of the possible exclusion. You only get $125,000." And the taxpayer, of course, argued against that. The IRS said, "Hey, we're done arguing. Here is the bill." And so the taxpayer had to go to court.

The judge there said, 'Section 121 has no such limitation that you cut the maximum exclusion in half because you only owned half the home. In fact, even the regs—and we'll see an example from the regs as well, and here is actually a site to the regs with the example showing that the IRS was wrong. It's kind of puzzling and unfortunate that they weren't able to convince the revenue agent or even the appeals officer. Maybe it hadn't gone to appeals, but it's very puzzling why they went to court.

The taxpayer did win in court. The owner interpreted the law correctly. If the other person owned half the home, each of them was entitled to, if they were single, $250,000. If they were married and both spouses met the requirements up to $500,000 exclusion. So it doesn't get prorated for what portion of a home that the client owns.

## STUDY QUESTION

---

**1.** The gain exclusion amount of $500,000 for a married couple filing jointly was selected because:

- **a.** The median home price in the U.S. in 1997.
- **b.** The earlier version of IRC section 121 allowed for a one-time gain exclusion of $500,000.
- **c.** The average gain on the sale of a principal residence in the U.S. was $500,000 in 1997.
- **d.** No reason was specified in the Taxpayer Relief Act of 1997 for the exclusion dollar amount.

---

# ¶ 105 WHAT IS A PRINCIPAL RESIDENCE?

## Rules of Section 121

Under Section 1.121-1(b), in additional to a freestanding house, townhouse, or condo, a principal residence may be a:

- Houseboat; or
- House trailer.

Under Section 121(d)(4)(B), a principal residence may be a house or apartment a taxpayer is entitled to occupy as tenant-stockholder in cooperative housing corporation.

Facts and circumstances considered in determining the principal residence is whether the dwelling has a bathroom, plus eating and sleeping facilities.

The taxpayer may have multiple homes, but only one is considered the principal residence under Reg. 1.121-1(b)(2) and (4). This is determined generally as the residence used for the majority of the time. Factors considered in determining which home is the principal residence include in addition to use of the property include but are not limited to

- The taxpayer's place of employment;
- The principal place of abode of the taxpayer's family members;
- The address listed on the taxpayer's federal and state tax returns, driver's license, automobile registration, and voter registration card;
- The taxpayer's mailing address for bills and correspondence;
- The location of the taxpayer's banks; and
- The location of religious organizations and recreational clubs with which the taxpayer is affiliated.'

## STUDY QUESTION

**2.** A boat or even a shed can be a principal residence if it has:
   **a.** At least one bedroom.
   **b.** Running water.
   **c.** A kitchen and a bathroom.
   **d.** Eating, sleeping, and toilet facilities.

## Multiple Homes

When sellers own more than one home that they're living in throughout the year, which one is their principal residence? Relevant factors a tax preparer (and the IRS) considers include but are not limited to

- The taxpayer's place of employment;
- The principal place of abode of the taxpayer's family members;
- The address listed on the taxpayer's federal and state tax returns, driver's license, automobile registration, and voter registration card;
- The taxpayer's mailing address for bills and correspondence;
- The location of the taxpayer's banks; and
- The location of religious organizations and recreational clubs with which the taxpayer is affiliated.

In today's world of automatic electronic payments and Internet shopping, figuring the locale of the principal residence becomes more complex.

    **EXAMPLE:** Taxpayer Leonard Hastings owns two residences, one in New York and one in Florida:

- From 1999 through 2004, he lives in the New York residence for 7 months and the Florida residence for 5 months of each year; and
- In the absence of facts and circumstances indicating otherwise, the New York residence is A's principal residence.

    Under Reg. 1.121-1(b)(4), Leonard would be eligible for the Section 121 exclusion of gain from the sale or exchange of the New York residence, but not the Florida residence.

    The tax preparer would just look back the prior five years from date of sale. Did the owner live in it at least 24 months, and here the seller would have to exclude the gain in the sale of the New York home.

But if a taxpayer moves out of a principal residence without selling it and into another, he or she has a time period when Section 121 applies to either home: the five-year lookback. Say that for two years the owners lived in their home in Virginia. For two years in the last five they lived in their home in New York. When they go to sell either one of those today, for both of them the tax preparer looks back on the five-year period and says, "Yes, they did use both for 24 months out of the prior five years."

Thus, under the five-year lookback rule, for taxpayers who may have more than principal residence during the period and move out of one without selling it and into another, there may be a period when Section 121 applies to either home, but not both.

**EXAMPLE:** If taxpayer moves out of a principal residence without selling it and into another, he or she may have time period when Section 121 applies to either home (but not both). Tilly Chatham owns two residences, one in Virginia and one in Maine:

- During 1999 and 2000, she lives in the Virginia residence
- During 2001 and 2002, she lives in the Maine residence
- During 2003, she lives in the Virginia residence
- Tilly's principal residence during 1999, 2000, and 2003 is the Virginia residence
- Tilly's principal residence during 2001 and 2002 is the Maine residence
- Tilly would be eligible for the Section 121 exclusion of gain from the sale or exchange of either residence (but not both) during 2003.

## STUDY QUESTION

**3.** Henry O'Rouke purchased a home in January 2007 and lived in it as his principal residence. In January 2011, Henry moved out of a house and had his father live in the house until July 2014 when Henry sold the home. Henry's gain on the home was $160,000.

    **a.** Henry may exclude the gain as he meets the Section 121 time requirements because the time his father used the home is attributed to Henry.

    **b.** Henry may not exclude the gain because he does not meet the 24 months out of 5 years use requirement.

    **c.** Henry can elect whether or not to use the Section 121 exclusion.

    **d.** Henry's father can claim the gain exclusion.

## Business or Rental Use of Part of a Principal Residence

If part of the home is used for rental, such as an office in the home, Reg. 1.121-1(e) applies.

The regulation applies if it's a separate structure from the dwelling unit or the owner may have a separate building outside that's rented. Then when the property is sold, only if it's a separate structure would the tax preparer need to do an allocation of the sales price. Obviously with that granny unit the seller has in the backyard that has been rented out—a separate structure—Section 121 would not apply to that because it's not a principal residence. So it's a focus of a separate structure.

How does the tax preparer allocate the purchase price? There's not a lot of guidance on that. How does the preparer separate what was tied to the principal residence versus to the granny unit? Of course, the seller may provide appraisals and maybe property tax bills that could help.

Under Reg. 1.121-1(e):

- If the property is a separate structure from the "dwelling unit," the preparer must allocate the amount realized, selling expenses, and basis
  - For a separate structure—assuming 2 out of 5 year use as a principal residence is not met, Section 121 does not apply and
  - As stated in IRS Publication 523, reporting depends on whether the property meets the "use" test and how it was used in the year of sale; and
- If the property was held for business use or rental is in same "dwelling unit" as residential portion, no allocation is needed
  - But the taxpayer must report depreciation claimed as taxable gain and
  - Publication 523 states that the seller need not report the non-Section 121 portion on Form 4797.

The preparer should refer to Schedule D instructions for reporting sales of such property.

Thus, if, instead of being a separate structure, the business use or rental is in the same dwelling as the residential portion, then there is no need to allocate. Basically, the tax preparer applies Section 121 to the entire item. But be aware for the seller's rental or office; the seller had been taking depreciation in prior years. Any gain representing depreciation, to the extent that that gain represents depreciation claimed on it, may not apply Section 121 exclusions. And that's clear in the statute and the regs. Of course, that amount picked up for the depreciation captured is also taxed to individuals at a 25 percent rate.

**Dwelling Unit.** Under Reg. 1.121-1(e) (2), the term "dwelling unit" has the same meaning as in Section 280A(f)(1), but does not include appurtenant structures or other property. Specifically

- Section 280A(f)(1)(A)—Dwelling unit 'includes a house, apartment, condominium, mobile home, boat, or similar property, and all structures or other property appurtenant to such dwelling unit.
- (B) Exception. The term "dwelling unit" does not include that portion of a unit that is used exclusively as a hotel, motel, inn, or similar establishment.

According to Publication 523 a duplex is separate part of the seller's home.

> **EXAMPLE:** In 2003, David McCulloch, an attorney, buys a house and dedicates one room as his law office. He claims $2,000 of depreciation for the office. In 2006 David sells the house.
> - His realized gain = $13,000:
>   - $2,000 recognized as unrecaptured section 1250 gain and
>   - $11,000 excluded;
> - There is no reason to allocate between home and office because the office is in the same dwelling unit.

**Method of Allocation,** If Needed. Under Reg. 1.121-1(e)(3), the tax preparer allocates basis and the amount realized between residential and nonresidential portions of the property employing the same method used to determine depreciation.

## Sale of Partial Interests

Section 1.121-4(e)(1) governs the sale of a partial interest in a principal residence. An exclusion applies if the interest sold or exchanged includes an interest in the dwelling unit.

Some caveats apply:

- Sales or exchanges of partial interests in the same principal residence are treated as one sale or exchange;

- The seller gets to apply only one maximum gain amount to all the partial interest sales;

- "Each spouse is treated as excluding one-half of the gain from a sale or exchange to which Section 121(b)(2)(A) and Reg.1.121-2(a)(3)(i)(relating to the limitation for certain joint returns) apply"; and

- For the two-year limitation, sales of partial interests in same principal residence are disregarded in the once-every-two-years limitation but are relevant if there is a sale or exchange of any other principal residence.

**EXAMPLE:** In 2004, Sarah Stern, who is single, buys a house for $400,000 to use as a principal residence. In 2006, she decides to sell half of that interest to her friend Bob Clybourn for $260,000 to use as a principal residence, and she has a gain on that of $60,000.

Sarah can exclude the gain. She sold half of a principal residence. And then a year later she sells the remaining 50 percent to Bob for $380,000 and the realized gain there is $180,000.

# Vacant Land

Can vacant land that's maybe next to the seller's home be a principal residence? Generally, Section 121 does not apply to vacant land; land itself is not going to be a principal residence because there is no residence on it. But there are exceptions. Reg. 1.121-1(b)(3) allows taxpayer owned and used vacant land to be considered part of the principal residence if it's adjacent to land containing a dwelling unit.

The regulation applies if the taxpayer sells or exchanges the dwelling in an exchange that meets the requirements of Section 121 within two years before or two years after the date of sale of exchange of vacant land. Plus, if the taxpayer sells just the vacant land in the tax year and reports the capital gain, then sells the related principal residence the following year, the preparer can amend the prior return to adjust the capital gains.

**EXAMPLE:** In 1991, Carol Donatello buys 10 acres of land with a home that she uses as her principal residence. In May 2005, she sells 8 of the acres not containing her principal residence:

- Realized gain = $110,000; and

- Because the principal residence was not sold, Carol must report the gain.

- In March 2007, Carol sells her principal residence and the remaining 2 acres:

- Realized gain = $180,000

Excluded under Section 121 is the sale of the 8 acres because the transaction was within two years from sale date dwelling. So Carol's preparer amends the 2005 return to consider the 2005 sale as a sale of her principal residence. The amended return excludes $70,000.

Under Reg. 1.121-1(b)(4), the $250,000 limit applies to any gain exclusion in total.

## Reconstruction

A demolition and reconstruction case, *Gates v. Comm'r,* *135 T.C. No. 1* (2010) dealt with the new home being ineligible for the Section 121 exclusion of gains. The seller owned a principal residence for two years and in 1999 demolished the residence and built a new home. The taxpayer never occupied it, but in the following year, 2000, sold the residence for $1.1 million. The realized gain was $591,406, which the taxpayer not only did not report but also did not file a timely return. The taxpayer later admitted that $91,406 was taxable gain, but the IRS held that it was not eligible for the Section 121 exclusion. The court agreed. The primary issue—aside from violation of reporting requirements—was the meaning of the terms "property" and "primary residence":

- Because the taxpayer never used new house as a principal residence, the gain on sale was not eligible for the exclusion;

- The ruling stated "Exclusions from income must be construed narrowly, and taxpayers must bring themselves within the clear scope of the exclusion"; and

- Further it was held "Our conclusion regarding the meaning that Congress attaches to the terms 'property' and 'principal residence' in Section 121(a) is also consistent with case law interpreting former Section 1034, as in effect before its repeal."

One judge in the case dissented with the ruling.

The first reaction of a lot of practitioners would be, "The gain falls under the Section 121 exclusion. The seller owned the whole thing for 24 months out of the prior 5 years." But what the seller actually sold was a brand new home actually never used as a principal residence. The lawful action would have been to occupy the new home for at least two years before it was sold, in which case the exclusion would have applied to the gains.

## STUDY QUESTION

---

**4.** Jane Clark is selling her home she has lived in for the past ten years. For the past five years, she has exclusively used one room in the home as a home office and claimed deductions for it on her Schedule C. Which of the following statements is true regarding the effect of the home office on the reporting of the gain on the sale of a residence?

- **a.** Jane must allocate the amount realized and basis between the portion of the home used for personal and for the home office.

- **b.** Jane must recognize gain equal to the depreciation claimed on the home.

- **c.** Jane may exclude all of the gain from the sale provided it does not exceed $250,000.

- **d.** Jane must treat part of the gain as attributable to nonqualified use of the residence.

---

## Owned and Used Time Periods

**Determining Who Is the Property Owner.** A major issue for tax preparers is consideration of the "owned" and "used" time periods under the regulations. Preparers must figure out who the actual owners of property are and what happens if they were temporarily absent from the property, relocated by their employer temporarily, or were absent due to health issues or unforeseen circumstances. Reg. 1.121-5 addresses suspending the five-year period for certain people—those in uniform services, foreign service, intelligence community (Section 121(d)(9), and the Peace Corps (Section 121(d)(12). So that's something to be aware of for clients working in one of those areas.

Who is the property owner? If it's a trust in which the taxpayer is treated as the owner of the trust under Section 671 of the trust rules, then the trust's holder is actually treated as the owner of that residence. If the owner is a single owner disregarded entity, that entity is, again, treated as owner of that residence, meaning that the owner, could use the Section 121 upon sale of the residence if all the other requirements are met.

**Determining the Period of Ownership.** How do the preparer and the IRS count the ownership period? Do sellers have 24 months of ownership in use? Sellers can aggregate periods. The two years do not have to be a consecutive period of use, so the exclusion applies if the total is 24 months or 730 days.

> **EXAMPLE:** Shamona Johnson owns and uses a condo as her principal residence from 2006 to 2014. In 2014, in she moves to another state and stops using the condo. She still owns it; her son moves into it. Then, almost four years later, Shamona sells the condo, realizing a gain of $220,000. Can she exclude any of the gain? Does she meet the requirements under the lookback rules? Her tax preparer knows she owned it for the whole time period. Did she use it as a principal residence for at least 24 months during that time period?

> Counting the days, Shamona certainly meets the ownership requirement, but she actually doesn't meet the use requirement because she doesn't use the condo for 24 months during that 5 years prior to sale. She waited too long to sell it. The key requirements are ownership *and* use of 24 months in the prior 5 years.

> So Shamona should have paid attention of the time limit if she wanted to exclude that gain. Of course, she also move back into the condo to chalk up the 24 months, which again, is part of tax planning because her capital gain was so large. To exclude would be the way to go.

Temporary absences, generally vacation, seasonal absence, will still count as a time of using it as a principal residence (Reg. 1.121-1(c)(32)(i), even if the owner rents it out. So when a person works in Germany because her employer sends her there for five months and she rented out her home while she was gone, the IRS counts that as a short temporary absence. She intended to return. It wasn't intended to be more than five months.

There was one example in the regs in which the person takes a one-year sabbatical abroad. The IRS held it not to be a temporary absence. It begs the question of where exactly that period falls.

Sellers cannot use the Section 121 exclusion more than once in a two-year period even when they have two qualifying homes.

**Safe Harbors.** Special requirements apply to failure to meet the Section 121 requirements when the sellers don't meet the 24-month ownership and use because of a change in place of employment, a health reason, or to the extent provided in regs some unforeseen circumstance related to a "qualified individual." Section 121-3—very important to figure out what this all means—provides some safe harbors. If sellers don't meet a safe harbor, they're still allowed to show based on facts and circumstances that the reason why they sold the home without having used it for the requisite 24 months out of 5 years prior to sale is because of a change in employment, health, or unforeseen circumstances. And the regs contain a good number of examples, plus there have been private letter rulings in court cases dealing with how this is interpreted as well.

Non-safe harbor factors under Reg. 1.121-3(b) include:

- The sale or exchange and the circumstances giving rise to the sale or exchange are proximate in time;
- The suitability of the property as the taxpayer's principal residence materially changes;
- The taxpayer's financial ability to maintain the property is materially impaired;
- The taxpayer uses the property as the taxpayer's residence during the period of the taxpayer's ownership of the property;
- The circumstances giving rise to the sale or exchange are not reasonably foreseeable when the taxpayer begins using the property as the taxpayer's principal residence; and
- The circumstances giving rise to the sale or exchange occur during the period of the taxpayer's ownership and use of the property as the taxpayer's principal residence.

In the law the word "qualified," involves a definition—an intricate one at that. Under Section 152(a)(1) – (a)(8) prior to a change in 2004, a qualifying individual is:

- A son or daughter of the taxpayer, or a descendant of either;
- A stepson or stepdaughter of the taxpayer;
- A brother, sister, stepbrother, or stepsister of the taxpayer;
- The father or mother of the taxpayer, or an ancestor of either;
- A stepfather or stepmother of the taxpayer;
- A son or daughter of a brother or sister of the taxpayer;
- A brother or sister of the father or mother of the taxpayer; or
- A son-in-law, daughter-in-law, father-in-law, mother-in-law, brother-in-law, or sister-in-law of the taxpayer.

Now what are some of the factors? If sellers don't meet a safe harbor—if they don't have a doctor's note documenting a health reason—might they still have one? The regs do list some factors (listed above) that may be relevant in determining the taxpayer's primary reason for the sale. Something major may apply regarding materiality of suitability for this home. Or maybe the owners' financial ability to maintain the home was materially impaired. So they're saying it might be some other unforeseen circumstance, such as health. The move has to be for a requisite minimum of 50 miles—just like the moving expense rule. For change in employment, there is a distance safe harbor here, which would be the best way to be able to use this. And the preparer can look at the factors here. If the seller's new place of employment is at least 50 miles farther from the residence sold or exchanged and was a former place of employment (see below), the tax preparer would prorate that amount based on the time the seller did own the home out of the 24 months.

Under Reg. 1.121-3(c)(3):

Employment includes the commencement of employment with a new employer, the continuation of employment with the same employer, and the commencement or continuation of self-employment.

**EXAMPLE:** The Smiths have lived in their home for 11 months. Ms. Smith has been asked by her employer to relocate to another state, so the Smiths sell their home, realizing a $40,000 gain. They owned the home for 11 months and it is their first home.

Their maximum possible gain would have been $500,000. This amount is reduced per Section 121(c) by this ratio:

Number of months actually used/owned (11)

$$\frac{24}{} \times$$

$500,000 = $229,167

Their gain is less than the $500,000 limit, so the Smiths may exclude the entire $40,000 of gain under Reg. 1.121-3(g).

A distance safe harbor may apply if:

- The change in place of employment occurs during period the seller owns and uses the property as his or her principal residence; and

- The qualified individual's new place of employment is at least 50 miles farther from the residence sold or exchanged than was the former place of employment, or, if no former place of employment, the distance between qualified individual's new place of employment and residence sold or exchanged is at least 50 miles

**EXAMPLE:** Ernestine Humbold is unemployed and owns a townhouse owned and used as her principal residence since 2003. In 2004, she gets a job 54 miles from her townhouse, and she sells it. Because Ernestine's new place of employment is at least 50 miles from her townhouse, the sale is within the safe harbor so she is entitled to claim a reduced maximum exclusion under Section 121(c)(2) according to Reg. 1.121-3(c)(4).

Another safe harbor applies for taxpayers experiencing unforeseen circumstances. Under Reg. 1.121-3(e), the safe harbor for gains applies if the primary reason for the sale or exchange is the occurrence of an event the taxpayer could not reasonably have anticipated before purchasing and occupying the residence. The circumstance cannot be simply a preference for another residence or an improvement in the seller's financial circumstances. Such unforeseen circumstances include:

- An involuntary conversion of the residence;

- Natural or man-made disasters or acts of war or terrorism resulting in a casualty to residence (even if not deductible under 165(h));

- In the case of a qualified individual
  - Death; or
  - Cessation of employment with the qualified individual eligible for unemployment compensation;

- Change in employment or self-employment status resulting in the taxpayer's inability to pay housing costs and reasonable basic living expenses for his or her household (including amounts for food, clothing, medical expenses, taxes, transportation, court-ordered payments, and expenses reasonably necessary to the production of income, but not for the maintenance of an affluent or luxurious standard of living);

- Divorce or legal separation under a decree of divorce or separate maintenance; or

- Multiple births resulting from same pregnancy.

Reg. 1.121-3(e)(3) states that the IRS may allow additional events as unforeseen circumstances because it

> may designate other events or situations as unforeseen circumstances in published guidance of general applicability and may issue rulings addressed to specific taxpayers identifying other events or situations as unforeseen circumstances with regard to those taxpayers (see Section 601.601(d)(2) of this chapter).

Examples of unforeseen circumstances include:

- Earthquake;
- The taxpayer being laid off and unable to pay mortgage and reasonable basic living expenses;
- Doubling of condo fees so that the taxpayer can no longer afford (not under safe harbor, but unforeseen);
- Certain reasons related to 9/11 terrorist attacks (Notice 2002-60); and
- Home too small once expecting another child (Private Letter Ruling 201628002).

On the other hand, examples of circumstances *not* unforeseen include:

- Buying a home on a heavily traveled road and then selling it due to traffic noise; and
- Getting a raise in pay so the taxpayer can afford a more expensive home.

## STUDY QUESTION

---

**5.** Bart Sysnik lived in home A for 18 months and was then transferred out of the country for 15 months. When he returns, he must live in home A for the next _____ months to qualify for the Section 121 gain exclusion.

    **a.** 0 (the time abroad is a temporary absence)

    **b.** 6

    **c.** 24

    **d.** 0 due to the special rule for travel abroad

---

# ¶ 106 MARITAL STATUS SPECIAL RULES

There are special rules in Reg. 1.121-2(a) for exclusion of capital gains based on the marital status of sellers. A key benefit for married couples filing jointly is that they may claim a maximum exclusion of $500,000 as long as one spouse meets the ownership requirements (the time and use requirements). The tax preparer should ensure that neither spouse is ineligible due to the one sale every two years rule. If either spouse fails to meet above requirements, then the maximum limitation amount to be claimed by the couple is the sum of each spouse's limitation amount determined on a separate basis as if they had not been married. For this purpose, each spouse is treated as owning the property during the period that either spouse owned the property.

## Qualifications for New and Remarried Spouses

Say a woman sells her principal residence, claims a Section 121 exclusion, and the next month marries someone who owns a home. She moves in and she uses it for 24 months and they decide to sell it. They should be aware of the timing because they won't get the $500,000 exclusion because the wife sold her home prior to getting married within less than two years. The husband will still be able to claim his individual $250,000 exclusion even though his wife is subject to the once every two years rule. The tax preparer, if consulted in advance of the sale, may suggest holding onto and using the home for an additional six months before selling it.

## Joint Owners

What about joint owners who are unmarried? It's kind of like the fact pattern with the *Hsu* case, where she owned 50 percent of the home and some unrelated party owned the other 50 percent. Or it could have been a sibling or a parent. It wasn't a spouse, though.

Joint owners in which the taxpayers jointly own the principal residence but file separate returns can get up to $250,000 of gain for their interest in the home, assuming they meet the ownership and use requirement, looking back 24 months of the prior 5 years.

> **EXAMPLE:** Sam Nolan and his grandfather Eddie are equal owners of a home in which they both resided in for 10 years. Both are single. The adjusted base is $100,000. They sell it today for $700,000, so it's got a total $600,000 gain. That means $300,000 of capital gain for each one. What's the tax treatment if they were to sell it?
>
> They each have a $300,000 gain. They each get full use of Section 121. This is where the IRS erred in sending the Hsu taxpayer in the original case. It's clear in the tax code and the regs that each one of them is assumed to have owned half a home. They get to each use the full breadth of Section 121, so they each have a $300,000 gain. They're single. So they each get to exclude $250,000—the maximum for a single filer—and $50,000 is then taxable.

At times, nonuse or ownership might still qualify for the exclusion. The taxpayer might be able to use somebody else's account toward that—for example, in a joint return. The husband and wife make a joint return for the tax year of the sale exchange of property. The general rules apply if *either* spouse meets the ownership or use requirements with respect to such property. But to get the $500,000 exclusion, both must meet the use requirements.

So it would be okay if only one met the ownership, but if they both meet the use requirement, they're going to get up to $500,000. And then we have the special rule for a deceased spouse, and there are a couple—actually, what also makes Section 121 a bit complicated is there are rules about joint filing a deceased spouse that show up more than once.

## Surviving Spouse

The ownership and use requirements cover an unmarried individual whose spouse is deceased on the date of sale exchange (Sec. 121(b)(4)). Then the period that such unmarried individual owned and used the property includes the period the deceased spouse owned and used the property before death.

> **EXAMPLE:** Jose Diaz, a single taxpayer, marries Cecilia Hernandez, who owned and used the principal residence to which Jose moves in. The following year Cecilia, the spouse owner—the original owner's spouse—dies and Jose, the surviving spouse, hasn't used it and owned it for two years. Jose can bring in the ownership and use of his deceased spouse under Section 121 (b)(2) on that year's return because of his wife's period of ownership and use.

However, a surviving spouse may still claim the $500,000 maximum exclusion if he or she sells the principal residence no later than two years after the spouse's death if the deceased met ownership and use requirements immediately before the date of death.

## Divorced Spouses

There is a special rule for time use by a divorced spouse. If the home is transferred from spouse or former spouse, and if the Section 1041 rule applies (a special rule regarding transfer) or it looks like gifting of property for which basis carries over, the ownership time will include the time of the transfer or ownership of the property, so again, special rules apply regarding divorced couples. For the time use by a divorced spouse, Section 121(d)(3) and Reg. 1.121-4(b) apply:

- For a home transferred from spouse or former spouse if Section 1041 applies— ownership time includes time transferor owned the property; and

- For property used by the former spouse per a divorce decree, an individual is treated as using property during any period of ownership while spouse or former spouse granted use under a divorce or separation instrument

## Unforeseen Circumstances for Married Couples Filing Jointly

Even in cases in which unforeseen circumstances apply to a sale, both spouses must meet the use requirement for the principal residence, although just one of the spouses needs to meet the ownership requirement. The one sale per two years rule and determination of principal residence rules still apply.

> **EXAMPLE:** In 1996, Giulio Campanelli buys a house, which he uses as his principal residence. On January 15, 1999, Giulio marries Constanza and she moves into Giulio's house. On January 15, 2000, Giulio sells the house due to a change in Constanza's place of employment. Neither spouse has excluded gain under Section 121 on a prior sale or exchange of property within the last two years.

- For $500,000 exclusion, both spouses must meet use requirement (okay that only Giulio meets the ownership requirement);

  — Thus, gain exclusion limit is the sum of each spouse's limitation amount determined on a separate basis as if they had not been married (Section 1.121-2(a)(3)(ii))

- Giulio must exclude up to $250,000 of gain;

- Constanza is not eligible to exclude maximum dollar limitation amount. Because the sale is due to a change in place of employment, she is eligible to claim a reduced maximum exclusion of up to $125,000 of the gain (365/730 × $250,000); and

- Giulio and Constanza exclude up to $375,000 of gain ($250,000 + $125,000) from the sale.

## STUDY QUESTION

**6.** Which of the following reasons qualifies as a sale due to "change in place of employment, health, or, to the extent provided in regulations, unforeseen circumstances" related to "qualified individual"?

    **a.** Employer requires California homeowner to move to Florida.

    **b.** New medical condition requires that homeowner live in a home without stairs.

    **c.** Birth of triplets while parents live in a 2-bedroom home.

    **d.** Increase in homeowner association fees leaves homeowner unable to afford to live in the home.

    **e.** Answers a, b, and c.

    **f.** All of the above.

# ¶ 107 LIMITATIONS AND SPECIAL RULES

## Circumstances Subject to Special Rules

A variety of limitations and special rules may apply under Section 121, including ones for remainder interests (Section 121(d)(8), cooperatives (Section 121(d)(4), and involuntary conversions of residences (Section 121(d)(5) and Reg. 1.121-4(d). Expatriates also should consider special rules (Section 121(e).

## The Limitation to Exclude Gain on Just One Sale or Exchange Every Two Years

Basically, Section 121(b)(3) and Reg. 1.121-2(b) state that no exclusion applies if the sale of the residence occurs during the two-year period ending on the date of sale, the taxpayer sold or exchanged other property for which the gain was excluded under Section 121.

> **EXAMPLE:** Astrid Bergdorf owned and used her townhouse as her principal residence for 2008 and 2009. In 2010, she buys a house that she owns and uses as her principal residence. In 2012, Astrid sells the townhouse and excluded the gain realized. In 2013, Astrid sells the house. Even though the house sale qualifies for the two-year ownership and use requirements, Section 121 does not apply to her gains on it because there was excluded gain within the prior two years on the townhouse. If the gain on the house sale was greater than the gain on the townhouse (but less than $250,000), Astrid can elect not to apply Section 121 to the townhouse gain.

# ¶ 108 REALIZED AND RECOGNIZED GAIN

Why would someone have a recognized gain? Whenever an owner sells or disposes of something, he or she has a *realized* gain. Then the next question is, "Does the seller have to recognize it all?" And if Section 121 applies to a principal residence sale, the seller might not need to recognize all of it. This is especially helpful—but not totally offsetting—in high-priced real estate markets.

> **EXAMPLE:** The Mazzaratis sell their home. They have an $800,000 gain. They're married filing jointly and lived in that home for 10 years. The $800,000 is their realized gain. All they are going to be able to exclude, assuming they meet the married filing jointly rule, is $500,000 and they'll have a $300,000 recognized gain. They also might have recognized gain because they had a period of nonqualified use.

When would that period of nonqualified use occur? Congress revised rules because tax practitioners issued planning advice to clients such as owning rental properties and converting each one sequentially to their principal residence, living in it for two years, then selling it to exclude much of the gains (other than depreciation claimed). Congress enacted the law that depreciation claimed after May 5, 1997, cannot be part of the gain included to the extent that the gain represents appreciation on the property claimed after that date. The rule changed going forward from 1997 for periods of nonqualified use of property (Section 121(b)(5). Thus, knowing the dates of purchase and sale ae very important in calculating the gain on the sale of a principal residence.

Tax preparers and planners must inquire of clients whether the purchase price (basis) of a residence they now sell included a rollover of gain under Section 1034. And if sellers had a period of using the residence as a rental property, they may have suspended passive rental loss that they are carrying forward. Regardless, the basis of the residence is affected by the costs of improvements (assuming the sellers kept receipts for their purchases). Also, basis is affected if the residence is acquired by gift or inheritance.

The following is a quick summary for the tax preparer of considerations and Section 121 rules affecting clients' recognition of gains upon sale of their principal residence:

- Common scenarios creating recognized gain;
  - Gain greater than dollar limit;
  - Nonqualified use (Section 121(b)(5));
  - Depreciation claimed (Section 121(d)(6))
  - Nonqualifying sale (not principal residence, too many sales, others)
- Also consider in calculation:
  - Basis affected by prior Section 1034 usage
  - Suspended passive activity loss and Section 469(g)
  - Improvements made to the property and special tax assessments
  - Property acquired by gift or inheritance
  - Involuntary conversion (Section 121(d)(5))
  - Like-kind exchange (Section 121(d)(10))

## Nonqualified Use

In July 2008 Congress revised legislation in the *Housing and Economic Recovery Act of 2008* (P.L. 110-289) for periods of nonqualified use of a principal residence to exclude gain allocated to those periods. A "period of nonqualified use" is any time after 2008 when the home was not used as the seller's principal residence or that of his or her spouse or former spouse, with the following exceptions:

- Any portion of five-year period ending on date of sale or exchange after last date used as a principal residence (except if the taxpayer moves out and rents it out while trying to sell it);
- Special rule for qualified official extended duty under Section (d)(9) of the act; and
- Temporary absence due to change in employment, health conditions or unforeseen circumstances (not to exceed aggregate period of two years).

The calculation is as follows:

$$\text{Ratio} = \frac{\text{Aggregate periods of nonqualified use while property was owned}}{\text{Period property was owned}}$$

The ratio starts with the total period of nonqualified use (when the sellers weren't using it as a principal residence but owned that property). The denominator is the total number of months the sellers owned the property. So for months of nonqualified use, no Section 121 benefit applies for that portion of the gain. The period of nonqualified use means any time after 2008 when the property is not used as a principal residence for the taxpayer, or taxpayer's spouse or former spouse.

Some examples for determining nonqualified use were provided from Congress by the Joint Committee on Taxation.

> **EXAMPLE:** Assume that an individual buys a property on January 1, 2009, for $400,000, and uses it as rental property for two years claiming $20,000 of depreciation deductions

- On January 1, 2011, the taxpayer converts the property to his principal residence;

- On January 1, 2013, the taxpayer moves out, and the taxpayer sells the property for $700,000 on January 1, 2014;

- As under present law, $20,000 gain attributable to the depreciation deductions is included in income;

- Of the remaining $300,000 gain, 40 percent of the gain (2 years ÷ 5 years), or $120,000, is allocated to nonqualified use and is not eligible for the exclusion; and

- Because the remaining gain of $180,000 is less than the maximum gain of $250,000 that may be excluded, gain of $180,000 is excluded from gross income.

**EXAMPLE:** Assume that an individual buys a principal residence on January 1, 2009, for $400,000, moves out on January 1, 2019, and on December 1, 2021, sells the property for $600,000. The entire $200,000 gain is excluded from gross income, as under present law, because periods after the last qualified use do not constitute nonqualified use.

**EXAMPLE:** On February 2, 2015, Samantha buys a home for rental purposes for $400,000. After renting it out for 5 years, she moves in, making it her principal residence. After living in the home for 3 years, Samantha sells if for $750,000. She claimed $40,000 depreciation on it before selling it. What is the tax effect?

Samantha must calculate gain allocable to periods of nonqualified use with this ratio:

$$\frac{\text{Period of nonqualified use: } 5}{\text{Total period owned } 8} * \$350,000 \text{ gain} =$$

$218,750—→ Section 121 not applicable (+ $40,000)
$131,250 excluded

Watching the dates is essential for accurately calculating the effect of periods of nonqualified use for the residence sold.

**EXAMPLE:** In 1990, Mr. and Ms. Delano purchased their first home at a cost of $30,000. In 2015 they sell the home. In one scenario, they have rented the house to renters for one year before selling it for $240,000, claiming $2,000 of depreciation before the sale. This constitutes a rental nonqualified use only after their qualified use. Section 121 still applies, but the $2,000 depreciation is taxable because the rental occurred after May 6, 1997. They had retained receipts for improvements to the residence over the nonrental years, which adds to their basis.

Alternatively, the Delanos rent out the house for two years. Prior to moving into it, the sales price is $240,000. The depreciation claim was $2,000. And in this scenario they rented the house out prior to moving into it, they bought this home in 1990, so their periods of nonqualified use were before 2009. That's not considered a period of nonqualified use because that's before the effective date of that provision. Plus the depreciation the Delanos claimed when they rented it out when they bought it in 1990, if the first time they rented it was 1990, 1991, and 1992, was not for a period of nonqualified use. It's before the effective date of that change in the law, plus because the depreciation they claimed back then was not after May 6, 1997, it will fall under Section 121 benefit as well.

The Delanos' tax preparer uses software that queries the date the home was acquired and when the period of nonqualified use occurred, which determines which law applies.

## Depreciation Recapture

Section 121(d)(6) and Reg. 1.121-1(d) govern recognition of gain attributable to depreciation. The rules prohibit exclusion for so much of gain from a residence sale as does not exceed the portion of depreciation adjustments (as defined in Section 1250(b)(3) attributable to periods after May 6, 1997, for the property.

## Section 1034 and Basis

The basis rules of Section 1016 as well as Section 121 apply to principal residences acquired using gains rolled over from the sale of a prior residence (before 1997):

(a) General rule. Proper adjustment in respect of the property shall in all cases be made—

— (7) in the case of a residence the acquisition of which resulted, under section 1034 (as in effect on the day before the date of the enactment of the Taxpayer Relief Act of 1997*), in the nonrecognition of any part of the gain realized on the sale, exchange, or involuntary conversion of another residence, to the extent provided in section 1034(e) (as so in effect);

— *Taxpayer Relief Act of 1997,* enacted August 5, 1997 with an effective date of May 6, 1997.

**EXAMPLE:** Mr. and Ms. Fiorino purchased their first home in 1980 for $25,000. In 1994, they sell the home for $125,000, so that causes them a $100,000 realized gain under Section 1034. The rule in 1994 was that if sales proceeds were reinvested within 24 months in a new principal residence, gain from the sale was deferred. The Fiorinos bought a home that cost $220,000, so they clearly bought a home costing more than what they spent on the one they sold. They got to defer that $100,000 of realized gain. They deferred it and believed the basis for tax is going to be $220,000 less my $100,000 deferred gain. Their Form 2119 attached to the return for the year of sale would have noted that basis.

In 2015 they sold the residence for $1 million. However, in 2015 their *tax basis* is not the $220,000 purchase price but $120,000, so their gain on the home was actually $880,000. After taking their $500,000 exclusion, they have a $380,000 taxable recognized gain. So if their tax preparer does not learn about the rolled over funds, he or she will incorrectly assume the basis was $220,000.

In addition, the Fiorinos rented out the home for a time period, generating rental loss, which is automatically a passive activity loss. However, they had no passive activity gain against which they could claim the loss (CCA 201428008) in 2015. However, under Section 469(g), a suspended loss is not triggered if the property was not sold in a fully taxable transaction. Thus, gain was generated but then excluded. The passive activity ended with the sale. The trigger rule in Section 469(g) states that to the extent suspended rental losses "exceed any net income or gain for the tax year of the disposition from all other passive activities, the losses will be treated as not from a passive activity." Thus, they can be used against nonpassive income.

Code Section 469's trigger rule became effective in 1987, and in a Chief Counsel Advice in 2014 the IRS held that gains from such residence sales are taxable transactions, but Section 121 nevertheless excludes the $250,000 (single filers) or $500,000 (joint filers) of gains.

## Like-Kind Exchange

What should sellers expect if their capital gains from the sale of their principal residence exceeds $500,000? What if they figured that if the gain would be more than $500,000, they should convert part of the home to rental property, rent it out for 12 months, exchange the home and, because the mandatory Section 121 applies to the exchange, use both that and mandatory Section 1034 to the property? Under both provisions, such a combination is permitted.

Rev. Proc. 2005-14 applies to such cases, stating:

> If a taxpayer acquires property in an exchange with respect to which gain is not recognized (in whole or in part) to the taxpayer under subsection (a) or (b) of Section 1031, Subsection (a) shall not apply to the sale or exchange of such property by such taxpayer (or by any person whose basis in such property is determined, in whole or in part, by reference to the basis in the hands of such taxpayer) during the 5-year period beginning with the date of such acquisition.

## Election Out of Mandatory Application of Section 121

Why would someone elect out of claiming a Section 121 exclusion? Possibly, the sellers would elect out of Section 121 because they had two sales in the two-year time period, and the second sale produced a larger gain than the first. Thus, electing out of the first transaction's exclusion under Reg. 1.121-4(g) would enable the sellers to claim the larger exclusion.

# ¶ 109 REPORTING THE SALE

Under IRS rules as detailed in Section 6045 and Reg. 1.6045-4, sellers do not have to report the sale of their principal residence on their federal return for the year of sale unless:

- They have a gain and do not qualify to exclude all of it;
- They have a gain and choose not to exclude it; or
- They have a loss and received a Form 1099-S.

The sellers report the transaction on Schedule D Form 8949 even though the losses are not deductible (Schedule D instructions describe nondeductible losses). If the sales price is less than $250,000, the real estate agent is not required to issue a Form 1099-S, *Proceeds from Real Estate Transactions,* and joint filers do not have to file it.

IRS tips and guidance for Section 6045 are provided on the IRS website, **www.irs.gov.** Rev. Proc. 2007-12 includes a sample assurance statement. Return preparers should check for updated guidance for reporting requirements of gains attributable to periods of nonqualified use.

# ¶ 110 FORGIVENESS OF DEBT

What if sellers have a principal residence for which they have cancellation of debt? Maybe the lender offers to reduce a $500,000 debt to $400,000—a workout.

Such a transaction produces cancellation of debt income, and that's taxable. The tax preparer checks Section 108 to see whether any exclusions might apply. If the taxpayer is in a title 11 bankruptcy, those provisions take precedence, and then the sellers could exclude the income as being under a title 11 bankruptcy proceeding.

If the amount meets the definition of qualified principal residence indebtedness, as defined under Section 108, and this discharge occurred before January 1, 2017—

because it's a temporary provision under the law—the sellers want to see if that exclusion applies, and that one takes precedence before any insolvency exception would apply.

Today, unless Congress renews it, that qualified principal residence provision is gone, but the preparer should not think their income is completely out under Section 108 because if the client is in a Title 11 bankruptcy, or they're insolvent, meaning the value of their debt is greater than the value of their assets, the insolvency exception will apply. The preparer should check whether Congress has renewed this qualified principal residence provision.

Also if instead of just a workout, the sellers may dispose of the property through foreclosure, short sale, involving filing some reporting forms for the cancellation of debt income.

## General Rules

As a brief review:

- Section 61(a)(12) covers gross income includes income from discharge of indebtedness;
- Section 108 provides for exclusion for certain cancellation of debt income if (ordering rule applies)
  - Discharge occurs in Title 11 case,
  - Discharge occurs when the taxpayer is insolvent,
  - Debt discharged is "qualified farm indebtedness,"
  - Non-C corporation's "qualified real property business indebtedness" is discharged, or
  - Debt discharged is "qualified principal residence indebtedness" discharged before January 1, 2017;
- Generally, tax attributes are reduced by excluded cancellation of debt income
  - Section 1017 discharge of indebtedness is also relevant and
- Several other special rules at Section 108 such as Section108(e)(5) applies when purchase money debt of solvent debtor treated as adjustment to property basis if certain requirements are met.

## Reporting Cancellation of Debt Income

The IRS guidance and filing paperwork include:

- Section 6050P, Returns relating to the cancellation of indebtedness by certain entities
- Section 6050J, Returns relating to foreclosures and abandonments of security
- Filing Form 1099-A, *Acquisition or Abandonment of Secured Property*
- Filing Form 1099-C, *Cancellation of Debt*
- Filing Form 982, *Reduction of Tax Attributes Due to Discharge of Indebtedness* (and checking Section 1082 Basis Adjustment).

## Recourse Debt Greater Than the Fair Market Value of Property

Rev. Rul. 90-16 and Reg. 1.1001-2 govern treatment of debt on a principal residence that exceeds the fair market value of the property.

**EXAMPLE:** Harold and Nancy Whitehead have $13,000 of recourse debt secured by their property. Their basis in the property when they become insolvent was $8,000. The fair market value of the property was $10,000. The gain realized on sale of the property equaled the fair market value minus their adjusted basis ($10,000 – $8,000). The cancellation of debt income was the debt minus the amount paid ($13,000 – $10,000 = $3,000). The income was excludable under Section 108 to the extent of insolvency (unless another provision applies).

**Foreclosure.** If the taxpayers' home is foreclosed upon—a nonrecourse debt—they don't have cancellation of debt income. The *Tufts* case, Rev. Rul. 91-31, says in that case the return claims the amount of the debt as the sales price less the basis of the home. The taxpayers have a gain or a loss. If it's a gain, Section 121 applies to help reduce the tax. If it's a loss, it's unusable loss.

**EXAMPLE:** Assume the same facts about the Whitehead property. Under Rev. Rul. 91-31 and the *Tufts* 1983 decision (461 U.S. 300), the gain realized equals the balance of nonrecourse debt ($13,000 – $8,000 = $5,000). The key factor is when the encumbered property was disposed of:

- Recourse debt: Use FMV to calculate gain. Any excess debt cancelled = cancellation of debt income; or
- Nonrecourse debt: Use debt balance to calculate gain; no cancellation of debt income (therefore Section 108 does not come into play).

For the foreclosure or short sale, the taxpayers are only going to have cancellation of debt income if it's recourse debt. So while the fact that exclusion for the principal residence debt under Section 108 has expired as of January 1, 2017, for some taxpayers if it's nonrecourse debt that goes away in the foreclosure or short sale, they wouldn't have had cancellation of debt income anyway.

**Reduction in Debt Without Property Disposition.** A workout situation:

- Generally produces cancellation of debt income whether the debt is recourse or nonrecourse;
- Rev Rul. 91-31 and Rev. Rul. 92-99 govern nonrecourse debt; and
- If seller is also lender and debtor is solvent, see Section 108(e)(5); the debt is generally treated as a purchase-price adjustment.

**Additional Cancellation of Debt Guidance.** The following provide guidance:

- Sections 108 and 1017 and regulations in the tax code;
- IRS Publication 4681, *Cancelled Debts, Foreclosures, Repossessions and Abandonments* (for individuals);
- Bankruptcy provisions;
- Section 1398; and
- Reg. 1.1398-3 for treatment of the Section 121 exclusion in individuals' title 11 cases.

# ¶ 111  PLANNING AND REMINDERS

A tax preparer or financial planner should be mindful of factors described here to help clients minimize capital gains from selling their principal residence.

## Property That Has Declined in Value

If the residence is worth less than the owner paid for it, he or she may sell it at a loss, but the loss is not allowed to reduce income. An alternative is to convert the property to a rental, but the seller and preparer should remember:

- The basis of rental = lesser of,
  - Fair market value at the date of conversion or
  - Basis;
- Does the owner expect the value to continue to decrease? If so, the owner and planner should discuss
  - Rental use versus cashing out and cutting losses,
  - Any other tax considerations.

## Appreciation of Property That Is Approaching the Owner's Gain Limit

Sometimes, marriage could be tax planning for these high gains situations (projected gains of more than $250,000 for a single taxpayer). And for married couples planning for a taxable gain greater than $500,000, that taxable amount is going to be subject to a net investment income tax, assuming the owners are within the dollar limits for that. They can consider the costs of selling and buying a new principal residence, but also consider the importance of tax planning versus other factors—perhaps they really like the home they own now. The planner should inform the clients about the 3.8 percent net investment income tax under Section 1411 that became effective in 2013.

Owners could consider installment sales. Installment sales could be good as far as getting a good return. Usually, sellers can charge greater interest than the bank's savings rate. Installments also might keep owners' income below the threshold for the net investment income tax.

For the planner and taxpayer, it's really just watching the timing of when the client is doing something affecting gains. For example, a couple gets married -Each one of them at the time they get married already owns a principal residence that has appreciation in it. Certainly when their gain will be more than $250,000 on both those homes, they want to see whether they can do the planning. They can plan that to maximize out up to the $500,000 as long as they sell no more than one every two years and they both meet the use requirements. For the $500,000, it's okay if only one spouse meets the ownership requirement, but both need to meet the use for 24 months requirement. So a lot of this is just planning to satisfy that. The planner can inform clients who consult him or her before selling.

Of course, recordkeeping is also important for planning. Clients should keep all the original papers. Hopefully, if they did have a Form 2119 on the home they still own, they kept that form, so the tax preparer can figure out the basis under Section 1034. If the owners made improvements, that's great—if records are maintained. Records substantiate costs the owners paid that increase their basis from their purchase price, especially when the gain will go beyond $500,000. Preparers and owners should calculate the effects of having a home office or using the residence as a rental property—before the home is sold.

And again, a lot of reminders apply to planners to be aware of effective dates, especially for depreciation and nonqualified use of the residence.

Owners of multiple homes should be able to substantiate the facts when the home they sell is their principal residence. Planners should advise owners to prove factors such as where their utility and tax bills are sent, where their driver's license address is listed, club or church membership records, etc.

# MODULE 1: INDIVIDUAL TAXATION—
# Chapter 2: Income Taxation of Trusts and Estates

## ¶ 201 WELCOME

Planning and implementing trusts and estates are growth areas for tax and attorney practices. More and more clients are using trusts, and more and more legal and tax practitioners are recommending use of these asset management tools. Trusts are created not just for tax issues, but primarily for asset protection, avoidance of probate, and for dealing with family members of the trustor.

## ¶ 202 LEARNING OBJECTIVES

Upon completion of this chapter, you will be able to:

- Identify basic tax issues for trusts and estates;
- Recognize the types of trusts;
- Identify the income reportable by fiduciaries and deductions available to them; and
- Recognize ways in which distributions in the year of termination are managed.

## ¶ 203 INTRODUCTION

Not every family member is as a mature, responsible individual ready to take on the responsibilities of wealth, and so a trust is a way to create wealth management, to delay outright distribution of funds, and to give the senior family members some comfort that while they are alive and upon their passing, the wealth and assets left to the next generation are being properly managed and handled. So planners are seeing more and more trusts being used.

This chapter explains how the income taxation of trusts and estates works—how trusts and estates are taxed, the fiscal or calendar year requirements, when returns have to be filed, and estimated payments. The chapter divides the types of trusts into the most common categories; simple, complex, grantor, and qualified revocable trusts. Additionally, the discussion explores the distinctions among trust accounting income, trust accounting principles, the essential components of trust and estate income taxation, the distributable net income (DNI) concept, and how all of them relate to taxable income, expenses, and deductions as reported on Form 1041. Finally, the chapter addresses the special consequences of the final year of a trust and estate and how the alternative minimum tax (AMT) applies to trusts and estates.

## ¶ 204 TAXING AUTHORITY

Trusts and estates are separate entities from individuals, from corporations, from partnerships. Trusts and estates are taxed under their own rules, and state law is going to be applicable here, so planners need to know individually something about state law, how the state defines income and principal, whether capital gains are only principal, and whether they can be associated with income. Those become some state law issues.

But it's the Internal Revenue Code that determines how trusts and estates are taxed for federal income tax purposes, and if state income taxes apply, the state may certainly dictate fiduciary income tax issues with respect to the planner's own state. State issues, of course, must be determined independently of this chapter.

# ¶ 205 COMMENCEMENT AND DURATION OF AN ESTATE

When does an estate start? It begins when someone dies. When a death occurs, the person's Form 1040 filing year ends on the date of death. And interestingly, the law says his or her estate's filing year begins the same day. A new taxpayer comes into being: the estate of the decedent. That new taxpayer needs an identification number. The estate can't use the decedent's Social Security number or income received subsequent to that person's death; the death closes out the 1040 filing year, and the Social Security number is no longer technically, at least, the identification for where income should be received.

The estate uses Form SS-4, which can be obtained online, by fax, or by regular mail from the IRS, to get a federal tax identification number. The sooner the identification number is obtained, the better for informing banks, brokerages, etc., about the existence of the estate. The practitioner must distinguish income received after the date of death to report on the estate's Form 1041, *U.S. Income Tax Return for Estates and Trusts,* rather than the decedent's Form 1040.

The duration of an estate depends on how complicated the assets are and how complicated the family issues prove to be. The more complications, the longer the estate lasts. Complications may involve:

- If the estate include assets that need valuation and appraisals, and if they exceed the federal filing threshold, filing a full Form 706, *United States Estate (and Generation-Skipping Transfer) Tax Return;*

- Marshaling and collecting the assets of the decedent and paying all of the legacies, bequests, debts, and taxes;

- Resolving claims by creditors; and

- Awaiting decision of any lawsuits against the decedent.

Thus, there is no set time for an estate to be resolved. Most estates without complication can be resolved in two years, but the factors listed above affect the estate's duration.

## STUDY QUESTION

---

**1.** In order to obtain a separate tax identification number for an estate, which of the following forms must be filed with the Internal Revenue Service?

    **a.** Form SS-4

    **b.** Form SS-5

    **c.** Form SS-8

    **d.** Form W-7

---

# ¶ 206  INCOME TAXATION OF AN ESTATE

## Subchapter J

Estates, as well as trusts, are taxed under Subchapter J of the Internal Revenue Code, and Subchapter J's theory or theme is that income has to be taxed one time. The opportunity for trusts and estates is that income might be taxed to the entity—the trust or estate itself. It may all be passed out to the beneficiaries and taxed to the beneficiaries with the trust or estate receiving an income distribution deduction, or some of it can be taxed to the entity and some taxed to the beneficiary, when some but not all of the income is distributed from the entity to the beneficiary. Practitioners have all those different possibilities in looking at how the fiduciary income tax rules work. The entity might be the payor, or the beneficiary might be the payor, with the entity deducting, or some income in both, depending upon how distributions are made.

## Basis

The basis of assets is important in tax planning. Most people will not be federal estate tax payors, but most people will be income tax payers. Thus, practitioners establish the highest basis for the client's assets so that when they are sold, they will have little or no gain, or even perhaps a loss. Certainly practitioners try to maximize basis.

When a person dies, generally the basis to the heir is the value of the property at date of death. Some assets don't get a stepped-up basis or a date of death basis. It could be a step down.

> **EXAMPLE:**  Harold Jefferson paid $100 for shares of a stock. If when Harold passes on, it's worth $40, his heir's basis is $40. Or if the stock is worth $175, his heir's basis is $175.

Some assets do not get a date of death value at basis. Those are income in respect of a decedent assets, commonly funds held in a retirement plan, IRA, or 401(k) account. Whatever that is worth at death, that's the amount that can pass to beneficiaries, and when they receive it, it is ordinary income to the heirs. There is no step up or down, there is no capital gain involvement, as a general rule, for those assets. So, the good news here is when a person dies, the heirs receive the date of death value as their basis, which heirs hope has been stepped up from the time the property was acquired. There is also another beneficial rule for heirs; they receive an automatic long-term holding period for inherited assets.

> **EXAMPLE:**  Jenny Chambers acquired property on June 1 and died on June 15. Jenny's grandson Brandon inherited that property and sold it on July 10. Even though the property was held for about 40 days in the family, Brandon's gain or loss is long-term because he inherited the property from a decedent. Both Jenny and Brandon's holding periods are irrelevant; the property becomes a long-term asset.

Distributions of income by an estate to its beneficiaries qualify the estate for an income distribution deduction, as explained later.

For tax years except for 2010, the estate's basis in property acquired from a decedent is the fair market value of the property on the decedent's date of death (or on the alternate valuation date). For 2010, if the estate elected out of the federal tax system, a modified carryover basis rule applies.

Regardless of their actual holding period by the estate, capital assets acquired from a decedent are considered to have been held by the estate for one year and thereby qualify for long-term gain or loss treatment.

## Accounting Methods and Tax Years

An estate may use either the cash or accrual method of accounting, regardless of the accounting method used by the decedent. Generally, estates use the cash method.

An interesting opportunity with estates is the choice of a fiscal year. Estates can use a fiscal year election, which is important because that opens up a lot of planning opportunities. The estate must choose the fiscal year when the first Form 1041 is filed. On Form SS-4, when the identification number is obtained, the filer is asked to state the end of the estate's accounting year. However, when the estate files Form 1041, a different fiscal year can be selected, but it may not be more than 12 months after the date it begins and must be at the end of the month. The fiscal year may be decided to be the same month as the death occurs. One of the advantages of the choice of the estate's fiscal year is that sometimes income can be deferred until a later year.

> **EXAMPLE:** Bethany Davis chose a January 31 fiscal year for the estate of her client who died in February of 2017. A significant payment—an IRA distribution—was made in February of 2017 to Fiona, the beneficiary.
>
> That tax year of the estate didn't end until January 31, 2018. Even though Fiona got the money in February of 2017, the estate's year end is used to determine the tax year for reporting of the beneficiary. So, that becomes 2018 income to the beneficiary. The tax on that is due April 15 of 2019. So, Fiona received a large check in February of 2017 but could pay the tax on it in April of 2019.

## Estimated Tax Payments

An estate is not required to make estimated tax payments unless it is open more than two years after the decedent's date of death. A short fiscal year counts as one tax year. But the fact that the fiduciary has the use of money for two years before the estate has to settle up with the IRS can be an advantage, considering the time value of money, the use of money, etc.

The estate need not make estimated tax payments if:

- There was no tax liability for the preceding full 12 month tax year; or
- The balance of tax due is less than $1,000.

In the final tax year of the estate, its estimated tax payments may be allocated to the beneficiaries per an election by the executor:

- Form 1041-T is used to make this allocation election; and
- Form 1041-T must be filed by the 65th day after the close of the estate's tax year.

A domestic estate must file Form 1041 if it has:

- Gross income in excess of $600 for the taxable year; or
- A beneficiary who is a nonresident alien.

The due date of Form 1041 is the fifteenth day of the fourth month following the close of the tax year. The estate may obtain an automatic five-and-a-half-month extension of time to file Form 1041 by using Form 7004, *Application for Automatic Extension of Time to File Certain Business Income Tax, Information, and Other Returns*. Penalties are avoided if the estate makes estimated tax payments equal to either 90 percent of the tax shown on the return for the current year or 100 percent of the tax shown on the return for the prior tax year. If the estate is distributing a significant portion or all of its income to the beneficiaries, even though it received income, the distribution deduction to beneficiaries will result in no tax liability for the estate, and therefore no underestimation penalty.

¶206

**EXAMPLE:** Emily Halverston paid significant estimated tax payments and then died having overpaid her estimates; she passed on before receiving enough income to cover those payments. Can those payments be moved to the estate? Unfortunately, the answer is no.

If Emily was not filing a joint return, then to claim a refund and to get that refund, the estate files Form 1310, *Statement of Person Claiming Refund Due a Deceased Taxpayer*. Form 1310 is filed by the representative of the estate to claim a refund for the decedent. A fiduciary has the requirement to do so.

When the adjusted gross income (AGI) of the estate exceeds $150,000, a special rule applies. The required percentage of the preceding year's tax that must now be paid in a tax year to satisfy the safe harbor provisions is 110 percent applicable for 2016 and 2017 estimated payments.

If there has been an underpayment of estimated taxes, the fiduciary should complete Form 2210, *Underpayment of Estimated Tax by Individuals, Estates, and Trusts,* which calculates the underestimation penalty. But in the final year of an estate, if the estate itself has overpaid its estimates, the fiduciary can move those overpaid estimates to the beneficiaries of the estate. A Form 1041-T can be filed within 65 days of the end of the estate's year with the IRS to allow movement of any estimated payments from the estate to the beneficiaries, but only in the estate's final year.

**NOTE:** Any estimated taxes paid by or on behalf of an individual prior to death may *not* be claimed on Form 1041.

**EXAMPLE:** Gerry Gleason closes out all the bank accounts for his client, and now it turns out there was a tax overpayment. To collect the refund, it might come months after Gerry has closed out all the bank accounts.

And where would Gerry deposit that refund check? The bank will not allow him to deposit it in the client's name; it's payable to the estate. The bank won't let Gerry deposit the amount in the executor's name; it's payable to the estate. The estate account is closed. The bank requires Gerry to reopen an estate account and go through all the procedures to open a new account, with new passwords and debit cards and all of the paperwork.

Then Gerry deposits the check, waits for it to clear, and then closes the account. It's a nuisance.

Alternatively, Form 1041-T is a nice way to wrap up the loose end of an overpayment in the estate accounts of the estate's estimated tax liability without going through some of the administrative aggravation that might otherwise be necessary.

The tax rates are the same for estates and trusts. Long-term capital gains and qualified dividends are taxed at the rate of 15 percent or the maximum tax rate of 20 percent when the entity's income exceeds $12,400 for 2016 ($12,500 for 2017), subject to special rules for the taxation of unrecaptured Section 1250 gain (25 percent) and gains realized on the sale or exchange of collectibles (28 percent).

## STUDY QUESTION

---

**2.** With respect to tax return filing requirements, an estate may obtain an automatic extension of _____ months by using Form 7004.

    **a.** Three

    **b.** Five and a half

    **c.** Six

    **d.** Nine

---

## Due Dates for Tax Payments

An estate has to file a tax return if it has gross income above $600 for the taxable year or if it has a beneficiary who is a nonresident alien. Any income payable to a nonresident alien requires the filing of Form 1041. But if the estate has only U.S. residents or citizens as its beneficiaries and has less than $600 of annual income, no Form 1041 is required.

Form 1041 is due on the 15th day of the fourth month following the close of the estate's fiscal tax year, so three and a half months after the end of that year. The tax return is due, typically, on April 15 for a calendar year. There can be different due dates because of holidays and weekends, but generally April 15 is the due date for a calendar year return.

Interestingly, the filing rules changed a couple of years ago, and now the IRS allows a five-and-a-half-month extension opportunity for the annual return. Form 7004 is filed if the estate requests an automatic five-and-a-half-month extension of time to file. The IRS does not provide an acknowledgment that Form 7004 was received, so it's wise to sometimes send two copies with a return envelope that's stamped and addressed, asking the IRS to return a copy of the form. That creates a record that the extension request was filed. But it's a five-and-a-half-month extension, so for a calendar year, the extension runs from April 15 to September 30 to file Form 1041. The extension doesn't extend to October 15, which is when the Form 1040 extension expires, or when a partnership or S corporation extended return would be due. Staggering some of these due dates makes tax preparation perhaps a bit easier.

Tax rates for estates and trusts are the same, and are discussed later in the chapter.

# ¶ 207 COMMENCEMENT AND DURATION OF A TRUST

A trust may be created by a transfer made during the lifetime of its creator (an *inter vivos* transfer) or by transfers made taking effect upon the death of the creator (a testamentary transfer). Transfers made during the creator's lifetime may be either revocable or irrevocable, depending on the terms of the trust document. A person today can sign a document creating a trust, putting a minimal amount of money or a whole lot of money in it, to create the trust. Thus, a trust created by a living trustor is an *inter vivos* trust or grantor trust. If it is created during his or her lifetime, the trust can be a revocable trust. That's the typical living trust that so many clients create, especially for families with a person moving into a retirement home. Or the trust might be irrevocable, a trust that technically can't be changed by the grantor who sets up that trust.

Multiple varieties of trusts are popular. Some clients may designate in their will that upon death, a trust is established for their spouse—a qualified terminable interest property (QTIP) trust. Trusts for children are called credit shelter trusts. Generation-skipping trusts are set up for grandchildren. If one client sets up all three types, three separate taxpayers with three identification numbers and three Forms 1041 are required. Or the client may prefer to set up one family trust with separate shares for each person. In that case, a single trust has multiple, separate shares. Just one Form 1041 would be filed for that trust, but the trust would have five Schedule K-1s, one for each of the five beneficiaries.

In summary, each trust created by a decedent's will is a separate and distinct taxpayer that requires its own identification number, recordkeeping, annual income tax return, and so on. The practitioner must read and understand clients' wills to know what the filing obligations are.

Trusts generally have a designated end date, for example, for the lifetime of the client's spouse or until the client's child reaches a certain age. The trust need not immediately end, but the practitioner should be in a position to wrap up the trust's provisions. When a trustee has discretion to distribute trust principal, the trust may end when the trustee, in the exercise of his or her discretion, distributes the balance of the principal, thus terminating the trust.

## STUDY QUESTION

---

**3.** Which of the following is another term for a grantor trust?

   **a.** Complex trust

   **b.** Simple trust

   **c.** Revocable trust

   **d.** Living trust

---

# ¶ 208  INCOME TAXATION OF A TRUST

Like estates, trusts are taxed under Subchapter J of the tax code that taxes income once—either to the trust that receives it or to the beneficiary to whom the trust distributes it within the trust's taxable year. If the trust does distribute all of the income it receives, it gets a distribution deduction for all of that income. The beneficiary gets a Schedule K-1 and reports all the income on the beneficiary's return.

## Simple, Complex, Grantor, and Revocable Living Trusts

Trusts may be classified generally as either simple trusts or complex trusts. What is a simple trust? The *simple trust* is one that is required to distribute all of its income currently. The trustees do not have discretion to hold back any income. A simple trust can't have a charitable beneficiary. If it does, it's not a simple trust and can't be distributing principal. A simple trust does get an annual income exemption of $300. Capital gain not distributed becomes taxable to the trust and therefore there is tax liability, and that's where that $300 exemption can provide a small amount of comfort.

*Complex trusts* are the typical discretionary trust, in which the trustee is given discretion to either pay income or accumulate income. A complex trust affords the trustee discretion and allows the client to include charitable beneficiaries. The fiduciary can distribute principal from a complex trust and is allowed a $100 annual tax exemption for the complex trust.

So, it is not required to make current payments of income to beneficiaries, but it certainly can. Under Code Secs. 661-663, distributions of income by a complex trust to its beneficiaries qualify the trust for an income distribution deduction, especially if the trust has charitable beneficiaries. A complex trust may allow the trustee discretion to distribute income or principal to the beneficiaries. Complex trusts have an annual exemption of $100.

The third broad category is a grantor trust. A *grantor trust* under Code Secs. one in which the grantor has retained certain rights, and if those rights fall within Code Secs. 671–679 of the tax code, if the rights retained by the grantor fall within the rights and opportunities described in those code sections, then the grantor remains taxable on the trust income. Even if the income is paid to someone else, the retention by the grantor of a grantor power leaves the grantor taxable on the income.

Grantor trusts are *inter vivos* trusts, or *living trusts,* created by a living person for his or her own use and benefit. The grantor will be taxed on the trust income, and the trust is disregarded as a separate taxable entity for federal income tax purposes. When the trust grantor dies, the trust typically becomes irrevocable, and the trust assets are administered according to the terms of the trust agreement. The revocable living trust is a common tax and estate planning document.

The trustee (generally, the fiduciary or person designated as holding the power of attorney) may not withhold or accumulate the trust income. The trust does not permit amounts to be paid, permanently set aside, or used for charitable purposes. No trust principal is distributed in the current year. The terms of the trust allow the trustee in its discretion to either pay or to withhold or accumulate current trust income so that it is not required to pay income currently to the beneficiary.

The client creating a revocable living trust is taxable on all the income. The trustor may allow children to get the income or his or her spouse to have the income. Because the client can revoke the trust, he or she is taxed on all the income regardless of who actually receives payments.

There are more subtle grantor trust powers that leave the grantor taxable on the income but may not require inclusion in the grantor's estate. If it's a revocable trust, Code Sec. 2038 states that if the grantor can revoke the trust when he or she dies, it's in the decedent's estate. But there are other powers that are not quite as large as revocation that still leave the grantor taxable on the trust income but do not require estate inclusion.

Again, the operative document should be checked. An attorney who drafts these documents may intend a trust to be a grantor trust, but the boilerplate of a 30-page document may bury a single paragraph, for example, giving the grantor the right to substitute trust property for other property.

The grantor is taxed on all that trust income. If a client has a grantor trust, then the grantor is taxed on all the income and the trust itself is disregarded as a taxpayer. The practitioner cannot ignore a grantor power that is meant to be there.

The grantor winds up reporting all the income of the grantor trust on his or her own Form 1041. The issue then becomes whether the grantor has to pick up all the income on the Form 1040 and whether Form 1041 is required. And the answer is: it depends.

The first consideration depends on is whether the grantor is the trustee. If the grantor or the grantor's spouse is the trustee, there is no need to file Form 1041; the practitioner just picks up all the income on the grantor's Form 1040.

If the grantor is not the trustee, the spouse is not the trustee—a bank, accountant, or attorney for the grantor is the trustee—the practitioner must obtain an identification number for the trust and file Form 1041.

On Form 1041, the practitioner checks the box grantor trust, and attaches a schedule claiming the items of income and deduction that the grantor will be reporting on his or her Form 1040, and provides the grantor a copy of the form. A couple of alternatives are mentioned in the Form 1041 instructions. The client can dispense with the Form 1041 and simply use a series of Form 1099 reports, making sure the grantor picks up all the income. A Form 1041 may be preferable because everything is on one document, on one schedule that the client and practitioner can always refer to make sure the grantor has been properly advised.

When the grantor of a grantor trust dies, the grantor trust becomes either a simple trust or a complex trust, if and when the trust is continuing. The practitioner examines the existing document. Does it require all the income to be distributed, or does it give the trustee ongoing discretion?

Certain costs of owning property, such management fees for condominiums and repair work, apply generally to their owners Any ownership costs are below the line expenses, subject to the 2 percent floor.

Services like preparation of a tax return only arising because of death or a trust or estate, to prepare Form 1041 or Form 706, certainly are above the line. A client wouldn't have to file those forms but for these situations.

Appraisal fees are deductible if they are involved appraising property in a trust or estate. So again, those are some of the reasons that they are allowed.

The big contention in this area after the ***M. J. Knight v. Commissioner*** case and the IRS regulations, is with respect to fiduciary fees. A client pays the trustee for a number of services, including investment advice and duties of being the trustee. Being the trustee is above the line. The investment advice is below the line. The IRS position is just to unbundle the fee.

## Estimated Tax Payments

General rules require a trust to file a declaration and make payments of estimated taxes if the trust is expected to owe $1,000 or more in tax liability. Form 1041-ES is used for the filing, usually on a quarterly basis. A sample voucher appears in Figure 2.1.

**Figure 2.1. Payment voucher used by a trust with quarterly estimated tax payment**

Form **1041-ES** Department of the Treasury Internal Revenue Service | **2016** Payment Voucher **4** | OMB No. 1545-0971

File only if the estate or trust is making a payment of estimated tax. Return this voucher with check or money order payable to **"United States Treasury."** Write the estate's or trust's EIN and "2016 Form 1041-ES" on the check or money order. Do not send cash. Enclose, but do not staple or attach, the payment with this voucher.

Calendar year—Due Jan. 17, 2017

Amount of estimated tax you are paying by check or money order. | Dollars | Cents

Fiscal year filers–enter year ending ________ (month and year)

Type or print:

Employer identification number

Name of estate or trust

Name and title of fiduciary

Address of fiduciary (number, street, and room or suite no.)

City, state, and ZIP code

-5-

Again, if the balance of tax due is less than $1,000, there is no estimation required and no penalty due. If the tax for the prior year was zero and it was a full 12-month year, even if the trust has tax liability for this year, the safe harbor applies.

If excess estimated tax payments are made for a particular year, they can be either refunded to the fiduciary, or applied against the tax liability for the next taxable year, or, by affirmative election, be distributed to the trust's beneficiaries via Form 1041-T:

- For trusts, this election may be made for any tax year; and
- This election to allocate estimated tax payments to the trust's beneficiaries must be made on or before the 65th day following the close of the trust's taxable year.

What about overpayments of estimated tax? Recall the rules of an estate: only in the final year can the estate take an estate's overpayment of estimates and use that Form 1041-T to move it to the beneficiaries. Trusts have a more generous rule. Trusts can do that for any tax year. So, if in any tax year of the trust, estimated taxes have been overpaid, they can certainly be applied to next year. Another option is to ask for a refund.

Or, within 65 days of the end of the trust year, assuming it's a calendar year, the trust has until March 6 of the following year to file Form 1041-T to move the overpaid estimates, or any of estimates—they don't have to be overpaid. The planner can move estimated payments from the trust to the individual by filing Form 1041-T, and now the individual picks up the estimated tax payments as if he or she had made them in the fourth quarter of the filing year.

## Due Dates for Tax Payments

In terms of taxable years, the trust—unlike estates—does not have the option, as a general rule, to select a fiscal year; trusts are calendar year taxpayers. The tax returns for trusts are due on April 15. There is an exception when a Code Sec. 645 election is made, as discussed later. But as a general rule, trusts must be calendar year taxpayers.

Form 1041 must be filed for a trust if it has:

- Any taxable income for the tax year; or
- Gross income of $600 or more regardless of taxable income; or
- A nonresident alien beneficiary.

Form 1041 must be filed on the fifteenth day of the fourth month following the end of the trust's taxable year.

A trust can obtain an automatic five-and-one-half-month extension of time to file Form 1041 by making a timely filing of Form 7004 (for 2016 and 2017 returns), i.e., filing Form 7004 on or before the due date of Form 1041.

When does a trust have to file a tax return? Again, notice how the rule is somewhat different than the rule for an estate. A trust has to file Form 1041 if it has any taxable income during the tax year. Although an estate requires $600 to file, if a trust that has *gross income* of $600 or more—even if it has no taxable income—has to file a return. So, again, the trusts have to do a bit more filing than estates.

Like an estate, if a trust has a nonresident alien beneficiary, it has to file a return. Like an estate, the Form 1041 for the trust is due three-and-a-half months after the end of its year, and because most are calendar year trusts, normally April 15 is going to be the required filing date.

Once again, there is an extension opportunity. That Form 7004 for estate filing extensions is the same form for trust extensions. There are coding differences. A practitioner codes an estate a little bit differently than a trust. The differences are all listed on the form. But the trust also gets that same five-and-a-half-month extension now. For a calendar year trust that would normally be due April 15, and the trust can get an extension until September 30 to file that return.

Practitioners benefit because a fiduciary entity that owns interests and partnerships or S corporations may not be getting an extended partnership or S corporation Schedule K-1 until the middle of September. So now the schedule allows at least have a little bit of breathing room for that two-week period between September 15 and September 30. Another extended tax season is awaiting the extended tax season—October 15—to get the extensions for Form 1040 done. But the IRS tried to stagger the dates to make it a bit less painful.

## Tax Rates for Trusts

The income tax rates for ordinary income of estates and trusts are extremely compressed. In terms of tax rates, as mentioned earlier, estates and trusts are handled in the same way, and at about a $12,500 threshold, tax is imposed at the highest rates for all the taxes—regular tax, tax on long-term gains and qualified dividends, tax on net investment income tax, etc. That number is indexed for inflation every year for trusts and estates, but the indexing went up $100 dollars from 2016 to 2017, so no major or significant adjustments have occurred.

Because income tax and estate/trust taxation may be in flux in 2017, the advice here is not to pay any tax or incur any tax liability that might be repealed. At least clients should get a little time to see what happens to tax law. And if a particular tax doesn't get repealed, clients would have paid it anyway. If it does get repealed, clients didn't pay it when they shouldn't have. So, everyone should see where all the legislation discussion is headed as Congress goes forward.

## Qualified Revocable Trusts

**What Is a QRT?** A qualified revocable trust (QRT) is a living trust, a revocable trust that the person establishes during his or her lifetime. When the person dies, the revocable living trust becomes a qualified revocable trust (QRT) for which an election can be made under Code Sec. 645. The heirs are allowed to treat that trust as if it were an estate for several years, which is preferable because estates under the tax code get a little bit better deal than trusts. Estates don't have to file estimated tax returns for two years, whereas trusts have to file them right away.

**QRT Election.** The QRT election must be made on Form 8855, *Election to Treat a Qualified Revocable Trust as Part of an Estate,* not later than the due date for filing the income tax return for the first tax year of the combined electing trust and related estate, if there is an executor, or of the first taxable year of the electing trust, if there is no executor. The election is irrevocable. The trustee of the trust signs the form and the executor of the estate signs the form. This election must be filed for the estate not later than the due date for the estate's income tax return. The estate's executor or personal representative is the responsible party. If there is no executor, then the trustee becomes the responsible party.

Once the election is made, the trust will be treated as part of and taxed as part of the estate for all tax years of the estate which end after the date of death of the decedent and before the date that is the later of two years after the date of the decedent's death, or the date that is six months after the date of the final determination of the estate tax liability (the "election period").

When a Section 645 election is made for a QRT, the trustee is *not* required to file Form 1041 for the short taxable year of the QRT beginning with the decedent's date of death and ending December 31 of that year. How long is this wonderful opportunity available? It's the later of two years after the person dies or when the estate tax proceeding is concluded. Now, in many cases there won't be any estate tax proceeding. There is no Form 706 to file if the client has less than $5.49 million in assets and is not married.

There's no reason to file the 706 when the assets are under the threshold and the person is single, but the trust will not get the benefit of portability. Two years from date of death is the duration of the qualified revocable trust election. If the estate does exceed $5.49 million in assets and Form 706 is filed, the trust may yet be concluded within two years. The later of two years and the conclusion is when this election period is over.

¶208

Once the Section 645 election has been made, an electing trust may select a fiscal year rather than a calendar year. The electing trust may claim a $600 annual exemption, be entitled to deduct up to $25,000 in real estate passive losses, and may deduct amounts paid or permanently set aside for charity.

The electing trust may hold S corporation stock in accordance with the broader rules allowing estates generally, but not all trusts, to be S corporation shareholders. An electing trust will be treated as a trust and not as an estate for purposes of the required minimum distribution (RMD) rules, such as those applicable to traditional IRAs. Once the QRT election is made, only one Form 1041 need be filed, rather than separate returns for the trust and the estate.

The executor of the related estate is responsible for filing Form 1041 for the estate and all electing trusts. Can Form 1041-T be filed to pay the beneficiaries tax out of the trust? No, the fiduciary has to show the estimated payments moving to the beneficiaries.

That should reduce beneficiaries' tax liability, but at the end of the day, if they owe tax, it can't be paid that from the trust. The beneficiaries need to be the actual payors; otherwise, there will be a big disconnection between Forms 1041 and 1040.

When the election period terminates, the combined estate and QRT are deemed to distribute all of their assets to a new trust.

## STUDY QUESTION

---

**4.** Which of the following statements regarding the election to treat a qualified revocable trust as part of the decedent's estate is correct?

  **a.** Once the election is made, the trust must apply calendar year reporting requirements.

  **b.** An electing trust may claim a $1,000 annual exemption and be entitled to deduct up to $15,000 in real estate passive losses.

  **c.** The electing trust may hold S corporation stock.

  **d.** Once a qualified revocable trust is made, separate returns for the trust and the estate are still required.

---

# ¶ 209 FUNDAMENTAL TRUST ACCOUNTING CONCEPTS

## Trust Accounting Income

Trust accounting income is an accounting concept that determines how much the trustee may or may not distribute to the income beneficiaries. It's not just a tax law concept, it is not the same thing as taxable income. Trust accounting income encompasses all the different types of income that a trust might receive: interest—both taxable and tax-exempt—dividends, rent, distributions from S corporations, and distributions from rental properties. Distributions from other trusts and estates, business income, everything considered to be income, with the exception of capital gain, are included. Capital gain is not part of trust accounting income; capital gain is part of trust accounting principal.

To summarize, generally:

- Trust accounting items include taxable interest, ordinary dividends, rental income, business (Schedule C) or partnership (Schedule E) income, and tax-exempt interest;
- Capital gains are not included in trust accounting income; and
- Trust accounting principal items include the proceeds of the sale or exchange of an item of trust principal that is capital gain property.

## Distributable Net Income

Distributable net income (DNI) is a tax concept used to ensure that an estate or trust acts as a conduit vehicle and avoids double taxation.

**Purposes of DNI.** The purposes of DNI include:

- To establish the maximum income distribution deduction that may be claimed by a trust or an estate;
- To establish the maximum amount of the entity's annual income taxable to the beneficiaries; and
- To determine the character of the items of income taxable to the beneficiaries.

   **EXAMPLE:** If a client's trust has DNI of $22,000 and the fiduciary doesn't distribute any of it, the trust pays tax on $22,000. If the trust distributes all of it to the beneficiaries, it deducts $22,000, and the beneficiaries pick up $22,000 of income. Or maybe the estate or the trust retains $10,000 and distributes $12,000. Now, the trust pays tax on $10,000 and the beneficiary pays tax on $12,000.

DNI refers to taxable income, plus tax-exempt interest, reduced by allocable expenses.

DNI *may* include capital gains when the trust instrument requires (or permits) the inclusion of capital gains in income and the distribution of capital gains to beneficiaries. Capital gains *are* included in DNI in the year of termination of an estate or trust. It also has a consistent character; DNI keeps the character of the asset from the entity to the beneficiary as the same. DNI constitutes the prorated distribution of income. If the income is all ordinary interest, then any distribution to the beneficiary is going to be all ordinary interest. If it's all qualified dividend, then the beneficiary gets all qualified dividend. If it's a mixture of different categories of income, then the fiduciary determines what percentage of each category to distribute to a beneficiary and that's how the beneficiary reports the income—it might be 10 percent long-term gain, 10 percent qualified dividend, 10 percent rental income, and so on, reported on Form 1041.

As a general rule, DNI does not include capital gains, but it might. What does the entity's document say about trust accounting principal? If the operative document—will, trust, whatever—says that principal can be distributed to beneficiaries, then the principal can be included in DNI. If the document says it must be distributed to beneficiaries, principal becomes part of DNI; otherwise, not.

The basic tax concept of trusts and estates is that distributions from an entity to a beneficiary carry out DNI to that beneficiary to the extent of the entity's DNI.

**Exceptions.** Specific bequests of property or specific bequests of a sum of money payable in not more than three installments do not carry out DNI. Also, payments of required bequests to charities do not carry out DNI. If beneficiaries receive distributions in excess of the entity's DNI for the taxable year, the balance of any distribution is treated as a nontaxable principal payment to the beneficiary.

**EXAMPLE:** A distribution beyond the DNI constitutes principal—a nontaxable principal distribution. So, Geraldine Chapham's trust got $20,000 of income, and her trustee is authorized in discretion to pay Geraldine's daughter Trisha whatever the daughter needs. Trisha needs $100,000, so the trustee gives her $100,000: $20,000 is income, $80,000 is principal. The trust gets a deduction for $20,000, Trisha pays income tax on $20,000, and the other $80,000 is a principal distribution, neither deductible by the entity nor taxable to the beneficiary.

## Revision of the Definition of "Income" of Trusts

IRS regulations have dramatically revised the definition of trust income and created situations when capital gains of a trust may be included in DNI.

The "prudent investor rule" requires a trustee to invest for total return and to allocate items of principal to income, or vice versa, to treat income and remainder beneficiaries more equitably.

Increasingly popular and widespread state legislation would allow a trustee to pay a unitrust amount (on a "total return trust" concept) to the income beneficiary to satisfy that beneficiary's right to trust income. The trustees have to be fair to all parties. The way a fiduciary can make that work is to allow capital gain to be distributed and allow principal to be distributed. So, today's rules and regulations have created tools like a total return trust, a trust that states that whatever amount is in the trust, beneficiaries are allowed 3, 4, or 5 percent payout per year.

If a trust's assets are $1 million and the beneficiary gets 5 percent annually, he or she is going to get $50,000. How does the fiduciary characterize that for trust accounting purposes? If it's ordinary income, fine. If it's capital gain, also fine. And if it's principal beyond any income, also fine. So, that $50,000 may be a blend of ordinary income, qualified dividend, or long-term and regular old principal to get the $50,000 to distribute.

The IRS has recognized all of that is permissible. The regulations allow acceptance of these distributions as not violating the rules that say trust accounting income is over on one side, trust accounting principal is on the other side, and never the two should meet. The law has been liberalized to allow a greater allowance of more generous and more appropriate distributions to achieve the goal of the person that establishes these trusts. In essence, the regulations allow the trust to include capital gains in trust accounting income. Reg. 1.643(b)-1 provides if local law permits a different allocation, trust provisions following that law will be respected for tax purposes if local law provides for a reasonable apportionment between the income and remainder beneficiaries of the total return of the trust for the year.

If the document is silent on this issue, state law may be applied. Most state laws now have something called a "power to adjust" that allows the distribution of capital gain if the trustee or executor has appropriate discretion to distribute principal. A safe harbor for a reasonable apportionment is stated to be a state law providing for a unitrust amount between 3 percent and 5 percent of the annual fair market value of the trust.

Further, Regulation 1.643(a)-3(b) allows the trustee to include realized capital gains in trust accounting income, and whereas Reg. 1.643(a)-3(a) states the traditional rule that ordinarily capital gain will be excluded from DNI, Reg. 1.643(a)-3(b) addresses capital gains under *Prudent Investor Act* practices by providing that capital gains may be *included* in DNI to the extent they are allocated to income, or if they are allocated to corpus.

## Taxable Income of the Trust

As a general rule, the taxable income of a trust or an estate is calculated in the same manner as that of an individual. The most important difference between an individual return and a fiduciary return is that the fiduciary return permits a distribution deduction for amounts of income distributed to beneficiaries. It is discussed next.

# ¶ 210 INCOME REPORTABLE BY FIDUCIARIES

## Interest

Using a current Form 1041, a practitioner first considers interest income. The same basic rules apply to trusts and estates as to an individual. They receive taxable interest income, they pay tax on it. Tax-exempt interest is also to be reported and accounted for but it's not taxable here as it would not be to an individual.

## Dividends

Dividends may be ordinary or qualified. If a dividend is shown as a proper qualified dividend, then it is taxed at the preferred rate of 15 percent (up to $12,500 taxable income) or 20 percent (for more than $12,400 for 2016, $12,500 for 2017), not the 39.6 maximum percent rate for ordinary income. So, it's not particularly generous, but the distinction between qualified and ordinary dividends certainly applies just as it would on the individual level.

An allocation must be made between the beneficiary's allocable share of qualified dividends and the trust or estate's allocable share of such dividends. For a beneficiary who falls in the 39.6 percent bracket and for 20 percent capital gain qualified dividends, long-term capital gain qualified dividend rules apply: an individual filing single, has a $418,400 threshold. For married filing jointly taxpayers, it's $470,700. Compared to $12,500, distributions sound better. For the 3.8 percent net investment income tax, singles with $200,000 adjusted gross income (AGI) or married filing jointly with $250,000 AGI are compared to $12,500. This is where there is pressure to make more distributions than not.

## Business Income

A trust or estate could have business income if managing the business of a decedent or it's running the business that's held in a trust. The fiduciary files a Schedule C from the 1040 series, or CEZ, whichever is appropriate. The entity is not required to pay self-employment tax and can make whatever elections and deductions that apply. The fiduciary is not bound by whatever the beneficiary, rather the grantor of the trust or the decedent, might have done. So, the fiduciary has the opportunity to take the number from Schedule C and add it to income on Form 1041.

## Capital Gains and Losses of a Business

For capital gains and losses of a business, the same concepts apply as for individuals: net short-term gains and losses, then net long-term gains and losses. Capital losses can offset capital gain. Excess capital loss above capital gains—the annual net capital loss deduction limitation of up to $3,000—is used to offset ordinary income, and any excess capital loss over and above that carries forward indefinitely. And so as long as the trust or estate is operative, any capital loss can be carried forward.

Schedule D of Form 1041 is used along with Form 8949, *Sales and Other Dispositions of Capital Assets*. The fiduciary must indicate on Form 1041 whether the capital gain or loss is to be allocated to the beneficiary or to the fiduciary. This will affect both DNI and the determination of whether the beneficiary or the entity will ultimately report the gain or loss.

## Income Tax Basis

Different income tax basis rules may be applicable to estate and trust situations:

- The decedent's estate receives a fair market value basis at the decedent's date of death (or alternate valuation date, if properly elected) Code Sec. 1014, and a deemed long-term holding period (Code Sec. 1223 (11)), regardless of how long an asset was actually held by the decedent;

- A trust that is a testamentary trust may receive a stepped-up basis from the decedent's death tax value; and

- An *inter vivos* trust that was funded prior to the decedent's death, that has continued thereafter, and the corpus of which was not included in the decedent's taxable estate, takes a carryover basis from the grantor-donor.

## Long-Term Gains

Net long-term capital gains realized by a trust or estate are taxed generally at the rate of 15 percent for 2016 and 2017, but a 20 percent tax rate applies when the entity's taxable income exceeds $12,400 for 2016, $12,500 for 2017. The rates apply for sales and other dispositions.

Capital gains are net investment income for purposes of the net investment income tax and will bear an additional 3.8 percent tax if the undistributed taxable income of the entity exceeds $12,400 for 2016, $12,500 for 2017. A trust or estate's net capital losses and unused loss carryforwards may not be passed through to the beneficiaries of an estate or trust, except in the final year of the entity's existence. So the losses terminate when the trust or estates terminates, and are only passed through in that final year.

The fiduciary shows on the Form 1041 Schedule D whether the capital gain, or for the final year the loss, is being allocated to the entity or to the beneficiary. One column on Part 3 of Schedule D is labeled Beneficiary and another column labeled Estate or Trust. The entry there will affect the rest of the return. Gain attributed to the beneficiary means the gain will be transferred to the beneficiary versus the entity. Different rules may apply. A decedent's estate gets the fair market value at date of death as its basis with that automatic long-term holding period, regardless of how long the property was held. If it's a trust and if it's a trust created at death, again, it's a decedent item with a basis equal to the fair market value at death.

But if the trust was created during a client's lifetime by a transfer from a grantor to a trust, that's a carryover basis. So, whatever the grantor's basis happened to be, that becomes the basis to the trust. So, the grantor might have paid $1,000 for something worth $25,000 when it was placed in the trust, and then 20 years later it's worth $100,000. The basis is still $1,000, whatever the grantor paid for it and then transferred it to the trust. Different basis rules can be applicable in a planning situation.

## Rents, Royalties, Partnerships, and Income from Other Estates and Trusts

The same general rules about at-risk rules and passive activity rules apply for trusts and estates as for individuals. Code Sec. 469 discusses passive activities, and Code Sec. 465 describes at-risk rules as they apply in the context of trusts and estates.

If an estate or trust has income derived from rents, royalties, partnerships, S corporations, and other estates and trusts, a completed Schedule E of Form 1040 is attached to Form 1041, reporting the net aggregate gain or loss.

¶210

Material participation by trusts is controversial. The IRS position is that the only way to call participation materially active is if only the fiduciary's participation is measured.

The taxpayer view is broader. If the fiduciary hires people in the course of managing an activity and that sum of all those people working is active versus passive, it should be active and the entity shouldn't be saddled with passive losses, and the income should not be considered passive income.

Taxpayers have won two cases on this argument, a 2003 case in a District Court in Texas, the *Mattie Carter Trust* case, and a 2014 U.S. Tax Court case, the *Frank Aragona Trust* case. In both of those cases, the courts found that a trust can materially participate as a trust and it may have situations in which the trust income is active and the losses are not passive.

The IRS still doesn't accept these positions, maintaining that the trust or estate is only the fiduciary. The IRS doesn't accept these positions, maintaining that only the activity of the fiduciary and not any employees or helpers should be tested as to material participation. More litigation in this area is likely, as the positions of taxpayers and the IRS remain significantly controversial. The issue is important because the entity could have a significant passive loss that can't be deducted against anything else, but if the loss turns out to be an active loss, it can offset the entity's other income.

Thus, unused fiduciary passive activity losses at the termination of the trust or estate lose their carryover potential and are not deductible by the beneficiaries. However, the benefit of the fiduciary's passive activity losses is not completely eliminated, because beneficiaries to whom a passive activity item is distributed may increase their basis in the activity by any unused (by the fiduciary) passive activity loss.

## Planning for Completion of Form 1041

**Depreciation.** There's a special rule that involves depreciation and depletion. Deductions for depreciation and depletion can be passed from the entity to the beneficiary during the operation of the entity. So, unlike other losses that can only get passed through in the final year, deductions for depletion and depreciation can be passed to beneficiaries as the entity is ongoing. The depreciation deduction is to be allocated between the fiduciary and the beneficiaries on the basis of the income allocated to each.

If the fiduciary is required to maintain a reserve for depreciation by the governing instrument or by local law, then the fiduciary receives the depreciation deduction to the extent of the reserve. Then any excess above the reserve can be distributed.

A Code Sec. 179 deduction for the acquisition of equipment, etc., cannot be claimed by trusts and estates, but they can use bonus depreciation. So, bonus depreciation is allowed. Section 179 depreciation not allowed for trusts and estates.

**Partnership or S Corporation Schedule K-1 Income.** When a trust owns an interest in a passthrough entity, such as a partnership or an S corporation, the trust must report its share of the entity's taxable income each year, regardless of how much the entity distributes to the trust. The entity may:

- Distribute more than enough for the trustee to pay its tax on the entity's taxable income;
- Distribute an amount less than the trust's tax on the entity's taxable income; or
- Distribute nothing.

The partnership delivers a Schedule K-1 to the trust. What does the trust do with that K-1?

¶210

Well, the question becomes does the K-1 have a check accompanying it? There are three possibilities. The first situation is that no check is received. The fiduciary has $100,000 of income from the partnership allocated to the trust. The partnership pays the trust nothing. The partnership letter says that the partnership reinvested all the money and has nothing to pay the trust. The trust's share of the income is $100,000.

In that case, the rules say that is principal to the trust. The trust does not distribute any income to its beneficiaries. The trust does not get an income distribution deduction, and the trust must pay the tax on $100,000. So, the trust gets no money, it still has to pay the income tax, and the trust doesn't get to lay off the income tax liability on the beneficiary. That's one problem.

The second situation is more beneficial. The trust receives a Schedule K-1 listing $100,000 of income, and a check for $100,000 is received. The trust includes $100,000 in income. If the trust document dictates to pay all the income to the beneficiary, the fiduciary does so. The trust gets a deduction, the beneficiary pays tax on $100,000.

Those are the two "easy" situations, either beneficiary pays nothing, trust pays all or trust receives it, deducts it, and the beneficiary pays the tax.

The middle ground is the hardest. The middle ground is when the trust receives some money from the partnership, but not everything that's on the Schedule K-1. So, now what happens? If the trust receives some money, it's income, it's supposed to distribute that to the beneficiary. A circular calculation happens. And this issue was studied by all kinds of smart people for a number of years, and about 10 years ago, the decision was made that an algebraic calculation is the proper result, the gist of which is:

When the passthrough entity distributes an amount equal to or greater than its taxable income, the trust or estate's tax attributable to the pass through entity's taxable income is zero, because the payments to the income beneficiary reduce the trust or estate's taxable income to zero.

This discussion does not solve the calculation; good software can do that. The fiduciary just needs awareness of the three circumstances for paying the income taxes of a passthrough.

## Farm Income

If the trust or estate has interest in a farm, the fiduciary completes Schedule F and attaches it to Form 1041. Does the farm have positive income? Great. Does the farm have a loss? The loss carries forward. There are no self-employment issues on farm income reported by an estate or trust. The fiduciary is not bound by tax elections made by the previous farm owner and is entitled to make new elections.

## Ordinary Gain or Loss

A trust or an estate reports the net ordinary gain or loss arising from the sale or exchange of property (other than capital assets) used in a trade or business and from condemnations and other involuntary conversions other than those arising from casualty or theft. A Form 4797, *Sales of Business Property,* is used to report the gain or loss and is attached to the Form 1041.

## Other Income

Other income could be compensation beyond the date of death. It could be—significantly—a distribution from a retirement plan. The qualified plan such as an IRA or 401(k) makes a distribution to a trust or to an estate. The distribution is other income and requires reporting on the Form 1041.

¶210

If the fiduciary distributes the income to the beneficiary, the beneficiary pays the tax, and the entity gets a deduction. If the entity doesn't distribute it, the entity pays the tax. Retirement plan benefits are ordinary income, and the fiduciary usually must decide what party is responsible for the tax.

# ¶ 211  DEDUCTIONS AVAILABLE TO FIDUCIARIES

## General Rules

Some general rules apply for deductions. The trust agreement or estate plan may state that certain deductions are to be taken from the principal and certain others from the income. A fiduciary does that when the client elects to charge half of the legal fee or fiduciary fee to principal, half to income. That's a trust accounting issue. That has nothing to do with taxation.

If the item is deductible, the fiduciary should take it all as a deduction whether it's allocable to principal or income. That's an action for accounting purposes, not for income tax purposes.

If tax-exempt income is involved, a "disallowance ratio" calls for allocating tax-exempt income to a variety of otherwise allowable deductions, and reducing those deductions. A schedule to the Form 1041 shows that has been done.

A trust or an estate may not claim a standard deduction. Instead, it may claim an exemption:

- $600 for an estate;
- $300 for a simple trust; and
- $100 for a complex trust.

As a general rule, deductions for expenditures that may be applicable to both a decedent's estate tax return (Form 706) and the income tax return of a decedent's estate or trust created under a decedent's will (such as fiduciary and professional fees) may be claimed only once, as the fiduciary chooses.

Funeral expenses may not be deducted on Form 1041; they may only be claimed on Form 706. Medical expenses can only be claimed on Form 706 or on the decedent's final Form 1040, not on the Form 1041.

## STUDY QUESTION

---

**5.** Which of the following identifies the exemption amount for complex trusts?

   **a.** $100

   **b.** $300

   **c.** $600

   **d.** $3,000

---

## Deductible Debts

An exception to the general rule is available for some items that constitute deductible debts of a decedent on Form 706 and also constitute deductible expenses on Form 1041 when paid by the fiduciary after the decedent's death. These items (such as business expenses, interest expenses, state income taxes, and real estate taxes owed at death and paid after death) are properly claimed as "double deductions."

## Unused Income Tax Deductions

A decedent's unused income tax deductions at the time of death do not carry forward to the fiduciary income tax return of the decedent's estate.

However, estates and trusts enjoy a "special" deduction known as the income distribution deduction.

## Allocation of Deductions

A deduction that is directly attributable to a category of income is where it is deducted.

> **EXAMPLE:** A trust or estate owns a rental property that generates $100,000 of rental income. The property has expenses against that income—management fees, insurance, repairs, and maintenance—all the items shown on a Schedule E.

> All of those deductions must go against the property's rental income. But the property management person has legal fees, accounting fees, and fiduciary fees. Where are those claimed? To what category of income does the fiduciary allocate those? The opportunity under the law says the fiduciary can allocate those expenses to any category of income. Although the client has an interest income tax rate of 39.6 percent, he has a qualified dividends tax rate of 15 percent or 20 percent. So the fiduciary wants to allocate as much of those legal, accounting and fiduciary expenses to the interest income and possibly wipe it out, and leaving alone the 15 percent qualified dividend.

> Such an allocation is allowed. The tax code and Regulation 1.6529(b) permit the choice when expenses are not attributable to a specific class of income. Once the fiduciary has appropriately allocated everything to the designated categories, expenses such as legal, accounting, and fiduciary fees can be allocated to whichever category of income is preferred.

# ¶ 212  SPECIFIC ITEMS OF DEDUCTION

## Interest Payments

Form 1041 lists specific items of deduction and categories of expense. Can a trust or estate claim interest paid as a deduction? It depends:

- Personal interest is nondeductible;
- Interest paid as qualified residence interest is deductible; and
- Interest payments made arising from federal or state tax deficiencies are nondeductible.

If the trust or estate is the owner of a person's residence, the Form 1041 can claim that interest expense home equity line, or a purchase of a home. However, the IRS is not generally generous in that situation. Interest payments incurred for underpayments of tax for deficiencies, both at the federal and state levels, are nondeductible.

## Tax Payments and Fees

However, many types of tax and fees are deductible on Form 1041, lines 10 through 21:

- State and local income, real estate taxes, and personal property taxes are deductible with respect to income earned and property owned by a trust or an estate, whereas state inheritance taxes and state estate and gift taxes are not;
- Fiduciary fees may be deducted if they are reasonable, and to the extent such fees are allocable to tax-exempt income, the deduction must be reduced proportionately; and

- If the entity has no tax-exempt income, fiduciary fees (whether executor or trustee) are deductible in full. If a percentage of the income is tax exempt, that percentage of the fiduciary fee will be nondeductible.

Recall that the fiduciary chooses whether to list the fiduciary fee on the Form 1041 or the Form 706. Normally if the entity doesn't have a Form 706 to file, the decision is simple. If Form 706 is required, then the decision depends on where the entity derives the most benefit. Attorney, accountant, and return preparer fees may *not* be deducted on Form 1041 if they were already claimed as deductible on Form 706.

The tax rate used for the Form 706 is a flat 40 percent rate. The tax rate on Form 1041 could be lower or higher, depending upon the client's tax rate—say, 39.6 percent plus the net investment income tax, or just 15 percent or 20 percent (on capital gains or dividends) plus the net investment income tax. So, again, these are decisions that have to be made.

If the fiduciary files both Forms 706 and 1041, a statement should be attached to Form 1041 claiming or showing where deductions are claimed, either on the 706 or the 1041. These and other administration expenses are noted on a waiver affirming that amounts being deducted on Form 1041 were not claimed on Form 706. There cannot be double-dipping.

## Charitable Deductions

Trusts and estates may claim an unlimited charitable deduction against their gross income. The governing instrument (will or trust agreement) must provide specifically for the charitable contribution in order for the deduction to be available. The governing instrument must provide for the gift to charity specifically. When a decedent dies and an heir donates the decedent's clothes and furniture to charity, if the decedent's will or trust doesn't say to do so as a bequest, the entity does not receive a Form 1041 deduction. Thus, if the fiduciary makes a voluntary payment to a charitable organization, such payment is not deductible. Also, what is given to charity has to be income. If the gift to the charity is property, the entity is not going to get a deduction anyway. So, for 1041 purposes, the deduction is unlimited, but it must come from income and the governing instrument must require it. The worth of the donation must also be substantiated under the IRS rules governing the contribution.

The will or trust agreement must state terms to actually pay it to charity or set it aside for charity. If the fiduciary is allowed to do that, then the entity can claim the appropriate deduction. The charitable deduction is listed on Schedule A of Form 1041. A legitimate deduction to charity is not claimed on a Schedule K-1; a K-1 is not given to a charity reporting a charitable contribution.

Schedule A's charitable contribution deduction then moves to line 13 on the first page of the Form 1041 and reduces the entity's taxable income. Simply giving charities Schedule K-1s doesn't reduce the taxable income of the trust or the estate.

> **PLANNING POINTER:** Payments to qualified charities made after the close of the current taxable year (Year 1) and before the end of the following taxable year (Year 2) may be treated as made in Year 1.

## STUDY QUESTION

---

**6.** Which of the following identifies the maximum amount of charitable donations that can be deducted against gross income for a trust or estate?

    **a.** $150,000

    **b.** $12,400

    **c.** $1,000

    **d.** Unlimited

---

## Other Deductions Not Subject to the 2 Percent Floor

This section of Form 1041 has been the subject of substantial controversy in the courts. General administration expenses, such as appraisal fees, probate fees, fiduciary bonds, judicially required accountings, and asset protection and distribution fees, all fall within these rules and are deductible on Line 15a of Form 1041.

What deductions are above the 2 percent line and what deductions are below it?

The big issue with the IRS and courts mentioned earlier arose over investment advisory fees (***M. J. Knight v. Commissioner***). Line 15a is above the line (i.e., not subject to the 2 percent floor), and 15c (for miscellaneous itemized deductions) is below the line. "Above the line" means deducted without regard to the 2 percent floor; "below the line" means deduct after applying the 2 percent floor of adjusted gross income. And if it is on line 15c, not only is the 2 percent haircut applied, but whatever is left is a tax preference for alternative minimum tax (AMT) purposes.

Naturally, the fiduciary tries to avoid the necessity of listing deductions on line 15c, and, of course, the government is trying to force deductions onto line 15C. So, the government concedes that deductions that are only involved with trusts and estates belong on 15a. Thus, costs on a fiduciary return for items such as appraisals, fiduciary bonds, probate and judicial accounting fees only arise because someone died or an executor or trustee must do certain reporting as part of estate or trust administration or compliance obligation. Those are all above the line deductions. However, the Supreme Court in ***Knight*** ruled that expenses "commonly" incurred by individuals are subject to the 2 percent of an estate or trust's AGI floor:

* Ownership costs;
* Investment advisory fees; and
* Trustee fees must be "unbundled."

Certain costs, if they're costs of owning property such as monthly fees for condominiums and repair work, are below the line expenses, subject to the 2 percent floor. Costs of expenses like tax preparation—if it's a tax return only arising because of death or a trust or estate such as Form 1041 or Form 706—are certainly above the line. The fiduciary wouldn't have to file those but for these situations. Appraisal fees are deductible if they are involved appraising property in a trust or estate. So again, those are some of the reasons that they allow.

The remaining issue after the ***Knight*** case and the IRS regulations concerns fiduciary fees. A client pays the trustee for both investment advice and actions taken for the trustee. Being the trustee is above the line. The investment advice is below the line. The IRS holds that practitioners must unbundle the feeds, but few fiduciaries maintain strict lines between the two types of service. Litigation will ensue.

**¶212**

## Income Distribution Deduction

The income distribution deduction is the unique feature of fiduciary income taxation. It permits the fiduciary to be treated as a separate taxable entity with passthrough characteristics:

- Income is received by the fiduciary entity;
- The entity deducts the income distributed to its beneficiaries;
- The beneficiaries in turn report the income distributions on their own tax returns; and
- This system prevents double taxation of the income received by the estate or trust.

Schedule B of the 1041 walks the filer through exactly how to calculate the income distribution deduction. And then that carries out the DNI to the beneficiary. The income distribution deduction also appears on the Schedule K-1 for the beneficiaries. Whatever the character is to the entity becomes the character of income to the beneficiary.

**Simple Trust.** For a simple trust, even if the fiduciary doesn't pay the beneficiary, the income nevertheless must be reported. So a simple trust gives a Schedule K-1 to the beneficiary reporting all the income, and the entity deducts it. Even if the trust or estate didn't pay anything to the beneficiary this year, a K-1 is still required. The fiduciary must claim the deduction on Form 1041 and pick up the income on the individual's Form 1040.

**Complex Trust.** All trusts not classified as simple trusts or grantor trusts are classified as complex trusts. The income distribution deduction available for complex trusts is equal to the sum of the income required to be distributed currently for the taxable year plus any other amounts of income properly paid, credited, or required to be distributed for such taxable year.

If it's a complex trust, as mentioned earlier, the fiduciary has choices of whether to distribute or not distribute, and where the resulting tax is paid. Here, planners can take advantage of what's called the 65-day rule. The fiduciary checks a box on the Form 1041 for a Code Sec. 663(d) election. Using this election, the fiduciary distributes money to the beneficiaries after the end of the year. So, if an entity uses a calendar year, the fiduciary make a distribution the first day of March. The beneficiary now has income for the prior tax year, and the entity gets a deduction for the prior tax year. If a fiduciary makes this election in 2017, the beneficiary would have 2016 income, and the entity gets a 2016 deduction.

> **PLANNING POINTER:** This advantage for the entity's income makes sense because of the entity's $12,500 threshold for paying the highest tax rates. Most beneficiaries will be in a preferable situation for tax brackets.

# ¶ 213 ESTATE TAX DEDUCTION

If the estate or trust includes an item of income in respect of a decedent (IRD) in its gross income that was also included in the decedent's estate for estate tax purposes, the estate or trust may deduct the portion of the estate tax attributable to the inclusion of the item of IRD in the decedent's estate. This double-tax situation is not as common as in the past, except for very large estates subject to estate tax when the distribution to the estate or to beneficiaries incurs income tax.

> **EXAMPLE:** Wilfred Halverston has a $20 million estate, with a $3 million traditional IRA as part of the total estate. His Form 706 lists the asset, so his beneficiary, Gerry, must pay death tax on that.

The IRD deduction is not subject to the 2 percent of AGI floor on miscellaneous itemized deductions.

Recall the exemptions: $600 for an estate, $300 for a simple trust, and $100 for a complex trust. In the final year the exemption is not used because all of the entity's assets are passed through.

# ¶ 214 TAX CALCULATIONS, CREDITS, AND PAYMENTS

Taxable income is handled for a trust or estate just as for individuals. Tax credits may be available. If the entity is subject to the net investment income tax, Form 8960, *Net Investment Income Tax—Individuals, Estates, and Trusts,* must be attached.

The fiduciary must determine whether any specific recapture taxes are due. Also, the trust or estate may be liable for household employment taxes, such as for home health aides and gardeners, reported on Schedule H. All the items that apply to Form 1040 thinking also apply to Form 1041 thinking.

Form 1041 returns are filed with the IRS service center in either Cincinnati, Ohio, or Ogden, Utah, depending on where the trustee is located. Fiduciaries submitting returns for beneficiaries should use the office to which the trustee files the forms. The instructions describe filing procedures.

# ¶ 215 DISTRIBUTIONS IN THE YEAR OF TERMINATION

## Passthrough Deductions

Recall that except for depreciation and depletion, deductions or losses never pass through to a beneficiary, except in the final year of the entity. For income tax purposes, an entity in its year of termination distributes to its beneficiaries a combination of:

- Current income;
- Previously undistributed income; and
- All remaining principal.

In that year, all of the entity's items of income and deduction pass directly to the beneficiaries and must be included on their respective income tax returns. How can the fiduciary most benefit the client in this situation? All those losses that were stuck within the entity now can move to the beneficiaries, and they can use them for as long as they remain alive, including:

- Net operating loss (NOL) carryovers;
- Capital loss carryovers; and
- Excess deductions for expenses.

If the entity has legal, accounting, or fiduciary fees all along that exceed its income, the fiduciary can't deduct them. They're not net operating losses. And the entity can't carry those forward. It's a mistake, if avoidable, to have big expenses when the entity can't deduct them. If the estate or trust has enough income, it's preferable to write them off against the income each tax period. But if the entity doesn't have a lot of income and can hold off on some expenses until the year of termination, those excess deductions can move from the entity to the beneficiary. Plus, the carryforward period for capital losses is unlimited.

But the beneficiary has to itemize deductions in that year as miscellaneous itemized deductions to the beneficiary, subject to the 2 percent floor. So again, there is another layer of complexity and not the most generous situation. But if the entity has multiple beneficiaries, based on their shares, they each get a share of that passthrough.

The items passed through to the beneficiaries in the year of termination are allocated to them based on their respective shares of the property of the trust or estate distributed to them that year.

## Unused Deductions

Some deductions are not usable:

- There is no personal exemption in the last year; and
- Excess charitable deductions are lost in the entity.

So, again, the fiduciary must exercise care in maximizing what can be passed through to the beneficiaries. But the good news is that NOLs and capital loss carry-overs, can go on for the duration of the NOL and for a lifetime—the capital loss carryover until it's used and the excess deductions in the year of termination.

# ¶ 216 TRUSTS AND ESTATES AND THE ALTERNATIVE MINIMUM TAX

The alternative minimum tax (AMT) rules have been applicable to trusts and estates since January 1, 1987. The rules are similar to those applicable to individuals, modified to take into account situations unique to the fiduciary entities.

The AMT exclusion is now indexed for inflation: $23,900 for 2016; $24,100 for 2017.

The same items as for individuals, like state and local taxes, are preferences. Certain items like private activity bonds are preferences. Thus, preferences for individuals are also preferences for AMT purposes. Miscellaneous itemized deductions are preferences.

A very small AMT exclusion applies in 2017: $24,100. However, not a lot of AMT applies in trusts or estates making big distributions to the beneficiaries, because the alternative minimum taxable income gets carried through to the beneficiaries. The only time the AMT liability is significant in the trust or the estate is when it has big expenses—the significant expenses subject to that 2 percent floor that wipe out all the income. Those expenses may result in AMT liability to the estate.

When a Schedule B of the 1041 must be completed, the fiduciary must complete Schedule I to show the AMT calculation. In most cases the estate or trust is not going to owe any AMT, but the allocation is required.

# MODULE 1: INDIVIDUAL TAXATION— Chapter 3: When Your Client Dies: Final Form 1040, Post-Death Elections and More

## ¶ 301 WELCOME

This chapter describes actions that the practitioner and clients representative (executor, trustee, or holder of a power of attorney) can take to navigate estate matters and official paperwork when a client passes away, as well as preventive moves a client can make to transfer wealth during his or her lifetime. Topics for executors or trustees include filing a final Form 1040 for the decedent, handling estimated tax payments, and processing and reporting income received after the client's death. The discussion addresses filing Form 706, *United States Estate (and Generation-Skipping Transfer) Tax Return* as well as Form 1041, *U.S. Income Tax Return for Estates and Trusts*. Clients and planners may wish to deal with the lifetime unused estate tax exemption to transfer wealth before death. Finally, the chapter describes a number of options, elections, and opportunities that could result in significant tax saving for the heirs of a deceased person.

## ¶ 302 LEARNING OBJECTIVES

---

Upon completion of this chapter, you will be able to:

- Identify information required to file a decedent's final Form 1040;
- Recognize proper management techniques for handling income in respect of a decedent; and
- Recognize elections to make postmortem to maximize estate or trust funds inherited by a client's beneficiaries.

---

## ¶ 303 INTRODUCTION

Obviously, a client's postdeath situation involves a sad discussion of death and taxes, but what practitioners often find in encountering the estate of a decedent is that planning wasn't always done too well during a person's lifetime. A lot of people leave their planning for the ultimate last minute. And then the last minute occurs before they got their planning done to a large extent. And what practitioners also find is that even if people did plan to distribute their wealth and bequests, a great deal of work still needs to be done once a person has died. A lot of decisions are required that, to be fair, the decedent could not have made prior to his or her death. But the hope was that the client lined up planning opportunities in a way to allow the survivors to have more options to save taxes, to make the correct decisions, and to address interesting and important tax issues.

For 2017 clients and planners can explore the larger exemptions from estate tax, the possibility that tax rates may soon be higher, and the need for flexibility in planning for estate management.

# ¶ 304  FIRST STEPS IN POSTMORTEM FINANCIAL MANAGEMENT

A client's final tax year ends with the date of his or her death. This means that:

- The decedent's tax year ends on that date, and his or her final Form 1040 tax return is due on April 15 of the following year;
- The executor or practitioner should expeditiously apply for a federal tax identification number for the estate using Form SS-4, *Application for Employer Identification Number,* because that number is used to handle income received after death, to inform investment firms and creditors about the death, subsequently complete and file Form 1041, etc.; and
- The practitioner should complete and file Form 56, *Notice Concerning Fiduciary Relationship,* to demonstrate the authority to handle estate and fiduciary matters.

A surviving spouse, executor, or trustee should be reminded that any income received following the decedent's date of death is estate income that will be reported on the first Form 1041, not the decedent's final Form 1040. The practitioner ensures that "constructively received income" prior to and following the death are separate, and all the deductions prior to death also will be reported on the final Form 1040. Deductible expenses that would have been claimed on Schedule A of 1040—medical expenses, interest paid, tax amounts—go on that schedule for the final Form 1040 if paid before the decedent died. The thoughtful client informed his or her finance-handling family member (or tax practitioner) how to access those records.

## Portability of an Unused Exemption

Portability is the opportunity to have a decedent's unused exemption, that $5.49 million exemption that all individuals have for transfer taxes during lifetime to death; if the client hasn't used it during lifetime or at death, it ports to the surviving spouse. If there is no surviving spouse, then there's no portability.

What portability says is if Spouse A leaves everything to Spouse B and the marital deduction says no tax applies at Spouse A's death, Spouse A in that example has not used any of his or her lifetime exemption. Spouse B now has in 2017 up to $10.98 million to work with: his or her own exemption, plus what's ported from the deceased spouse. In 2017 the IRS provided a very favorable revenue procedure for estate management: Revenue Procedure 2017-34. It states that if a married couple is eligible to make a portability election and has not done so, even if the spouse files late, he or she now has until January 2nd of 2018 to file for the exclusion election by filing Form 706.

The other benefit of Rev. Proc. 2017-34 is it says that the estate gets the later of January 2 of 2018 or two years after a person's death to file the portability election. So a person who died within the last two years may file for the exclusion up to two years from date of death. So that is a very favorable determination. People formerly spent $10,000 in user fees to be granted the opportunity to make a late portability election; now the user fee is not necessary if Form 706 is filed within two years.

## STUDY QUESTIONS

1. In general, when a client dies the practitioner should apply for a federal identification number for the estate as soon as possible using which of the following forms?

   a. Form SS-4.
   b. Form 56.
   c. Form 1040.
   d. Form 706.

**2.** Each of the following statements with respect to a decedent's final tax return is correct, *except:*

   **a.** Income through the date of the death should be included in the return.

   **b.** Deductible expenses include state and local income tax but not property taxes.

   **c.** Deductions appropriate through date of death include those that are actually and constructively received.

   **d.** A court appointed executor or representative is responsible for filing the final tax return.

## Content of the Final Form 1040 Tax Return

Even if the decedent passed away early in 2017, his or her final Form 1040 is not due until April 17, 2018, because the usual due date falls on a weekend. If the client passed away early in 2017 or had received an extension to file in October, and did not submit a 2016 return, that, too, must be filed. The fiduciary—tax preparer, surviving spouse, executor, etc.—is responsible for representing the decedent's interest.

**Filing Status.** A joint return may be filed for the decedent's year of death as long as the surviving spouse did not remarry by the end of 2017. If a remarriage occurred, the final Form 1040 must use the married filing separately status. A surviving spouse who remarried in 2017 may be able to file a joint return with the new spouse but certainly not with the deceased spouse.

The final Form 1040 should show the word "deceased" on the top. The signature block should indicate the date of death. The return is filed where the filer lives. For example, if a parent dies in New York but the executor lives in Florida, the return is filed with the IRS Service Center where Florida taxpayers file—that is, where the personal representative files.

**Special Income and Deductions Situations.** Perhaps the client was a shareholder of an S corporation. How does the practitioner report S corporation income in the final year? The interesting answer is there is a choice in that circumstance:

- Taking the full year's income for the S corporation and then allocating that income based on the number of days that the decedent lived. If the decedent died on the 183rd day of the year, then 183 over 365 would be the fraction multiplied against the income for the full year and that's how much income would be reported; or

- Doing a hypothetical closing of the books on the decedent's date of death, which allows an exact allocation. If the client died August 1 of 2017, how much income did the decedent receive or was entitled to receive as of that particular date? That amount goes on the final 1040.

The same approach applies to a partnership or limited liability company (LLC) taxed as a partnership: the interim closing of the books or a proration of income to the days that the person was living in the short tax year. However, the practitioner should check the partnership agreement to determine what it states should be done if a partner or LLC member dies. Only if the agreement is silent on the issue does the practitioner have a choice.

Perhaps the client was the beneficiary of a simple trust and the agreement provision says to pay all the income to the decedent but he or she dies before receiving the income. Does the return still claim or report the income as received? The answer is no; only the trust income that was actually received is reported on the decedent's final 1040. If there is an entitlement to income that had not yet been received, that would be income in respect to the decedent when it's paid out and that would go on an estate's Form 1041. Even if it's a simple trust, which might not be paying all the income to the beneficiary but the trust still has to give a Schedule K-1 to the beneficiary saying that all the income is taxable, the practitioner still has to ask the question: As of date of death, had there been a receipt of income?

What happens when a person is entitled to wages and salaries? Obviously everything received through date of death would be on a final 1040 and probably on a Form W-2. The problem is sometimes the employer lists amounts on a W-2 that were received after death. Maybe the client was entitled to a bonus and maybe he or she died having earned the bonus but before the bonus was paid. For example, large brokerage firms typically pay their bonuses early in the next tax year. If the deceased got the check in December but died in August, there is a proration. The client's W-2 indicated income received after death, and some of that belongs on a Form 1041. It's always awkward because there is a Form W-2 the employer filed with the IRS and that income number doesn't agree with income on the final Form 1040. The IRS may flag the mismatch and issue a deficiency notice. Then the practitioner must send an explanation letter to straighten the discrepancy out.

IRA and retirement plan distributions can also trigger issues with the final Form 1040. A client may have had an IRA or qualified plan and got nothing during the year because a required minimum distribution (RMD) was not required. The client was not yet age 70½, so no distribution amount goes on the final Form 1040, of course. Had the client lived and taken no RMD, it wouldn't have gone on the 1040 anyway. But maybe the client was older than 70½, required to take those RMDs every year. Then if he or she did take it, it would be listed on their final 1040 because the client took it while alive. If the client did not take the RMD for 2017, it is not listed on the final 1040. It is not an item of constructive receipt. Instead, the beneficiary has to take that RMD and report it on his or her tax return.

**EXAMPLE:** Julia McCoy, a child, is the beneficiary of Joe McCoy, the decedent. He died in August before he had taken his 2017 RMD. The rule provides that Julia has to take that RMD and report the income on a Form 1040, based upon the amount that Joe should have taken in the year of death.

These rules are very complicated for retirement planning issues. The practitioner doesn't start using the beneficiary's life expectancy for withdrawals until the year following the participant's year of death. In the participant's year of death, the question is: was any required minimum distribution not taken by the decedent? If the answer is yes, then the beneficiary has to take it and report it on his or her return.

Another issue involves installment sales. Maybe the client was in the midst of an installment sale. He or she sold something using a 10-year note and died in year six. So the client has received years one through five. Was the income received for year six? If it was, of course it's included on the final Form 1040, the portion of the year six payment that represents income. It might be interest. It might be capital gain. It might be both.

But the good news here is that death is not a disposition of the installment sale note. So the fact that the client is still owed four or five years of payment doesn't prompt an immediate realization anywhere. It doesn't appear on the decedent's final 1040. And the person who inherits the note doesn't have an immediate realization, assuming of course there's no immediate payment. So an heir doesn't have to report the unrealized gain in his or her adjusted gross income.

**PLANNING POINTER:** Imagine that the decedent entered into an installment sale transaction in the year of his or her death. The practitioner considers electing out of installment sale treatment and reporting 100 percent of the gain on the decedent's final Form 1040. Does the decedent have a long-term capital loss carryover perhaps or even a short-term loss carryover, a capital loss carryover of some type? Or did the decedent incur significant medical expenses in the last year of life that will not be deductible if he or she didn't have income? It'll just be wasted. So the thought is to increase the reportable income by electing out of installment sale treatment and then offset that income with some type of loss carryover—something to offset the loss or significant itemized deductions that can reduce that income and think of it that way. Every now and then practitioners encounter a situation when a planning option turns out to be better than just allowing normal procedures to prevail.

If a client who, based upon medical opinion and observation, is sadly not likely to live out the year, once again the experienced practitioner considers options. Is the client incurring major medical expenses? Does the client have a loss carryover deduction? If so, the planner can find a way to get more income—take money out of an IRA, withdraw money from the IRA beyond the RMD. If the taxpayer has all these losses to offset it, the tax effect will net to either zero or a lower number than would have been the case without the losses.

And now that IRA money has been income taxed, so when it passes by inheritance to heirs, it's not subject to income tax to them. And so it's not income in respect of a decedent if the decedent already reported the income.

An issue that often arises is whether to sell the decedent's residence. Well, if the client sold it before death and it was his or her principal residence, the seller gets $500,000 exclusion of gain on a joint return or a $250,000 exclusion if a single person. As long as a surviving spouse doesn't remarry before the home is sold, he or she has a two-year opportunity beyond date of death to still get that $500,000 exclusion.

**EXAMPLE:** Harriet Tillson, who is 97 and alive but in very poor health, bought her home for $38,000 sixty years ago, and her son Jeff believes it could be sold for $1.2 million now. And her improvements over the years, Harriet kept records of them, wouldn't stretch to more than $100,000. So there's an enormous gain should she be a seller while alive. But if she passes and the basis steps-up to date of death value, hopefully there'll be little or no capital gain for Jeff.

So the advice there of course is to hang onto the home. Pay the property tax. Make sure the place doesn't fall down and maintain and, given Harriet's bad health, there'll be a significant tax saving if the heir is going to pay income tax on about $800,000 versus zero; tax planning steps in.

If a person has savings bonds—probably not too many E type bonds left but lots of EE bonds are still around—most of the E bonds have reached their 30-year maturity and the owner should have cashed them in. But if an heir holds those bonds, what happens when the person dies? Is the accrued income taxable? And the answer is no. A client can leave the bond to the heir and the heir now owns the bond. The heir will have to report all the accrued income when the heir cashes in the bond or it matures because the savings bond is not a stepped-up basis item. It is income in respect to the decedent, considered ordinary income. Another opportunity here suggests reporting all the accrued interest on savings bonds on the decedent's final Form 1040. So if the person dies in October 2017 and the final 1040 is filed in April of 2018, an election on that form is available to report all the accrued interest on the savings bonds as income on the 2017 return. Why do that? Well, because when the heirs receive the bonds, the income through the decedent's date of death has been reported, so the heirs won't have to pay tax on it. And again, maybe the practitioner has the opportunity to take a deduction there to offset this choice of income by a deduction.

**¶304**

What about medical expenses? Many times persons in their last year of life may have significant medical expenses. The practitioner may claim them on the final 1040 of the decedent or claim them on the Form 706 for the estate. The practitioner may not claim them on a fiduciary Form 1041. On the Form 1040, the client is subject to the decedent's 10 percent floor for the medical deduction, but the other opportunity is to claim the decedent's medical expenses paid up to one year following the decedent's date of death.

The practitioner may conclude NLLs die with the decedent. And there's a rule that's very technical that people often ignore that says: for a married couple, the loss belongs to the person who sustained it. So if it's jointly held property, both spouses sustained it. As community property, each one has a half-interest.

But say Spouse A was the entire loser or the person who sustained the capital loss. If Spouse A dies, even though he or she has filed a joint return with Spouse B, the correct rule under the tax code and regulations is: Spouse B can't claim that loss. It was not his or hers. On joint returns that that little nicety is often ignored but incorrectly so.

Another area that is unhappy in this loss situation is: What happens if the client has a passive activity loss? If the decedent had been renting property for 20 years and incurred a massive loss carryforward because the property is rented, it's considered a passive asset. Can the practitioner take that loss and move it to the heirs? The answer is no.

What the planner can do on the final 1040 however, is a two-step process. First, the practitioner allocates the unused losses and adds that amount to the basis of the property passing to heirs. So that may cover all of the loss. It may not, because the amount can't go above fair market value to make that basis adjustment. So the planner adjusts the basis to fair market value. If excess losses remain, the practitioner can use those excess losses on the final Form 1040 against other income, to offset some portfolio income for example.

But if the filer doesn't have enough of other income, after the practitioner adjusts basis, the consideration is other income. Any remaining losses are just lost. They do not carry over to heirs, the Form 1041, or anywhere else. No unused deductions that go to the 1041.

A client may have been very charitable, made a significant gift to charity beyond the adjusted gross income (AGI) allowed percentage. At the date of death the client had a five-year charitable contribution carryover. And if the client didn't use it all, can any of that go to beneficiaries or on the Form 1041? No; the client has to use it or lose it during his or her lifetime.

One of the advantages of dying is wiping out the recapture problem. A client bought property many years ago, and it was residential real estate. It appreciated over 27½ years. And then aside from the land portion, the value is zero and then the client dies. And guess what? The heirs get a stepped-up basis equal to fair market value at death. And they start all over again. No one pays tax on that recapture.

So depending upon the client's situation, a passing can be egregious from the tax side with great despair. His or her tax planner didn't get to claim all the losses; or it may be a great celebration from the tax side, because all that recapture never got paid.

If the client has a charitable contribution, it cannot be carried over from a decedent to someone else. So, the advice is this: If the person is quite elderly and ill and wants to make a gift to charity, ask whether he or she trusts someone to make the gift to charity after the person's death. Then the client can leave the property to the trusted person to make the charitable contribution. That way, one of the decedent's children can get the income tax benefit of the deduction.

If the client has a dividend declared and paid prior to death, it's included on the decedent's final 1040, even if not deposited in the bank yet. But if it's declared before death—such as declared July 25 to be payable August 20 but the person died August 1—it's income in respect to the decedent because it wasn't payable yet, as of the date of death. The client was entitled to it but it was something that came after death.

Another issue that comes up is about estimated taxes. Are these taxes required once the person has died? And the good news is no. So the executor or heir shouldn't be charged a penalty. If the client dies midyear having made the first two quarters' estimated payments in April and June, the executor or practitioner doesn't have to make that September payment.

But extra care is due if the client filed a joint return. Because the survivor, not having died, is still responsible for estimated taxes. And if all the decedent's income on a joint return involved jointly held property, it now becomes income of the survivor and all the estimates should stay the same. So again it's something to discuss with clients. In some cases, it's often safer to at least make one more estimated payment after the person dies and then get a refund for any overpayment.

It's always awkward as a representative of clients to deal with the family of the decedent, because maybe the family the practitioner didn't work much with before must be told why Mom or Dad has an underpayment penalty for estimates. Maybe it's better to make another payment or so, just to make sure that issue doesn't arise with the heirs. Sometimes just being a little safer is better practice.

**Debt.** If the client left a Form 1040 for which there's money due, that is a debt of the decedent. Was the client filing Form 706? If he or she has a 706 estate tax requirement because the wealth exceeded the exemption amount; then the balance due on that final Form1040 is a debt. And the practitioner can claim it as a debt on the appropriate schedule, usually Schedule J and sometimes Schedule L of Form 706.

What if the client files a joint return? Technically, the practitioner is supposed to allocate the refund between the spouses, depending upon how much income Spouse A made. How much did Spouse B make? And the appropriate percentage of each spouse's income on the joint return is how to allocate the refund, if it needs to be allocated separately. Or if the deceased has a liability, same thing; for a joint return, Spouse A earned 80 percent of the money; then the liability is 80 percent debt on Spouse A's Form 706. But if there's a surviving spouse, chances are if the marital deduction is involved, maybe there's no tax due on that Form 706 anyway. But these are aspects the practitioner has to look at on a case-by-case basis.

**Refunds.** An awkward possibility is what happens if spouses are not filing a joint return and the decedent is entitled to a refund? Who's going to get the refund? The personal representative files the Form 1040 and requests the refund. The practitioner adds a Form 1310, *Statement of Person Claiming Refund Due a Deceased Taxpayer,* to the tax return. The 1310 establishes that there is a duly appointed representative of the estate and the check should be made payable to that person in his or her capacity as the fiduciary.

And Form 1310 is simple; basically, it asks for some information. The problem is the IRS never seems to figure it out; does the IRS want the form e-filed or not?

**Investments and Unearned Income.** If Form 1099s are received for the year of death, technically the practitioner is only supposed to report what the decedent was entitled to as of his or her date of death. When did the banks, brokerage firms, etc., learn that there was a death and the client has a new ID number? Some brokerage firms are on top of such situations. As soon as they learn there's been a death, they immediately segregate money into an estate account. Even if the estate doesn't have an ID number immediately, the firms suggest getting one, but meanwhile the firm segregates the account and that will help with the reporting—but that doesn't happen that often.

Usually the bank or the brokerage house leaves everything under the Social Security number (SSN) of the decedent and then sends a Form 1099 for everything that was under the decedent's SSN. If that was income earned post death, it doesn't belong on the 1040.

So what does the practitioner do? If only what was earned and received through death is reported and that amount mismatches with the 1099, the IRS will issue one of those computer letters that notes the discrepancy. That prompts a postal exchange between the practitioner and the IRS. But often the client's family member gets the letter and the client is a surviving spouse who has no tax experience and may mail a check immediately.

And typically the notice comes in July or August, after the practitioner has done all the tax return work. And the next time the practitioner sees the family member and the deficiency letter turns up. In this case the practitioner should do the following: Everything that shows up on a Form 1099 in this client's SSN should be listed on Schedule B of Form 1040. So the practitioner lists all the interest and dividends that the 1099 mentions, then does a subtraction accompanied with a statement—a simple statement saying that as a result of taxpayer's death, on Form 1041 for the taxpayer's estate, an amount equal to X reported there. And the ID number of the 1041 Form is listed to show the amount as a subtraction. Tax software will do that and accept the subtraction on Schedule B.

So again these are steps the practitioner needs to do. If the client's personal representative doesn't change the SSN to the ID number until the following tax year, the practitioner doesn't file a new 1040 for a year after a person died. The preparer wouldn't file a 2018 1040 for a 2017 decedent, regardless of how much income got reported on 1099s or W-2s as 2018 income for a 2017 decedent.

All that information goes on the estate's Form 1041 and a statement is attached to it, basically saying that all of this income was reported under the SSN of the decedent is the income of the decedent's estate. Indicate what the SSN is and indicate the ID number of the estate. And if the practitioner is ever questioned, he or she can show it matched the 1099s or W-2s to what appears on the 1041 and go from there.

One of the nastier issues is income in respect to the decedent (IRD). It's a nasty issue because there's no adjustment for the basis when a person died. And it's surprising how many clients don't know this. So the practitioner gets into a situation where Mom or Dad died and left the child a $600,000 IRA. And the child thinks: Well, because Mom or Dad died, there's no income tax due on that. Well, unless it was a ROTH IRA, it is ordinary taxable income.

Again, it's important for clients to understand that retirement plan distributions, compensation received after death for services rendered prior to death, just a variety of undistributed income that comes later—all these things are income in respect to the decedent. And so the tax professional needs to make sure that the recipient respects the IRD aspects of what they're getting. A retirement plan might be payable to an estate, for example. Terrible planning. People do it. So the estate now has to pay income tax.

When the estate is the beneficiary, the practitioner has to withdraw all the money from the retirement plan not later than either five years after death, if the client died before age 70½ or based upon his or her actuarial remaining life expectancy if they died after 70½, as opposed to being allowed to stretch the money out to the beneficiaries.

So it's not a great situation. But the estate would pick up the income on a Form 1041 and then hopefully distribute it to beneficiaries who are presumably in lower income tax brackets. They certainly can't be in higher ones when the cap of the top bracket for a trust or an estate is reached at $12,500 and individuals are at hundreds of thousands of dollars more than that.

In the rare case when a client actually has a federal estate tax to pay and some of the assets on the Form 706 are IRD assets; the planner should make sure to appropriately take a deduction on the income recipient's tax return. So a parent dies, has an estate over the threshold, pays estate tax, has IRD items like retirement plans; then the beneficiaries who are going to pay income tax on that retirement plan item get an offset in deduction of the estate tax that was paid. It's a rare case because well below 1 percent of all decedents are paying federal estate tax.

To summarize, the final Form 1040 should include:

- Income through date of death;
- Deductions appropriate through date of death
  - — Actually received
  - — Constructively received;
- Expenses paid; and
- Deductible expenses
  - — State and local income tax
  - — Property taxes and business expenditures.

## STUDY QUESTION

**3.** Which of the following types of income or deductions should be included on the final Form 1040 tax return?

    **a.** Payments for wages and salaries received after death.

    **b.** Retirement plan distributions received after death.

    **c.** Unrealized gain from installment sales.

    **d.** Actual distributions of trust income received through the date of death.

# ¶ 305 ELECTIONS THAT AFFECT THE FIDUCIARY INCOME TAX RETURN

## Selecting a Fiscal Year

An estate is not required to be a calendar year taxpayer. So the estate can choose a fiscal year. Fiscal years can't go longer than 12 months. They have to end at the end of a month. An estate can use short years. If a client died August 1, 2017, the shortest year to select would end August 31, 2017. The longest year would end July 3, 2018. The tax preparer or executor can choose any month end in between.

The estate selects its fiscal year when it files its first federal income tax return adopting that year and files Form SS-4. Beneficiaries report their shares of income from an estate in their own tax years with or within which the estate tax year ends. The planner should consider the adoption of a fiscal year for an estate if doing so allows deferral of income for the estate. However, with a fiscal year the planner has to calculate end-of-the-month allocations of dividends, income, etc., which may add time and costs of handling the estate. Although estates can select fiscal years, trusts have to employ calendar years.

## The Qualified Revocable Trust Election of Code Sec. 645

Code Sec. 645 was enacted to enable people who established revocable living trusts to elect to treat their trusts as if they were estates. The election is made on the first Form 1041 filed for the estate and by filing Form 8855, *Election to Treat a Qualified Revocable Trust as Part of an Estate.*

The executor of an estate and the trustee of a "qualified revocable trust" (QRT) can elect to treat the decedent's revocable trust as part of the estate rather than as a separate trust for income tax purposes. The term "qualified revocable trust" refers to any trust that was treated as owned by the decedent at death as the result of the decedent retaining a power to revoke the trust under Code Sec. 676.

If no estate tax return is filed for the decedent's estate, this election applies for two years from the date of the decedent's death. There are a number of valuable benefits arising from making this election:

- Estate administration expenses can be deducted on either the estate income tax return (Form 1041) or on the estate tax return (Form 706);
- Certain expenses incurred by an estate may only be deducted on Form 706— and not on Form 1041; and
- Medical expenses of the decedent paid within one year of the decedent's death may be claimed on either the decedent's final Form 1040 or on Form 706, but may not be claimed on Form 1041.

The election enables the trust to be treated as an estate for two years or until Form 706 issues are resolved—quite helpful for complicated estates or ones with pending lawsuits. The trust treated as an estate can use a fiscal year and defer estimated tax payments for two years, benefits unavailable to trusts normally. Further, passive losses can be listed on the Form 1041 if the decedent was actively engaged in an otherwise passive activity, with up to $25,000 deductible against other income if the decedent's adjusted gross income (AGI) doesn't exceed $150,000. Trusts cannot capitalize on these benefits unless they make the Code Sec. 645 election.

If the estate is treated as a trust, it gets an exemption of either $100 (for a complex trust) or $300 (for a simple trust). It gets an exemption of $600 as an estate. So, not life changing here, but better. The other advantage is having to file just one tax return during this election period—a return for the estate, not for a trust. When the time is up, then the trust goes forward and files its own tax returns thereafter. So the trust needs an ID number. The estate needs an ID number. If the planner was using the decedent's SSN because it was a grantor revocable trust, as many of them are, the planner instead must get an ID number for the trust and an ID number for the estate.

There's nothing to lose by filing the Code Sec. 645 election. Even if no one takes advantage of any features for which trusts are less advantageous than estates, it doesn't hurt to have options. Maybe the fiscal year, maybe the $600, not having to pay estimated taxes right away; maybe just filing one tax return is an advantage for the client. Maybe the practitioner doesn't have to file multiple tax returns in the situation like that.

At the end of the Code Sec. 645 applicable period, does the surviving trust need to obtain a new federal ID number? Generally, no. If the practitioner obtained one at the beginning of the 645 period, he or she basically just doesn't use it for a couple of years. But the planner got an ID number because the decedent died and had a trust. So that trust becomes the ongoing engine for tax reporting for two years or the estate has ended.

## Electing Where to Claim Estate Administration Expense Deductions

Estate administration expenses can be deducted on either the estate income tax return (Form 1041) or on the estate tax return (Form 706). Certain expenses incurred by an estate may only be deducted on Form 706—and not on Form 1041. Medical expenses of the decedent paid within one year of the decedent's death may be claimed on either the decedent's final Form 1040 or on Form 706, but may not be claimed on Form 1041.

If the practitioner is filing a nontaxable Form 706, everything goes to the surviving spouse. It is preferable not to claim these expenses on a Form 706 if the client is entitled to claim them on a Form 1041. However, if the practitioner is filing a 706 and has got legal fees, accounting fees, or fiduciary fees, where may they be claimed? The client can take them either on the 706 or on the 1041 but not both places.

Then the practitioner should look at the tax rates. The tax rate on Form 706 is a flat rate of 40 percent. Form 1041, depending upon what the practitioner is doing about making or not making distributions to beneficiaries, has a maximum rate of 39.6 percent, plus the net investment income tax. So that raises the rate to 43.4 percent. And is there a state income tax? Well, that makes it higher. Is there a state death tax? That might make the estate tax discussion more helpful.

The pros and cons must be weighed. Funeral expenses cannot be claimed anywhere except on Form 706. So if the client files a nontaxable 706, the funeral expenses become nondeductible. Medical expenses, as mentioned earlier, can be claimed on either Form 706 or Form 1040 but not on the 1041. There is an opportunity to deduct something on both the 706 and the 1041: interest payments, state and local income taxes, real property tax, personal property taxes, and trade or business expenses. It's a short list. But when something is double deducted, it can be claimed it as a debt on the 706 and as a payment of one of these categories just mentioned: interest, state and local tax, etc., on the 1041. Claiming them in two places is smart where that is allowed.

## The 65-Day Election for Distribution Allocations

Estates and trusts may elect to treat all or part of distributions made to beneficiaries within the first 65 days of the taxable year as if they were paid on the last day of the preceding taxable year. The election is made by having the fiduciary simply check the appropriate box on Page 2 of Form 1041. Then the beneficiaries do not have to report the income until this year's return, perhaps saving clients substantial currently taxable income.

This election may be a valuable choice for several possible reasons.

## Estimated Tax Payment Elections

Besides postponing payments on distributions for beneficiaries, perhaps the deceased made large estimated tax payments in the year Form 1041-T was due. The estimated payments not required for the deceased's tax liability can be moved to the trust beneficiary. The election is made by completing Form 1041-T and filing it within 65 days after the end of the trust's taxable year. The election applies to estimated taxes paid by the trust for any tax year and by the estate only in its final year.

## Election to Deduct a Charitable Contribution on the Prior Year's Tax Return

Another opportunity for the planner concerns charitable contributions. A trust and an estate have the opportunity to elect to deduct a charitable contribution made in one year on the income tax return for the prior tax year.

¶305

A situation could arise where there is insufficient taxable income in a particular year to use the benefit of the charitable deduction. The planner can make the gift to charity in year two and deduct it in year one. The IRS regulations explain the process; it's not that complicated. If the practitioner hasn't yet filed for year one, the return simply includes the deduction as a deduction and goes from there. The planner files a statement with the return, meeting the IRS requirements and Regulation 1.642(c). And the planner tells the IRS to apply the year two contribution as a year one deduction.

If the year one return has been filed, again, not a big deal. The planner amends year one's return and claims the deduction as a year one deduction. If beneficiaries can benefit from the year one deduction and they've already received their Schedule K-1s, the planner amends their tax returns because now they get less income because the client has a bigger deduction. So now the planner amends the beneficiaries' returns and gets them a refund.

But if the first trust year is a significant income year, the client will owe a penalty if payments didn't address estimated taxes. So for trusts the planner has to act very quickly. For estates, there is that two-year grace period before the planner has to revise paperwork. So the charitable contribution is an opportunity.

## Election to Recognize Gain on the Distribution of Property

Another possible choice is making an election on your Form 1041 to recognize gain on the distribution of property. And so here is a situation when the planner doesn't have to do this. The general rule is you distribute property to a beneficiary and there's no recognition of gain to the entity.

As a general rule, an in-kind distribution of property by an estate or trust to its beneficiaries does not result in the recognition of gain or loss to the distributing entity. A special election is available to enable the estate or trust to treat the property distribution as a sale of the property at its fair market value, and recognize the gain at the level of the trust or estate

> **CAUTION:** The practitioner should be careful about the net investment income tax thresholds here.

The distribution of property carries out distributable net income (DNI) to the beneficiaries, but the amount of DNI depends on whether the Code Sec. 643(e) election was made.

> **EXAMPLE:** Marissa Colburn, the beneficiary, takes her value of the property left her by grandma Emily as the value of property; the lower of the basis of the fair market value on the date of distribution. So Emily's estate distributes the Black Acre real estates and there's no gain or loss to the trust or estate in doing the distribution. The value of the Black Acre to Marissa is the lower of the estate or trust basis or the fair market value and then that carries over to her—a carryover basis. The value of the lower basis or fair market value and the basis carries to her.

So that's a normal case. But Emily's estate is given the opportunity under Code Sec. 6439(e), and the planner checks a box on the Form 1041 to voluntarily report gain. Why would the planner do that? What if the estate has a significant capital loss carryover? Emily had also established a trust for a younger granddaughter, Natalie, who is 15 years old and is set to receive her trust money when she's 35. So the planner can carry that capital loss for 20 years, hoping to use it one day. But maybe the trust will never get to use it but it will carry to Natalie at age 35.

Why wait 20 years? If the trust has a property that has appreciated significantly, it can pass to the beneficiary so gain is recognized at the trust level. Then the planner can offset it by the loss carryover to get a zero result. So there's no income to Natalie now. And now she can use the full fair market value as her basis. So Natalie sells the property and has no gain or loss at the beneficiary level. And because she is a young person, she can use the money for college, creating a business, or hang onto it for a couple years until she is more mature.

The Section 643(e) election is often attractive when there has been a capital gain property with a capital loss carryover or a capital loss in the current year. Can a practitioner make the election to treat it as a sale to the beneficiary if the sale would result in a loss? The answer is no. Because transactions between entities and beneficiaries if the estate realizes a loss, they are considered related taxpayers and so the planner can't do that.

# ¶ 306  ADDRESSING THE FINAL YEAR OF THE TRUST OR ESTATE

A very special year of estate administration is the final year or trust administration as well—the final year of the entity. Because now finally the practitioner can pass money or other property through from the entity to the beneficiary on the Schedule K-1. Up until the final year, the only deduction ever allowed to pass from entity to beneficiary is that for depreciation, depletion, and amortization and only if those deductions follow distributions of income to the beneficiary. If that's the situation, then the planner can do that.

The final year however, when there is a capital loss carryover, that passes to the beneficiary who can use it indefinitely. A net operating loss (NOL) having remaining years can pass to the beneficiary and be used for those remaining years by him or her.

One of the best things in the final year, if there are excess deductions in the year of termination, is that they may finally be used. It's a shame when an estate has a situation where the taxpayer has big expenses in the trust or the estate for legal fees, accounting fees, fiduciary fees. Once the practitioner exhausts the income with those losses, those expenses, they're done. They can't be carried forward any further within the entity. They are not NOLs. The practitioner can't pass them to the beneficiaries because it's not the final year.

When the estate finally gets to that final year, any excess deductions in the year of termination go to the beneficiary. He or she has to itemize to be able to use them, and they are miscellaneous itemized deductions subject to the 2 percent floor. So unless tax laws change to the point where that itemized deduction disappears, this can be a valuable opportunity for claiming an itemized deduction in the final year of the entity only.

So again if the practitioner can defer some of legal, accounting, and fiduciary fees until that final year, then the beneficiary gets to use the writeoffs. And maybe the practitioner has a slightly happier client who gets to use some of those expense deductions based on any or all three types of fees.

Passive losses, as mentioned earlier, can't carry to the beneficiary, even in the final year. So if the Form 1041 has had a lot of rental property and the 1041 is done, can the passive loss pass to the beneficiary? No. All the planner can do at this point is adjust the basis of the assets passing to the beneficiary, which is not terrible. The beneficiaries would have smaller gains now if they sell those assets or more depreciation if they keep them and they're depreciable assets. So it's not terrible but it's not nearly as good as it could have been had those losses offset more. The goal is to try to use as much of the losses that arise as can be.

Another tricky issue on fiduciary income tax returns is: Is an expense deductible with or without regard to the 2 percent floor on miscellaneous itemized deductions for the entity? Lines 15a ("Other deductions **not** subject to the 2% floor") and 15c ("Allowable miscellaneous itemized deductions subject to the 2% floor") of the Form 1041 pertain here. The 15a deductions are allowed without regard to the 2 percent floor. The 15c deductions are allowed after applying the 2 percent floor.

This whole issue was hotly litigated for years between taxpayers and the IRS. And the case of *Knight v. Commissioner* was decided by the U.S. Supreme Court in 2008. And in that case the justices found that if an expense was commonly incurred by individuals, as well as trusts and estates, it is not available for deduction above the line. It only can be used below the line. And so that's where the planner wants to be looking for those expenses.

The IRS issued regulations that became effective in January 2015 that estate managers have yet to see pushback from taxpayers on because the filings were done in 2016. And if there are issues to be litigated, they should begin in the next couple of months. But the IRS took the position that if an estate has what is called an ownership cost that is subject to the 2 percent floor. That means it is subject to the miscellaneous deduction rules and the 2 percent floor threshold.

If, however, an estate has costs that are only incurred with respect to trust and estates—a judicial accounting, a probate fee, things of that nature—they are above the line, that is, listed on line15a, not subject to the 2 percent floor. A fiduciary bond would be another example; paying for death certificates another example. If there is an investment advisory fee, clearly that is subject to the 2 percent floor. That was the issue specifically addressed in the *Knight* case. The client pays an investment advisor for the trust and estate. Nondeceased taxpayers can pay those without trusts and estates; therefore, such costs are subject to the 2 percent floor.

The real controversy is going to arise as the IRS requires trustees to unbundle their fees—to make an allocation between the amounts charged as a trustee, which those are deductible without regard to the 2 percent floor, and those actions trustees take that are more in the nature of being an investment advisor. And the IRS rules are vague, telling practitioners to use any reasonable method to distinguish the two types of service. One suggested approach is just to use time charges. Well, most banks and trustees don't keep time records. So this will be interesting to watch play out in court.

But the IRS has a lot of incentive to force estates to list items on line 15c with the 2 percent floor because not only does that reduce the deduction by the 2 percent of AGI but because it's on line 15c, it automatically becomes an item of tax preference, which then gets added back for alternative minimum tax calculations. So it makes it more likely the estate will have an AMT problem on everything else.

## STUDY QUESTION

---

**4.** Which of the following statements with respect to elections that affect the fiduciary income tax return is correct?

- **a.** A trust is required to make annual payments of estimated taxes and can elect to treat any portion of the estimated taxes it has paid as made instead by a trust beneficiary.
- **b.** An estate has the option of choosing to report its income on a fiscal reporting year, so long as the year ends on the first day of a month.
- **c.** If no estate tax return is filed for the decedent's estate, this election applies for three years from the date of the decedent's death.
- **d.** Estates and trusts may elect to treat all or part of distributions made to beneficiaries within the first 45 days of the taxable year as if they were paid on the last day of the preceding taxable year.

---

# ¶ 307 DISCLAIMERS

A disclaimer is an act by a beneficiary whereby the beneficiary declines, refuses, and renounces an interest in property otherwise bequeathed to the beneficiary. When a disclaimer satisfies the requirements of a "qualified disclaimer," the disclaiming beneficiary is treated as not having made a gift.

## Requirements for a Qualified Disclaimer

Code Sec. 2518 contains the requirements for a qualified disclaimer, effective for all transfers made after 1977, including:

- Must be in writing;

- Must be unqualified and irrevocable;

- Must be signed;

- Must identify the interest disclaimed;

- Must be delivered to the personal representative of the estate or to the transferor of the property or to the holder of legal title to the property within nine months after the creation of the instrument;

- The nine-month period commences with the "transfer creating the interest";

- For transfers made during lifetime, the period begins when the transfer is complete for federal gift tax purposes;

- For transfers made at death, or that become irrevocable at death, the decedent's date of death is the date from which the nine-month period is measured;

- Unawareness of one's right to an interest in property does not extend the time to make a qualified disclaimer under Code Sec. 2518;

- The timing requirements provided under federal law are intended to create a uniform standard for federal law purposes, notwithstanding whether or not a disclaimer will be considered timely as a matter of state law;

- Extending the time to file the federal estate tax return does *not* extend the time to make a qualified disclaimer; and

- The person disclaiming must not accept the property interest or any of its benefits prior to the disclaimer.

## STUDY QUESTION

**5.** Each of the following identifies a requirement for a qualified disclaimer as prescribed by Code Sec. 2518 *except*:

    **a.** Must be in writing.

    **b.** Must identify the interest disclaimed.

    **c.** Must be qualified and revocable.

    **d.** Must be delivered to the personal representative of the estate.

## Interest in Jointly Held Property May Be Disclaimed by the Surviving Joint Tenant

The disclaimer may be used to overcome the failure of a married couple to adequately separate their assets during life, so as to be able to take full advantage of the applicable exclusion available at the death of the first of the spouses to die.

The regulations adopted the general rule that transfers must be disclaimed within nine months from the date of the transfer creating the disclaimed interest.

Joint accounts (such as bank accounts, brokerage accounts, mutual funds, and other investment accounts) that are revocable during the decedent's lifetime may be disclaimed in their entirety by the surviving joint tenant within nine months of the death of the deceased co-tenant.

The key to disclaimers under Code Sec. 2518 is that the person who disclaims is neither the gifter nor the donor and does not include the property in an estate or generation-skipping trust because the person is not making a transfer.

> **EXAMPLE:**  Sheryl Johnson is left rental property by her maiden aunt's estate. She cannot accept months of rent and then make a qualified disclaimer. Her aunt also left Sheryl shares of stock. She cannot cash dividend checks and then disclaim the gift.

> **EXAMPLE:**  Jerry and Harold Albany are spouses when Harold dies. Jerry can still reside in their home and use the property because it was a jointly held residence but still disclaim the half-interest inherited from Harold.

Bank accounts are a broader issue because an heir can disclaim the entire interest in the bank account because it is a revocable transfer in a joint account. Either owner could have gone to the bank and withdrawn all the money; so either can disclaim 100 percent of a joint account. That allows that all to pass to the potential beneficiary. So, accounts offer a lot of planning opportunities here if the plan is to avoid having the disclaiming party be a donor.

Disclaimers are really excellent opportunities because a lot of times the person who is the heir doesn't need the property. Alternatively, the heir may have no cash to pay the tax bill when the estate tax comes due.

> **EXAMPLE:**  Marie White leaves property equally to each of her four children, two of whom are very wealthy through their own success as hedge fund operators; the other two are school teachers. So maybe the hedge fund operators disclaim their shares, so their siblings who are the school teachers will get a bigger inheritance. If that's possible in the family, no one's making a gift. If the hedge fund operators each got their quarter interest and gave it to their siblings, they'd have made a gift. They'd also have used some of their lifetime gift tax exclusion.

> **EXAMPLE:**  The Stemples are twin clients with an interest in a closely held business and they have no liquidity. They don't have any cash. The business is very valuable. They have a taxable estate. And the Stemples' parent who owns the business dies, wanting the twins to inherit the business. The question is whether the value of the business is greater than 35 percent of the decedent's estate. If so, Code Sec. 6166 becomes available to use. And so if the decedent was a U.S. citizen or resident at death and the value met that 35 percent requirement, the twins can pay some of the federal estate tax in installments.

If clients don't owe any federal estate tax, this is of no interest. But if a client owes federal estate tax and doesn't have the dollars to pay it and 35 percent or more of the estate is represented by one or more closely held businesses, now this opportunity to defer is available.

So that can be obviously very valuable for planning. The twins have to make their decision within nine months of death. They make the election and here's what the planner helps them do: They get five years of interest only and then nine years of interest and principal. So it's a 14-year deferment basically after the client dies; they pay interest only for the five years and then interest and principal for the balance. But they can only defer the tax on the business interest. So if the business interest is 60 percent of their estate, they can defer 60 percent of the federal estate tax, using Code Sec. 6166. The other 40 percent is due the normal day, nine months after death.

The twins have to pay interest on the unpaid balance of their tax but the interest rate is very favorable. It's 2 percent on the first $1.49 million of deferred tax and then it's 45 percent of the IRS underpayment rate on the balance. The IRS underpayment rate is around 4 percent now. So it's effectively another 2 percent. So the twins pay 2 percent up to $1.49 million and a little more than 2 percent but that's adjusted every year; so they may end up paying more or less on the other piece.

The whole reason this provision is in the tax code is to allow people to keep the business in the family and have enough time to pay the tax. The good news is the interest rate is low. The bad news is none of the tax is deductible anywhere. It's not an administration expense on the Form 706. It's not deductible on the Form 1041. So that's the bad news. But if the rates are low, clients can live with that.

The twins make the election on Form 706. But they have to add the appropriate information that the IRS is looking for. They are allowed to aggregate their businesses to get to that 35 percent. Do they own at least 20 percent of every business they want to aggregate? If the answer is yes, the twins can aggregate them. The IRS allows this for proprietorships, partnerships, LLCs, S corporations. Anything that's a closely held business, it can be done.

The IRS does not allow use of passive interests here, however. So if the twins have a rental property that they don't actively manage, that can't be part of the 35 percent calculation to reach their percentage. It can be complicated, especially if payments are late and the IRS accelerates them of if either of the twins wants to sell more than half of the family business. If the IRS dislikes something reported for the estate, the twins can be asked for a fiduciary bond to ensure taxes are paid.

Finally, the whole approach results in an extension of the statute of limitations on assessment of deficiencies for the period of the extension of time granted for payment of the tax.

# ¶ 308 MARITAL DEDUCTION PLANNING

The way to plan the marital deduction is to have a client with a spouse who leaves the spouse money. That's an easy one. A spouse can be left money outright—it's not a big deal. A few intricacies can develop in estate planning for married couples, though.

## The Portability Election

Portability is extremely important in this discussion because if the estate files a timely Form 706, it has made a portability election. That means that the unused wealth exclusion of the deceased spouse ports to the surviving spouse. If the client is not a married person, there's no portability issue; couples have to be married to have portability.

Portability applies to deaths occurring in 2011 and later. Is it required? No, spouses don't have to bother. But it's a mistake to do nothing. The practitioner should file portability elections in virtually every estate of any married clients. Because one never knows whether sometime down the road, the surviving spouse becomes wealthier than expected.

Very fortunately there's a new law in town. Rev. Proc. 2017-34 allows an estate to extend the election period until January 2, 2018, or until two years from the decedent's date of death, whichever is later. So if a client died in 2011, and the practitioner realizes the surviving spouse is now cashing in with the booming stock market or perhaps launched a high-tech business or became an heir of an unexpected relative or won the lottery. Whatever the heir did, he or she is wealthy.

Enacted in June 2017, the revenue procedure offers the surviving spouse who timely files the portability election to have an extra $5 million exemption from his or her first deceased spouse. Previously, a spouse had to pay a $10,000 user fee to ask the IRS for this extension. But now the return is not late and taxes properly filed, this exemption is available to the surviving spouse.

## QTIP Marital Deduction Election

Typical estate planning for married couples suggests use of the estate tax marital deduction at the death of the first spouse to die. When property is left in trust by a decedent for his or her surviving spouse, such a conveyance may qualify for the estate tax marital deduction if the special trust—a QTIP—is written in a qualifying manner, if certain mandatory requirements are observed, and if the personal representative of the first decedent's estate makes a qualifying election.

To qualify for this marital deduction:

- The surviving spouse must be given a qualifying income interest for life in the QTIP property;

- The effect of the QTIP election is to defer estate tax liability from the death of the first spouse until the death of the surviving spouse;

- The QTIP election must be made on a timely filed the Form 706 estate tax return (including extensions) or on the first return following the due date if a timely return is not filed; and

- The QTIP election is selected on Schedule M.

But what the QTIP election allows clients to do is to have a trust that says the surviving spouse is entitled to all the income; the surviving spouse can get principal in the trustee's discretion. And when the surviving spouse dies, all of the property passes to the chosen heirs of the first decedent. So though the surviving spouse gets an outright distribution at the decedent's death, the decedent's heirs can receive what is left when the surviving spouse passes away. This option is a perfect plan for blended families that want to ensure the current spouse is taken care of but to leave the ultimate disposition of property to the first decedent's family.

The marital deduction is disallowed where the surviving spouse is not a United States citizen, with one exception: if the surviving spouse becomes a U.S. citizen before the estate tax return is filed and provided he or she was a U.S. resident at all times after the date of decedent's death and before becoming a U.S. citizen.

The marital deduction will apply, even if the spouse is not a U.S. citizen, when the property passes to a qualified domestic trust (QDOT).

## Reverse QTIP Election

In a reverse QTIP situation, the estate of the transferor decedent (or the donor spouse) is permitted to treat the property transfer as if no QTIP election was made only for purposes of the generation-skipping transfer (GST) tax and is accomplished by making a "reverse QTIP election" (Code Section 2652(a)(3)).

> **CAUTION:** The GST exclusion is not portable.

The election must be made on Schedule R of the Form 706 tax return on which the QTIP election is made. A partial reverse QTIP election is not allowed. Alternatively, it is possible to use the funding of the credit shelter trust as the vehicle to achieve full use of the GST exemption.

Wealthy families want to use it twice. They want to use the $5.49 million GST exclusion when A dies and when B dies. How does that magic happen? It happens by making sure to have the GST election at each death. A wealthy grandparent can just leave property outright to the grandkids. Spouse A decides to leave $5.49 million to the grandkids. Spouse B objects that the plan doesn't leave enough to him or her. So they create a plan that says: Spouse A leaves property in trust for Spouse B: the QTIP election.

But the grandparents make the reverse QTIP election. They simply fill in a section on Schedule R of the 706 and we say that Spouse A is the transferor to the skipped persons. Spouse B, the survivor, gets the benefit of the QTIP income principal if needed. Spouse B dies. Property goes ultimately to the grandchildren. A is the transferor because A, we made the reverse QTIP election. B can now leave his or her own exempt amount to the grandchildren and therefore the couple used both exemptions. That's what the reverse QTIP offers.

# ¶ 309 ELECTING THE ALTERNATE VALUATION DATE

Another postmortem opportunity is the alternative valuation date. Here the property owner has a choice:

- Value everything as of the decedent's date of death, end of discussion;
- Value property six months after the decedent died.

But the planner can only do that to reduce the value of the decedent's assets that are taxable and the tax liability. If the decedent has no tax liability, the alternate date is unavailable. If a client has tax liability and the values on the alternate date are higher and the client want to have a higher basis to the heirs, he or she cannot do that. The planner can't use the alternated date. It can only be used to reduce the size of the estate and reduce the tax liability.

The election for the alternate date is very simple. The practitioner checks a box on Form 706 and completes all the columns on the 706 for the alternate date. The planner would fill in the date of death and the alternate date and go from there. So few estates are taxable now that use of the alternate date is not as popular.

## STUDY QUESTION

---

**6.** Which of the following statements about electing the alternate valuation date is correct?

    **a.** The alternate valuation date is irrevocable once the election is made.

    **b.** An estate has the option to report the value of the decedent's assets as of the date of death or as of the date that is nine months after the decedent's date of death.

    **c.** In order for the alternate valuation date election to be used, the gross estate must increase in value and the combined estate and generation-skipping tax liability must increase as the result of making the election.

    **d.** The election must be made by checking a box on Form 1040 and completing the form indicating the alternate valuation information where appropriate.

---

# ¶ 310 ELECTING SPECIAL USE VALUATION FOR REAL PROPERTY USED IN FARMING OR CLOSELY HELD BUSINESSES

First, the technical requirements to qualify:

- The decedent must have been a U.S. citizen or resident at the time of his or her death;

- The real property must be considered "qualified real property";

- The maximum value reduction for 2017 is $1,120,000; and

- 50 percent or more of the adjusted value of the gross estate must consist of real or personal property that was being used for a qualified use by the decedent or a member of his or her family on the date of the decedent's death and that was acquired from or passed from the decedent to a qualified heir of the decedent.

How does this election work? A client owns a farm or has real estate used in a closely held business. The normal rule says the practitioner has to value everything at its highest and best use. So maybe the farm is in a location where the community would love to build a new airport or a shopping mall or a sports stadium. Well, the highest and best use might be that, rather than the farm. But if the planner makes a special use valuation election because the decedent was a farmer and the heirs are going to be farmers, then the property's worth can be set at a reduced value. An appraisal is required and then the planner can reduce the value of the property by up to $1,120,000 in 2017.

That number is indexed for inflation every year. So it varies from year to year. But the current number is $1,120,000. So if the property would be sold for $10 million; now it's going to be about $8.8 million through that reduction. But there are a lot of requirements to make the election. The property has to be used as a farm by the decedent. It has to be used as a farm by the qualified heirs. And if the heirs fail to use it as a farm on an ongoing basis, they lose the benefit of the election and there is recapture.

# ¶ 311  SECTION 754 ELECTION TO ADJUST THE BASIS OF PARTNERSHIP ASSETS

Another postmortem opportunity is the Code Sec. 754 election. This applies to a partnership, an LLC taxed as a partnership, or a general or a limited partnership. The general rule is when a person dies, the heir takes as his or her basis of the partnership interest, the fair market value of the decedent's interest. So that's pretty straightforward. But the interesting issue is the inside basis (under Code Sec. 743(b)) of the partnership assets does not change when a person dies. If that's the case, a person who dies may have a partnership interest worth $1 million dollars and all the assets within the partnership depreciated to zero. The partnership sells something. The heir to that partnership interest is going to have a share of the gain, even though he or she just got this very valuable interest with a high basis.

The Section 754 election is made by the partnership by attaching a statement to its Form 1065, *U.S. Return of Partnership Income,* by the due date (including extensions) or within 12 months thereof for the year during which the partner died (or a partnership interest is sold).

The downside to the tax benefits offered by a Section 754 election is the additional costs and administrative burdens of computing and tracking the basis adjustments applicable to every item of partnership property, as Section 754 requires.

# ¶ 312  SPECIAL ELECTIONS TO PROTECT AN S CORPORATION ELECTION

When a shareholder with an S corporation interest dies, frequently the interest passes to a trust. Did it pass through an electing small business trust (ESBT) or a qualified Subchapter S trust (QSST)? If the interest went into one of those categories, did the planner make the election? There are just 2½ months after the person dies or actually until the stock is transferred to the trust to make an election.

These forms of trust protect the S status:

- A QSST may only have a single current-income beneficiary who must be a United States citizen or resident; and

- An ESBT may have multiple beneficiaries and is permitted to either distribute or retain its income in the discretion of the trustee.

The election is one the planner should file as a notice with the IRS Form 1120S, *U.S. Income Tax Return for an S Corporation,* that now there are trusts as shareholders. If the election was not filed within 2½ months of the trust becoming a shareholder, the corporation has lost its S status—not good news. So when the client dies and leaves property in trust to his or her children, the S corporation shares are now in this trust. The planner funds the trust with the shares and makes no election. The corporation lost its S election.

So what can the incoming practitioner do to resurrect this situation? A late election can be filed within 3 years and 75 days of the date it should have been filed. Rev. Proc. 2013-30 says: it allows a 3 year plus 75 day grace period. If the client died in 2016 and the trust was funded in 2016, the current practitioner didn't know anything about making an election. The current practitioner can file the election now, so long as everybody was treated as an S corporation shareholder from the time he or she got the shares and everything was filed on time. Reasonable cause is required to maintain the S status. Rev. Proc. 2013-30 avoids the requirement to obtain a private letter ruling.

# MODULE 1: INDIVIDUAL TAXATION—
# Chapter 4: Proving Material Participation for the Passive Loss Rules

## ¶ 401 WELCOME

This chapter examines how an individual materially participates in a trade or business activity and why the level of participation matters for tax purposes. The concept is the subject of numerous IRS regulations and audit guidelines. Next, milestone decisions in case law are described that shaped how an individual currently can prove he or she materially participates in a trade or business.

## ¶ 402 LEARNING OBJECTIVES

Upon completion of this chapter, you will be able to:

- Identify how regulatory tests of material participation aim to curb abuse of business loss claims;
- Recognize the guidance principles the IRS provides for audits under the antiabuse rules; and
- Identify ways taxpayers can plan to prove material participation in their business activities.

## ¶ 403 INTRODUCTION

About 40 years ago, tax shelters—especially the real estate variety—were running amuck in the United States. Thus, in 1976 the at-risk rules were devised with the idea that these rules would deny losses unless a taxpayer was actually at risk for the investment. And most folks who wanted tax losses really didn't want to be at risk. Real estate activities were exempted from the at-risk rules, with the result that investors changed their shelter focus from fields such as oil and gas ventures or equipment leasing to real estate.

In response, in 1986 regulators created the passive activity loss (PAL) rules targeted specifically to real estate investors. Rental activities are almost always passive. So the at-risk rules were expanded to encompass real estate activities—the popular tax sheltering opportunities. Today, the passive loss rules governing real estate have proven so effective that such real estate tax shelters have declined.

## ¶ 404 WHY MATERIAL PARTICIPATION MATTERS

### Avoiding the Net Investment Income Tax

If a taxpayer can satisfy one of the current tests for material participation, a loss activity can be categorized as active, so that associated losses from the activity are not limited by the bounds of Code Sec. 469 and may be deductible. Satisfying one of the tests and relating the activity to a trade or business, income may be exempted from the 3.8 percent net investment income tax (NIIT) created in 2013 as a funding mechanism for the Affordable Care Act health programs. That tax on an individual applies to

- The net investment income; or
- The excess of modified adjusted gross income over the following threshold amounts:
  - $250,000 for those married filing jointly or qualifying widow(er) with a dependent child,
  - $125,000 for those married filing separately; and
  - $200,000 in all other cases.

The IRS defines "net investment income" to include

- Interest, dividends, certain annuities, royalties, and rents (unless derived in a trade or business in which the NIIT doesn't apply);
- Income derived in a trade or business that is a passive activity or trading in financial instruments or commodities; and
- Net gains from the disposition of property (to the extent taken into account in computing taxable income), other than property held in a trade or business to which NIIT doesn't apply.

## Qualified Joint Ventures

Material participation is also used in qualification for the Code Sec. 761(f) qualified joint venture. That statutory provision says if a joint venture operates a trade or business between a husband and wife who both materially participate in it, the couple can choose tax treatment of the venture as either a partnership or a disregarded entity. For couples in community property states who own an interest in an unincorporated business entity as their community property, they too have the choice between status as a partnership or disregarded entity. Those in the other states must both materially participate to have the choice.

If a more favorable tax rate is adopted for qualified business income, such as that of passthrough entities, the issue will become how the Treasury Department will define qualified income.

Another issue is proposed regulations that are now about 20 years old that deal with self-employment tax for members of a limited liability company (LLC) that in certain situations may subject members to self-employment tax: working in an activity for more than 500 hours annually. The regulations don't actually use the terminology stating the members materially participate, but that more than 500 hours is the first test of material participation.

## Qualified Real Estate Professionals

In 1993, the "qualified real estate professional" (QREP) came to be. The qualified real estate professional is not subject to the rule that rentals are automatically passive, and that means that material participation is now in play for those folks. They have an opportunity to show that they materially participate and therefore not have a passive activity.

And it also means that today, in a period of low interest rates and longer lives for depreciation purposes, there are a lot more rental properties that are throwing off income. And the issue then becomes the investors not wanting that income to be subject to that 3.8 percent Medicare surtax; it's only the qualified real estate professionals who can maintain the 3.8 percent surtax doesn't apply because their rentals are not automatically passive, and they can demonstrate material participation.

Who qualifies as a qualified real estate professional? He or she is someone who:

- Spends more than half time in real estate activities;
- Spends more than 750 hours in real estate activities annually;
- May elect to aggregate all rental activities; and
- Can help support material participation criteria for all aggregated activities.

# ¶ 405 DEFINING THE ISSUES FOR PASSIVE ACTIVITIES

The preceding just defined the exemption from the passive activity strictures for qualified real estate professionals. But other definitions are crucial to the discussion of material participation.

## What Is a Passive Activity?

The rules define a "passive activity" as:

- A trade or business activity in which the taxpayer does not materially participate
  - "Trade or business," for this purpose, includes the Code Sec. 212 investment activities, and
  - It also includes start-up business operations;
- Code Sec. 469 does not apply to an activity until the basis and at-risk basis limitations are first satisfied.

## What Is an Activity?

Similar to Code Sec. 465, a facts-and-circumstances determination is used to define "activity":

- Real estate professionals have special aggregation rules for rentals;
- What scope is applied to the term
  - A broad definition may allow for material participation, but
  - A narrow definition may help when the investor has a disposition.

Taxpayers should not underestimate the importance of grouping activities to meet the requirements for annual hours. Proper groupings can be very helpful in meeting the criteria for material participation. Reg. 1.469-4 allows some flexibility in the facts-and-circumstances used to define activity.

## What Constitutes Material Participation

Reg. 1.46905T(f)(4) maintains that the extent of an individual's participation in an activity may be established by any reasonable means, such as:

- Contemporaneous daily time reports (ones written at the time of the activity), logs, or similar documents are not required if the extent of the participation may be established by other reasonable means; and
- Reasonable means for these purposes may include but are not limited to the identification of services performed over a period of time and the approximate number of hours spent performing such services during such period, based on appointment books, calendars, or narrative summaries.

The background for this regulation is the auto log, a 1984 requirement that auto expenses of people who drove extensively for a trade or business be proven with contemporaneous logs of every related trip. Taxpayers objected so strenuously that in January 1985 the IRS announced it would relax the rules for substantiation. In April 1985 Congress retroactively repealed the auto log requirement, replacing it with a rule requiring "adequate" records and "substantial corroborating evidence." When the PAL rules were enacted, they did not required logs of hours for applying Code Sec. 469.

So now different requirements exist for businesspeople and tradespeople.

**For Investors.** The threshold for material participation is based on hours of annual participation. The criteria ignore the hours the taxpayer spends as an investor unless he or she is also active in management of the activity. The criteria also ignore work not customarily done by an owner if performed simply to satisfy the material participation baseline. Further, unless the investors are qualified real estate professionals, hours of spouses for the activity are aggregated.

**For Limited Partners.** A limited partner is generally assumed to be a passive participant. However, limited partners can use the following to establish material participation:

- The 500 annual hours criterion (test 1);
- The 5-out-of-10 years criterion (test 5); and
- Any 3 years (test 6).

**For LLC Members and LLP Partners.** By statute, the members and partners fall into the limited entrepreneur category and are arguably subject to the limited partner tests (above). By case law, however, with the acquiescence of the IRS in one of its actions on decision (AOD) memoranda, the members and partners may use all seven tests for material participation.

## STUDY QUESTION

**1.** The passive activity loss (PAL) rules are applicable to each of the following types of taxpayers *except:*

    **a.** Closely held S corporations.

    **b.** Individuals.

    **c.** Trusts.

    **d.** Estates.

---

# ¶ 406 TESTS OF MATERIAL PARTICIPATION

There are seven standard tests described in IRS Publication 925, *Passive Activity and At-Risk Rules,* to determine whether a taxpayer may claim to have materially participated in a trade or business activity. Figure 4.1 summarizes the tests.

Test 1. The taxpayer participated in the activity for more than 500 hours.

Test 2. The taxpayer's participation was substantially all the participation in the activity of all individuals for the tax year, including the participation of individuals who did not own any interest in the activity.

Test 3. The taxpayer participated in the activity for more than 100 hours during the tax year and participated at least as much as any other individual (*including individuals who did not own any interest in the activity*) for the year.

Test 4. The activity is a significant participation activity, and the taxpayer participated in all significant participation activities for more than 500 hours. A "significant participation activity" is any trade or business activity in the taxpayer participated for more than 100 hours during the year and in which he or she did not materially participate under any of the material participation tests, other than this test.

Test 5. The taxpayer materially participated in the activity for any 5 (*whether or not consecutive*) of the 10 immediately preceding tax years.

Test 6. The activity is a personal service activity in which the taxpayer materially participated in any 3 (*whether or not consecutive*) preceding tax years. An activity is a "personal service activity" if it involves the performance of personal services in the fields of health (including veterinary services), law, engineering, architecture, accounting, actuarial science, performing arts, consulting, or any other trade or business in which capital is not a material income-producing factor.

Test 7. Based on the facts and circumstances, the taxpayer participated in the activity on a regular, continuous, and substantial basis during the year.

**Figure 4.1. The Seven Tests of Material Participation**

**CAUTION:** Publication 925 warns that taxpayer did not materially participate in the activity under test 7 if he or she participated in the activity for 100 hours or less during the year. Participation in managing the activity does not count in determining whether the taxpayer materially participated under this test if:

- Any other person received compensation for managing the activity; or
- Any individual spent more hours during the tax year managing the activity than the taxpayer did (regardless of whether the individual was compensated for the management services).

A common issue is how to meet the 500-hour stipulation if a taxpayer becomes involved in an activity late in the year. The 500 hours minimum is not prorated, so an individual does have to meet more than 500 hours, even if it means the last month. But the good news is that he or she may satisfy one of the six other tests. So, if the taxpayer buys an interest in an activity late in the year, it could be that he or she only has an opportunity to spend 62 hours on that activity. Under the terms of test 2, if the taxpayer performs substantially all of the work, he or she materially participates. So, for somebody who acquires a property late in the year, the 500 hours is really kind of off the table, but the acquirer does have the other tests that he or she may satisfy.

One of the issues with a trust is who has to materially participate. And the IRS has taken the position that the trustee has to satisfy the requirement and the courts have not been so harsh about that. If the trustee is hiring somebody else, then in certain cases, the taxpayer can use those hours.

Now, this issue happens to say it's a grantor trust. If it's a grantor trust, the IRS looks through the trust and it doesn't really have a trust as the taxpayer; in a sense, an individual is the taxpayer.

Not all seven tests use hours, but the tests that don't use hours are antiabuse rules. And so, they're kind of designed to target investors. These taxpayers don't really want to rely on those types of definitions of material participation.

If the taxpayer is involved in management, he or she is going to look at financial statements as a manager. So, looking at the financial statements counts if the individual is also managing, but it doesn't count if all he or she does is sort of passive investment.

The IRS ignores work not customarily done by an owner if done to satisfy material participation. There's actually an example in the regulations in which the owner of the business, at the end of the year is just a few hours short of material participation. So, what the owner does is send the janitor home and the owner ends up doing the janitorial work. That's not a common approach!

As mentioned earlier, spousal hours are aggregated. There are two exceptions to this practice. The general rule is that if the taxpayers are spouses, they are thrown them together, they're one taxpayer. The first exception is qualified real estate professional. In defining whether someone is a qualified real estate professional, each spouse stands alone. One of them could be a qualified real estate professional and the other one is not. The second exception is the husband and wife who run a joint venture, as described earlier. Each spouse's participation is separate. Otherwise, for purpose of the PAL rules' definition of material participation, spouses' hours are aggregated.

For the test 3 requirement, which sounds easy to satisfy, the taxpayer must spend more than 100 hours in a significant participation activity (a SPA). Now if the taxpayer has a SPA and does not less than anyone else (i.e., at least as much), not less literally means exactly what it says. If the taxpayer works 105 hours and somebody else works 105 hours, they both materially participate because their hours tied. But if the taxpayer spends 105 hours and somebody else spends 110 hours, the taxpayer doesn't meet this test. The individual who spends 110 hours, if that's the most work of anybody, does materially participate. "Anybody else" includes nonowner employees, so it's not just the people who have an ownership interest.

Test 4, again a SPA, may satisfy material participation if the taxpayer doesn't meet any other test. He or she can aggregate these SPAs that do not meet any other test and, if combined they exceed 500 hours, the taxpayer has materially participated.

**EXAMPLE:** Chris Regan has one activity that she spent 200 hours on, another one that she spent 200 on, and another one that she spent 150 hours on in 2017. So 200 + 200 + 150 hours = 550 hours for the year. As long as none of those three activities meets another material participation test, Chris can throw them all together. She gets to 550 hours and test 4 says she materially participate in all three of them.

Now if it turns out that the 150 hours spent on her third activity was more time than anybody else, and so Chris met test 3, more than 100 hours and not less than anyone else. Then in that case, she materially participated in number three, the 150-hour activity. She can only aggregate the 200 and the 200, thus not exceeding 500. So, by materially participating in that third activity under test 3, she must discount the other two activities.

Now a taxpayer may or may not want that aggregation, depending on whether activities earned income or had losses, but that's the result. So those first four tests have very mechanical applications. Nothing is particularly difficult about meeting those first four tests, except for ways to show the number of hours spent. How does the taxpayer prove that he or she spent more than 100 hours and, moreover, how does the taxpayer prove that he or she spent not less than anybody else?

Tests 5 and 6 deal with participation over multiple years, not one year's hours. Test 5 requires material participation in 5 of the preceding 10 years—and not necessarily 5 years in a row. Test 6 deals with material participation in a personal service activity in any 3 preceding years. They are both antiabuse tests. Taxpayers had used the criteria to manipulate their income and expenses to produce income loss in year 1, year 2, and year 3, and by timing the income, push it into one year and deductions in the other direction. They avoided material participation in the years in which they had income, and would materially participate in the year with losses. Their income vacillated between passive income and nonpassive losses. So the tests require that the taxpayer who materially participates in 5 of the 10 preceding years is materially participating (for tax purposes) in the current year.

Test 6 addresses abuses of personal service activity with the provision of *any 3 preceding years.*

**EXAMPLE:** Joe O'Reilly was a partner in an accounting firm for 20 years, then retired. He draws some retirement pay from the firm but no longer performs accounting work. Code Sec. 736 holds that as long as Joe is receiving retirement payments, he is still a partner. He maintains that he is not materially participating so his income is passive and can be sheltered. The IRS responds that if it's a personal service activity, it produces income considered to be active income because Joe participated for far more than the preceding 3 years.

Test 7, the criterion to have regular, continuous, substantial involvement, is essentially useless. It depends on the facts and circumstances of participation, and the IRS is not particularly friendly about satisfying it.

## STUDY QUESTION

**2.** Which of the following types of material participation tests are based on statute and difficult to satisfy?

    **a.** Substantially all participation.

    **b.** Regular, continuous, substantial involvement.

    **c.** Material participation in any 3 preceding years.

    **d.** More than 100 hours and not less than anyone else.

## Application of Tests 1 Through 4

Tests 1 through 4 look at the number of hours a taxpayer participates. In grouping material participation activities, the focus is showing the number of hours that he or she spent in an activity.

**Limited Partners.** When the tests were written, limited partners were the folks who were taking these passive losses. They were the ones who were getting these tax shelter benefits. Maybe the rules targeted the physician who had substantial income, didn't want to pay tax on that, and so the physician was investing as a limited partner.

The tests were aimed to make sure, as a general rule, that limited partners' activities were going to be passive. The general rule was that limited partners are passive. But there are a couple of exceptions to that. The IRS had the two antiabuse rules and wanted limited partners to circumvent them simply by becoming limited partners. So, tests 5 and 6, the antiabuse provisions, apply to everybody.

And then under test 1, if a limited partner works more than 500 hours, it doesn't matter what kind of a partner he or she is, the participation is material. So, for the most part, limited partners are limited to that more than 500-hour test.

## STUDY QUESTION

**3.** Although a limited partner is assumed to be passive, a limited partner may use each of the following tests to establish material participation, ***except:***

    **a.** More than 100 hours and not less than anyone else.

    **b.** More than 500 hours.

    **c.** Material participation in 5 or the preceding 10 years.

    **d.** Material participation in any 3 preceding years.

**Members of LLCs and Partners in LLPs.** When the tests were written in 1986, very few taxpayers had limited liability companies, so the IRS didn't really build LLCs into the program. So members of an LLC or partners of an LLP partner, had questions as to whether they can qualify. Those questions have largely been resolved through a variety of court cases. The courts have said the members should have the opportunity to see whether they materially participate. How to do that? The IRS uses facts and circumstances in addition to the tests.

The IRS has now acquiesced using actions on decision of court rulings. The IRS lost five cases on this issue and acquiesced to one of them. Thus, from a litigation standpoint going forward, the IRS is not going to prevent those in an LLC or LLP from using all seven tests for material participation.

**Real Estate Professionals.** Real estate professionals are not subject to the rule that rentals are automatically passive, and that means that real estate agents have the opportunity, again, to use all seven tests. So, it's really, really important to determine whether somebody is a real estate professional. A real estate professional is somebody who, in a sense, is in real estate.

But being in real estate encompasses lots of different activities. Real estate professionals are not necessarily just homebuilders or real estate brokers. They also invest in real estate. They also purchase land and hold it for investment. They develop land sometimes. They do a lot more than sell houses.

Thus, the IRS said real estate professionals have to prove that they spend more than half of their time in these real estate activities. So, primarily, they must show they are in real estate. And second, the total annual time must be more than 750 hours. That's kind of an arbitrary test that's actually in the statute but not in the regulations, so criteria real estate professionals satisfy is not just to prove the number of hours for material participation but also that more than half of their time is spent in real estate activity. One step is documenting their hours and recording more than 750 hours in real estate activities. And then beyond that, they go back to the regular old material participation tests.

Somebody who was not a real estate professional in the past and now becomes a real estate professional who materially participates may have carryover suspended passive losses. Qualified real estate professionals have a problem. If they had losses suspended in years where they were not qualified real estate professionals, they can't suddenly say now they're qualified real estate professionals so they get to apply those rules with respect to every activity they've ever been involved in.

One of the problems with losses being suspended under the passive loss rule is they get frozen at that third hurdle, the hardest one to clear. The basis hurdle and the at-risk basis hurdle, are a lot easier to clear because taxpayers can simply establish basis and they're over those hurdles.

But when taxpayers get to that third hurdle, the passive loss hurdle, the only way to clear that hurdle is to have passive income or to completely dispose of the activity's property in question.

**Contemporaneous Recordkeeping.** Proof of hours of participation in an activity would seem to require activity logs prepared close in time to when the activity occurred. But such detailed notetaking is something taxpayers hate to do. So for tests 1 through 4, many taxpayers resort to after-the-fact counting of hours and employ confirmation bias to find results that support their position. But material participation is an inherently factual, hours-based issue, so many taxpayers and tax practitioners turn to a detailed review of the facts and decisions in case law. Court decisions, covered next, can be annoying because they don't always confirm the positions taxpayers would like.

## Indicators of Lacking Material Participation Under Any Test

The IRS Audit Guide lists indicators that a taxpayer does not have material participation in an activity under any of the seven tests:

- The taxpayer is not compensated for services;
- His or her residence is hundreds of miles away from the activity;
- He or she has significant W-2 wages requiring more than 40 hours per week;
- The taxpayer has numerous other activities, including hobbies, requiring significant time;
- The activity has onsite paid employees;
- The taxpayer is elderly or has health issues; and
- The work claimed by taxpayer does not materially affect the operations of the trade or business.

# ¶ 407 JUDICIAL DECISIONS ABOUT MATERIAL PARTICIPATION

Although there are a lot of court cases debating the issue of material participation and the PAL rules, none of the cases involved detailed, contemporaneous logs of time spent recording activities. This section minimizes the inherent confirmation bias in using only decisions that support the taxpayer's position by examining:

- Four suits with taxpayers winning the decision; and
- Four cases in which the IRS won the day.

All eight cases are Tax Court memorandum decisions that were not specially selected here; material participation cases are heavily slanted to Tax Court memorandum cases. This prevalence reflects the fact-specific nature of the issue.

> **CAUTION:** Taxpayers and tax practitioners are wise not to rely on using just one or two specific cases as their position's authority. It is more useful—and preventive of courtroom surprises—to examine a multiplicity of cases such as those summarized here.

Comparing favorable and unfavorable decisions is instructive. Are the taxpayer's facts similar enough to apply favorable decisions as precedents? Can the facts of unfavorable cases be distinguished enough so the decision does not apply to the taxpayer's case?

## Goshorn, TC Memo 1993-578

**Winner of Proof Offered.** IRS.

**Facts Summary.**

- Taxpayer bought a sailboat while living in Dallas;
- UPS (employer) moved him to Connecticut;
- Hired marina to rent the boat in Texas;
- Visited Texas 14 times for UPS work
  - Made side trips to marina to inspect boat,
  - Did budgeting work at home in Connecticut;

- Taxpayer claimed
  - Monthly budgeting work (8 hours per month),
  - Inspection of boat when in Texas (8 hours per trip),
  - All travel time between CT and TX (needed to get over 500 hours); and
- Marina did all work connected with boat rental.

**Basis of Court Ruling.**

- Work considered to be investor work;
- Hours not well documented; after the fact estimates of fixed budget time per month, fixed "inspection" time per trip;
- Court said material participation substantiations "by no means allow the type of post-event ballpark guesstimate that petitioner used." This will become the most-used Tax Court quote on this issue.

## *Speer,* TC Memo 1996-323

**Winner of Proof Offered.** IRS.

**Facts Summary.**

- Controlling shareholder of Home Shopping Network (HSN);
- Involved in 30 or so family-owned businesses;
- Spent most time on HSN; and
- Three loss-generating businesses.

**Basis of Court Ruling.**

- Claimed test 4—aggregation of SPA totaling more than 500 hours;
- Reported 150-250-150 hours in three operations (testimony);
- Claimed his testimony was a "narrative summary"; and
- Otherwise no records provided of time.

## *Carlstedt,* TC Memo 1997-331

**Winner of Proof Offered.** IRS.

**Facts Summary.**

- IRS and taxpayer flip sides
  - Activity produced income
  - Taxpayer wanted passive income
  - Taxpayer argued he spent less than 500 hours; IRS said he spent more than 500 hours;
- Taxpayer had a contemporaneous calendar and a supplemental diary of activities; and
- Times were assigned years after the fact.

**Basis of Court Ruling.**

- Taxpayer had a contractor job and 2 passthrough entities (including the one at issue);
- The operations of the three businesses were interrelated; and
- He seemed to allocate time to the contractor job and away from the activity that he wanted to be passive.

**¶407**

## Fowler, TC Memo 2002-223

**Winner of Proof Offered.** IRS.

**Facts Summary.**

- President of heating and air conditioning company;
- Kept detailed electronic calendar of his planned activities, scheduled a month in advance;
- He did not adjust the (estimated) time until 6 to 7 years later when preparing for trial;
- Thus there were no contemporaneous records of time;
- Taxpayer had 4 rental properties;
- Claimed to be a QREP with material participation;
- Said heating and air conditioning business was a real property business; and
- Claimed more than 750 hours but lacked proof because his records were after-the-fact ballpark guesstimates.

**Basis of Court Ruling.**

- The taxpayer tried to distinguish his case from the other "losers" by flashing his calendar to the IRS and Tax Court;
- But this calendar was detailed only as a prework planner and did not record activities as they were actually done, or even record activities shortly thereafter, and provided no actual times spent on activities; and
- So in the end it was no better than the ballpark guesstimate of others, and led to the same result.

## Harrison, TC Memo 1996-509

**Winner of Proof Offered.** Taxpayer.

**Facts Summary.**

- Taxpayer owns trucking and waste removal business;
- Lives in New Jersey;
- Developed an interest in gold mining and later met someone in Las Vegas who was involved in treasure hunting;
- Taxpayer invested in 3 treasure hunting ventures, none of which was successful;
- Taxpayer did no research before investing, but did communicate with a well-known, and successful, treasure hunter;
- He spent 35 to 40 days on a ship for one of the ventures, working as a crew member;
- He sent considerable other time working with a joint venture partner; and
- He also continued to run his NJ business with daily phone communication.

**Basis of Court Ruling.**

- He claimed more than 1,200 hours based on description of activities and time estimates;
- Joint venture partner supported his description of his involvement; and
- Tax Court did not accept all of his time estimates but believed he spent more than 500 hours.

## *Adeyemo,* TC Memo 2014-1

**Winner of Proof Offered.** Taxpayer.

**Facts Summary.**

- Taxpayer was a sales representative; unemployed for 5 months of one year at issue;
- Owned and managed 7 rentals; taxpayer did management work;
- Claimed QREP status and material participation;
- Had a logbook that was very thorough (activities), although time was entered after the fact;
- There was inconsistent evidence whether logbook was contemporaneously prepared;
- Tax Court accepted the logbook because
  - There is no requirement it be contemporaneous,
  - It was quite detailed, and
  - The accepted logbook was the "winning" part of this case;
- The logbook showed 800 rental hours one year and 715 the other.

**Basis of Court Ruling.**

- Tax Court found taxpayer was *not* a QREP
  - QREP must spend more than 50 percent of his or her total time in real property trade/business activities,
  - His sales rep responsibilities were found to be 1,500 hours in one year, and
  - Less than 750 total real estate hours made issue not relevant in year 2 (partial unemployed year); and
- Taxpayer claimed added hours after the fact that were unreliable "ballpark guesstimates."

## *Tolin,* TC Memo 2014-65

**Winner of Proof Offered:** Taxpayer.

**Facts Summary.**

- Sole practitioner attorney in Minneapolis;
- Documented law work 1,200 hours-1,100 hours-1,000 hours in three years at issue;
- Involved in horse racing and later breeding;
- Owned "Choosing Choice," (CC) a race horse with some success in shorter races;
- Activity primarily holding CC out to stud;
- Boarded CC at several places, but settled on Louisiana;
- Spent time in Minnesota marketing CC and also made many trips to Louisiana; and
- Stayed with owned of horse farm when he visited LA and travelled to other farms to push stud services to mares at other farms.

**Basis of Court Ruling.**

- Narrative summary with about 168 hours for LA travel; Tax Court accepted 150;
- The narrative summary was supported by phone records, third-party witnesses;
- With the hours spent in Minnesota marketing CC and administrating the activity, the Tax Court accepted he satisfied material participation;

¶407

- Taxpayer devoted considerable time to networking with the state breeders association and with horse farm owners and owners of mares;
- These parties supported his narrative; and
- Court cited **Bartlett,** TC Memo 2013-182, that narrative summary needs supporting documentation.

## Kline, TC Memo 2015-144

**Winner of Proof Offered: Taxpayer.**

**Facts Summary.**

- Taxpayer was captain with Southwest Airlines;
- Lived in Arizona;
- Business chartering boats in British Virgin Islands;
- Hired a charter management company that would allow him to be involved in management;
- Taxpayer advertised charters, primarily to other airline pilots;
- Taxpayer and his wife worked some charters where he captained the boat and also worked a total of 12 hours per day (as did his wife); and
- A log of hours was created at the time of the audit.

**Basis of Court Ruling.**

- The charter company had detailed records of time/activity spent by its crews for charters where taxpayer/wife not in charge;
- Tax Court accepted material participation under test 3 (more than 100 hours and more than anyone else); and
- Taxpayer time record was
  - Email records used to estimate time spent when not in BVI,
  - Invoices of his charters with his time estimates consistent with charter company records of other trips,
  - The invoices in particular were supporting evidence, and
  - Charter company used many employees, so none worked more than taxpayer.

## STUDY QUESTIONS

**4.** Which of the following identifies a court case in which the IRS prevailed with respect to disputes arising related to material participation?

    **a.** *Harrison,* TC Memo 1996-509.

    **b.** *Adeyemo,* TC Memo 2014-1.

    **c.** *Kline,* TC Memo 2015-144.

    **d.** *Goshorn,* TC Memo 1993-578.

**5.** Which of the following identifies a court case in which the taxpayer prevailed with respect to disputes related to material participation?

    **a.** *Tolin,* TC Memo 2014-65.

    **b.** *Goshorn,* TC Memo 1993-578.

    **c.** *Speer,* TC Memo 1996-323.

    **d.** *Fowler,* TC Memo 2002-223.

## Lessons Learned from Both Winners and Losers

These eight case summaries offer valuable insight into the applications of the seven tests and the uses of facts and circumstances in reaching rulings about material participation. It is clear that one need not have contemporaneous time records; the Tax Court accepts the statement in Reg. 1.469-5T(f)(4) about substantiation. However, a contemporaneous record of time is a very good idea; electronic means (e.g., a cell phone or laptop scheduling calendar) of capturing time and activity are prevalent now.

A "typical" taxpayer will re-create time and activity logs when the issue is raised, but this on-the-fly substantiation does not go well as documentation in court. Exceptions to these caveats about recordkeeping apply when there is some other supporting evidence to corroborate the after-the-fact time and activity records:

- Kline had invoices of boat charters;

- Tolin had various parties who met with him about his stud horse who could support his activities and times spent; and

- Harrison had a joint venture partner (treasure hunting) who supported his claimed involvement.

General logs of activities without precise time allocations are not very helpful as court evidence. Tax practitioners can provide clients with copies of the IRS Audit Manual activity log to use each year. Those last three columns in the IRS audit logs are the important ones. If the taxpayer also records the date there, then the log provides contemporaneous records and the records are not going to have any question at all. If the taxpayer completes all four columns, the record is perfect. If he or she is going to miss one of those four columns, the date is the one to miss because contemporaneous records, by definition, are not required. But it's ideal to have the activity, have the hours, and have third parties who can substantiate it.

Time allocations that are incredulous actually hurt a taxpayer's credibility; it's preferable not to inflate the hours just to satisfy one of the tests' criteria. Records should describe specific activities performed in addition to just the time spent. Having the names of people with whom the taxpayer performed the activity provides valuable corroboration, as in the *Bartlett, Tolin,* and *Harrison* cases.

Having a full-time job makes it hard for the taxpayer to support time in other activities.

Many of the lessons gleaned from the cases are negative—what not to do to prove material participation. As much as Congress devised rules that did not *require* contemporaneous written records of activities and time spent, the wiser course for taxpayers is to maintain contemporaneous written records of time spent by activity. The regulations under Code Sec. 274(d) state that written evidence is more credible if it was provided close in time to the activity.

On an unrelated issue, Reg. 1.274-5T(c)(1) offers guidance on the credibility of records:

- Written evidence is more credible;

- "Probative value of written evidence is greater the closer in time it relates ... ";

- The proactive taxpayer completes an "IRS log" of dates, times, and activities to supplement the receipts and other documents given to his or her tax preparer after year end.

Strategies taxpayers need to understand are the types of triggers the IRS keys in on to launch an audit of investors and how to build a case in advance for their material participation in their trade or business activities.

## STUDY QUESTION

6. Based on the various cases presented as examples, which of the following identifies one of the key lessons learned?

    **a.** Written evidence is more credible.

    **b.** A taxpayer is required to keep contemporaneous time log of passive activity.

    **c.** Typical taxpayers create time and activity logs before potential issues are raised.

    **d.** Having a full-time job makes it easier to support significant time in other activities.

# MODULE 1: INDIVIDUAL TAXATION— Chapter 5: Sharing Economy: Tax Issues for the Gig Economy

## ¶ 501  WELCOME

This chapter covers the rules for those who are engaged in the gig economy—a system characterized by workers who are engaged for short-term ("gig") projects. This chapter provides an overview of recent tax developments and highlights planning tips and techniques to help tax practitioners in their practice.

## ¶ 502  LEARNING OBJECTIVES

Upon completion of this chapter, you will be able to:

- Identify where to report income and expenses earned in the gig economy;
- Recognize how self-employment tax affects gig economy earnings; and
- Identify the limitations on deducting rental losses.

## ¶ 503  INTRODUCTION

Workers in the gig economy are primarily freelancers or independent contractors engaged in contingent, alternative, or on-demand work arrangements. According to one study (The Rise and Nature of Alternative Work Arrangements in the United States, 1995–2015), 95 percent of net employment growth in the United States between 2005 and 2015 was in the gig economy Another study reported by McKinsey Global Institute in 2016 (Independent Work: Choice, Necessity, and the Gig Economy) found that between 20 percent and 30 percent of workers are engaged in some independent contractor work.

And, according to yet another study (Intuit 2020 Report: Twenty Trends That Will Shape the Next Decade), it is expected that by 2020, 40 percent of the U.S. workforce will be independent contractors. The Bureau of Labor Statistics started collecting new data on the gig economy in May 2017, but it is unclear when the information will become available.

Along with the gig economy is the sharing economy, which is essentially a subset of the gig economy. The sharing economy is characterized by renting out the use of property—such as a home or business tools—on a short-term basis.

## ¶ 504  THE GIG ECONOMY

The gig economy has vast effects on workers and businesses. From the worker perspective, freelance work offers flexibility. Only gigs of interest need to be accepted. This work arrangement also offers work-life balance, with scheduling up to the freelancer. The work may be full time or part time (to supplement a full-time job or work fewer hours).

## Worker Perspective

The gig economy connotes freelance writers and web designers sitting by their computers at odd hours to complete a project. The reality is that the gig economy affects all type of workers in all types of industries:

- Professional workers in accounting, law, and engineering;
- Office workers in bookkeeping, website design, and social media; and
- Construction workers in the trades.

## Business Perspective

The hourly rate of pay for an independent contractor may run higher than the rate for a comparable employee, but the overall cost is lower:

- The business pays for labor only on an as-needed basis;
- The business avoids payroll taxes; there are no FICA or FUTA taxes on payments to independent contractors;
- The business does not have to provide to independent contractors health coverage, retirement benefits, or any other fringe benefits offered to employees; and
- Using independent contractors may avoid the need to pay for office space if the workers work from remote locations, such as from their homes.

## STUDY QUESTION

1. A company engages a graphic artist through an online platform to design a logo. The artist is an independent contractor. Typically the company saves money on all of the following *except*:

   a. Payroll taxes.
   b. Fringe benefits.
   c. The hourly rate of pay.
   d. Office space.

## Categories of Independent Workers

There are four general categories of independent contractors:

- Those using the gig economy for their primary income out of choice (because they like the work arrangement);
- Those using the gig economy for their primary income out of necessity (because they cannot obtain satisfactory employment);
- Those using the gig economy for supplemental income as casual earners; and
- Those using the gig economy for supplemental income because they are financially strapped.

Whatever the motivation for working in the gig economy, the tax results are the same.

One of the features of the gig economy is that many workers obtain their projects through online platforms. Some of the most popular gig economy platforms are:

- Uber and Lyft: drivers use their own vehicles to taxi riders. Other driving platforms include Turro (renting out personal vehicles) and HopSkipJump (driving children to afterschool activities);
- TaskRabbit and Postmates: performing various chores (e.g., delivering dry cleaning). Amazon Flex is a delivery service of Amazon. Dolly is a platform specifically for movers (e.g., providing a vehicle or doing heavy lifting);
- Care.com: babysitting and other caregiving;
- Freelancer, HelloTech, and Spare Hire: professional services (e.g., website design, tech assistance, finance and consulting); and
- Etsy and eBay: selling personally created items.

Of course, there are still many other workers who obtain gigs directly from those for whom they provide services. They may have ongoing work relationships, receive referrals, or find opportunities in other ways.

As a general rule, a worker engaged in the gig economy is self-employed and must contend with all that this status implies. Of course, a worker could set up a corporation and become an employee of his or her corporation. Or a worker may be an employee of a temporary employment agency helping him or her find gigs. But this chapter focuses mainly on self-employment.

Self-employment means:

- The worker is responsible for paying income taxes and self-employment tax. There is no wage withholding so paying these taxes usually means paying estimated taxes;
- The worker must obtain his or her own insurance. This insurance may be liability coverage (errors and omissions or malpractice insurance), health coverage, and special auto insurance; and
- The worker usually cannot receive workers' compensation or unemployment benefits. This means the worker doesn't have a safety net if the gigs dry up or if he or she is injured on the job. Of course, some states allow sole proprietors to opt in for coverage for workers' compensation.

The IRS is interested in this sector. In 2016, the IRS launched a Sharing Economy Resource Center (IR 2016-110, 8/22/16) accessible through the IRS website, irs.gov. This landing page provides links to information for:

- Individuals providing personal services;
- Individuals who are renting out their homes; and
- Company concerns.

## STUDY QUESTION

**2.** Which is *not* a factor in determining whether a worker in the gig economy is an employee or independent contractor?

- **a.** Whether the worker works full time or part time.
- **b.** The ability of the service recipient to dictate when, where, and how the work gets done.
- **c.** Which party pays for expenses
- **d.** The subjective belief by the service recipient and the worker that the worker is a contractor.

## Sharing Economy

A compliment to the gig economy is the sharing economy in which money is earned by sharing property that's owned, such as a home or business equipment. There are platforms for sharing property. These generally do not entail personal services but rather rental fees for short-term rentals. Some examples of platforms for sharing property include:

- Airbnb and OneFineStay: renting out personal residences;
- ToolLocker: renting light and heavy equipment;
- ParkingPanda: renting out a parking space; and
- OpenAirplane: renting a plane.

Some, but not all, of the tax issues for workers in the gig economy apply as well for those renting out property in the sharing economy. These tax issues will be addressed later in the chapter.

# ¶ 505 TAX ISSUES FOR SERVICE WORKERS

Many of the tax issues for performing services may be familiar to tax practitioners. The point of this section is to cover information that is not necessarily familiar to those engaged in the gig economy. Practitioners working with those engaged in the gig economy should share this information to ensure that their clients are tax compliant.

Also, this section addresses federal tax obligations. There may be additional tax obligations for workers at the state and local levels.

## Recordkeeping

Much as for sole proprietors or pass-through entity shareholders/partners, for their business organization gig workers are required to keep books and records. If the self-employed worker performs solo services, income and expenses may be tracked in simple Excel spreadsheets. Additionally, today's software, cloud, and mobile accounting options make recordkeeping easier.

## Worker Classification

Perhaps the first tax issue for someone performing services involves a determination of worker classification. Is the worker an employee or independent contractor? In some cases it is clear that the worker is an independent contractor because he or she has a business of providing services for multiple customers and controls all aspects of this business.

In some cases it is clear that the worker is an employee. For example, individuals who obtain placements through a temporary agency are employees of the agency even though they perform services for third parties. As such, the worker receives wages, which are subject to withholding and reported on Form W-2. The worker may also receive certain benefits, such as sick pay accrued under state law.

**Reporting Expenses.** If the worker is an employee and has any job-related expenses, deductions are reported on Form 2106 (or 2106-EZ) and then claimed as a miscellaneous itemized deduction on Schedule A of Form 1040. This means that only expenses in excess of 2 percent of adjusted gross income (AGI) are actually deducted. And if the taxpayer is subject to the alternative minimum tax, he or she gets no benefit from the deduction.

This chapter does not discuss tax issues for employees working in the gig economy; rather, the discussion focuses on self-employed individuals.

**Unsettled Law.** Worker classification may not be so clear. There have been lawsuits testing whether Uber drivers are employees. The Third District Court of Appeals in a Florida case refused to allow a driver dropped by Uber to claim unemployment benefits; he wasn't considered an employee. Class action suits in California and Massachusetts resulted in agreements by Uber to make some changes, while continuing to treat drivers as independent contractors. However, new lawsuits continue to be filed.

If worker classification isn't clear, it's important to apply the three-factor test to determine worker classification:

- *Behavioral control* covers facts that show whether the business has a right to direct and control what work is accomplished and how the work is done, through instructions, training, or other means;

- *Financial control* covers facts that show if the business has a right to direct or control the financial and business aspects of the worker's job. These include facts showing who can make the profit, who pays for expenses, and how the worker is paid; and

- *Relationship of the parties* covers facts that show the type of relationship the parties had, such as a written contract evidencing that both parties wanted to create an independent contractor agreement.

A determination of worker classification isn't dependent on whether the person works full or part time or how much he or she earns.

No single factor is controlling when it comes to worker classification. For example, the mere fact of having a written agreement stating that the worker is an independent contractor does not nail down worker classification; the IRS is not a party to the agreement. More details about worker classification can be found in IRS Publication 1779, *Independent Contractor or Employee,* and IRS Publication 15-A, *Employer's Supplemental Tax Guide.*

## Tax Ramifications of Being an Independent Contractor

**Reporting Income.** The first tax issue concerns reporting income. All income must be reported on Schedule C of Form 1040. Schedule C-EZ, *Net Profit from Business,* can be used, but this form is barred if the worker is claiming a home office deduction, as explained later.

When it comes to reported income, it does not matter whether the income is paid in cash, property, or barter. Payment by digital currency, such as bitcoin, is treated as payment in property, not cash.

There is no minimum income below which income need not be reported on a worker's income tax return. This is so even though income may not be reported to the IRS.

If a company receives services of the gig worker, it must report payments of $600 or more for the year on Form 1099-MISC, *Miscellaneous Income.* And this information is also provided to the IRS. If the worker provides services to consumers, there is no information reporting.

**PLANNING POINTER:**    To help contractors prepare their tax returns promptly, Form 1099-MISC with an entry in box 7 showing nonemployee compensation must be provided to the worker and transmitted to the IRS by January 31. This is the same deadline as for W-2s.

**CAUTION:**    The IRS is looking for unreported income. Tax gap estimates released in 2016 (a press release detailing the gap for 2008–2010 can be found on irs.gov) stated that much of spread between what the government collected and

**¶505**

what it thinks it should have collected is because of self-employed individuals underreporting income, overstating deductions, and not paying self-employment tax.

If the IRS suspects that income is not reported or is being underreported, the IRS may examine a taxpayer and check on income reporting through:

- Cross checking reporting against Forms 1099-MISC;
- Cross checking reporting against Forms 1099-K, Payment Card and Third Party Network Transactions; and
- Examining bank account records.

There is considerable litigation on businesses that fail to report income. In a recent case, a jewelry maker who sold his wares at craft shows and online failed to report all of his income. The IRS used Form 1099-Ks to reconstruct his income, and he couldn't show that the IRS was wrong (**Kahmann,** TC Summary Opinion 2017-35).

**Reporting Expenses.** Those working in the gig economy do not pay tax on their gross receipts—the fees or other payments received for their services. They pay tax on their *net earnings from self-employment*, which is the net profit that results after subtracting allowable deductions for business expenses from these gross receipts.

Expenses that are deductible are listed in Part II of Schedule C. There are many that are enumerated, such as advertising and car and truck expenses. Examples of other expenses likely to be relevant to a worker in the gig economy include:

- Insurance other than health insurance;
- Legal and professional fees, such as fees for accounting or bookkeeping services;
- Repairs and maintenance;
- Supplies;
- Taxes and licenses; and
- Utilities.

However, even if there is no special line for a particular deduction, it can be claimed as "other expenses." For example, Uber drivers who provide water and magazines for riders can treat these costs as other deductible expenses. These other expenses are listed in Part V of Schedule C.

Some expenses unique to those in the gig economy may be fully deductible. These include fees paid to the platform through which they work. For example, there's a $20 nonrefundable fee charged by TaskRabbit to run a criminal background check.

Some expenses may not be fully deductible. Many in the gig economy drive their personal vehicle for business, either as the gig itself (such as Uber or Lyft) or in connection with the gig. These workers can deduct their actual expenses or use the IRS-set standard allowance (53.5 cents per mile in 2017). If the standard mileage allowance is used, it covers lease payments or depreciation, insurance, registration and tags, gas and oil, car washes, repairs and maintenance, and tires.

**Figuring Full Versus Partial Deductions.** To take any deduction for a vehicle, it is essential to keep track of business mileage and other elements of the travel (e.g., dates and destinations). This can be done with a written log or a mobile app for this purpose. Lack of substantiation is a key area of litigation, and the courts are loathe to allow writeoffs without proper records, no matter how credible a taxpayer's testimony may be.

Whether the actual expense method or the IRS standard mileage allowance is used for business driving, tolls and parking fees are also deductible.

To substantiate business use of a vehicle on Part IV of Schedule C, the worker should:

- Allocate mileage between business use and other use;
- Determine whether the vehicle was available during off hours;
- Note whether another vehicle is available for personal use; and
- Keep evidence to support the mileage deduction and costs such as parking.

Another key deduction is the cost of a mobile phone . . . the cost to buy it as well as the monthly service plan. If the phone is used exclusively for business, such as a rideshare driver having a dedicated phone for riders, determining the writeoff is easy. The cost of the phone likely can be deducted through expensing (the Section 179 deduction) or the *de minimis* rule, as explained later. The full cost of the monthly service plan is deductible.

If a personal phone is used sometimes for business, an allocation of expenses should be made. The IRS doesn't say exactly how to do this. An allocation based on the relative time that the phone is used would be ideal. The carriers can provide itemized bills listing the calls and text messages for phone usage.

The same can be said for tablets with Internet access.

One of the key deductions for many who work in the gig economy is a home office deduction. It is listed as a separate deduction on line 30 of Schedule C. It is not included with other business deductions in Parts II or V of Schedule C.

The home office deduction applies if two conditions are met:

- The home office is the principal place of business, a place to meet or deal with customers and clients in the normal course of business, or it is a separate structure. For the freelance writer or web designer working from a home office, this condition is easy to meet. For those who perform chores or do other activities at customer locations, this condition can be met by showing that the home office is used for substantial administrative activities, such as keeping books and records, scheduling appointments, and ordering supplies; and
- The space must be used regularly and exclusively for business. This can be a full room or a part of an area, whether or not partitioned for business use. However, the space cannot be used part of the day for business and another part for personal or family activities.

A home office can encompass multiple areas within a home, such as part of a garage to store supplies used in the second bedroom that's the home office.

The deduction can be the actual costs related to the home office or an amount determined under an IRS-created simplified method:

- If the *actual expense method* is used, the home office deduction is figured on Form 8829, *Expenses for Business Use of Your Home;* and
- If the *simplified method* is used, the deduction is limited to $5 per square foot up to 300 square feet of space (the maximum deduction is $1,500). The deduction can be figured on a worksheet in the instructions to Schedule C.

   **PLANNING POINTER:**  Some taxpayers fear that claiming a home office deduction is an audit red flag. However, there is no evidence to support this, other than some anecdotal evidence in the past, and taxpayers eligible to claim the home office deduction may be missing out on an important tax-saving opportunity.

## STUDY QUESTION

3. Which statement about the home office deduction is correct?
    a. It is an audit red flag.
    b. A deduction can only be claimed if an entire room is devoted to business use.
    c. An Uber driver can claim a home office deduction for a home used to keep her books and records.
    d. A deduction can be taken for a family den used during the day for family and at night for business.

## Reporting Costs of Fringe Benefits

How do "fringe benefits"—health coverage, retirement plans, and other benefits—relate to the gig economy? For the most part, self-employed individuals pay for any benefits they desire. For example, health coverage can be a big expense for self-employed individuals. Some may have coverage through a job if the gig economy is their part-time endeavor. Some may have COBRA coverage for 18 months following the departure from a job, although they have to pay for this in most cases. Some may enjoy coverage through a spouse. Otherwise, the self-employed person needs to find coverage.

> **PLANNING POINTER:** Self-employed individuals must use the individual marketplace (not the small business marketplace) under the Affordable Care Act to shop for coverage. However, those who are not eligible for the premium tax credit may be better advised to shop elsewhere.

**Listing Deductions for Benefit Costs on Form 1040.** The cost of health coverage, contributions to health savings accounts, and contributions to retirement plans are not treated as business expenses. They are personal expenses deductible as an adjustment to gross income.

More specifically, deductions for fringe benefits of self-employed individuals are claimed in the Adjusted Gross Income section of Form 1040:

- 100 percent of health insurance is deducted on line 29;
- Contributions to health savings accounts are deducted on line 25; and
- Contributions to SEPs, SIMPLE-IRAs, or other retirement plans are deducted on line 28.

**Portability of Benefits for Service Workers.** There is focus today on the matter of portability of benefits. These are benefits that workers can take with them when they leave employment or belong to them when they're self-employed. These benefits provide a safety net for workers.

Some benefits, such as vested benefits in retirement plans and amounts in health savings accounts, are portable. But many other benefits are not. Some other areas of focus for portable benefits include:

- Disability coverage;
- Life insurance; and
- Sick pay.

One gig platform—Care.com—is already offering its contractors who are babysitters and other caregivers a fringe benefit (see care.com). It is up to $500 per year that can be used to pay for health care, transportation, or other needed benefits. The benefit is funded by imposing a surcharge on customers using the platform. Whether this becomes a model for other gig economy platforms remains to be seen.

¶505

Pending legislation called the Portable Benefits for Independent Workers Pilot Program Act (S. 1251) would create a $20 million fund for the Department of Labor to give to state and local governments and nonprofit organizations to create pilot programs on portable benefits. Some states—California, New Jersey, New York, and Washington—are also exploring legislation supporting portable benefits.

## Tax Credits

Two tax credits may be especially relevant to workers in the gig economy. If earnings are modest, the worker may be eligible for the earned income tax credit. The amount of the credit is determined in part on earned income, which includes both compensation from a job and net earnings from self-employment.

The worker may also be able to claim a dependent care credit. This credit is designed to help pay the cost of caregiving for a qualified person in order to work, including working at self-employment.

## Self-Employment Tax

Self-employment tax is a major issue for those working in the gig economy. Self-employed individuals who are profitable must pay self-employment tax. Essentially, this works out to encompass the employer and employee shares of FICA. Self-employment tax covers Social Security tax and Medicare tax obligations for a self-employed person.

The tax is imposed on net earnings from self-employment—profit—from a full-time or part-time business activity. It is reported on Schedule SE of Form 1040. If spouses each have self-employment income, each must complete a separate Schedule SE.

The tax for the Social Security portion is 12.4 percent. However, it is imposed only on net earnings up to the annual Social Security *wage base* (the maximum amount of annual income subject to Social Security tax). For example, for 2017, the wage base is $127,200.

The tax for the Medicare portion is 2.9 percent. There is no ceiling on this portion of the tax; it applies to all net earnings from self-employment.

Thus, the total self-employment tax rate is 15.3 percent.

One-half of self-employment taxes is deductible as an adjustment to gross income. This is deducted on line 27 of Form 1040.

Unlike businesses that can deduct the employer share of FICA against business income, self-employed individuals cannot treat self-employment tax—even one-half of it—as a business expense. Over the years there have been proposals in Congress to change this tax treatment, but nothing has happened to date.

If a person working in the gig economy also has a job, then self-employment tax must be coordinated with FICA payments. This prevents any overpayment of the Social Security portion of self-employment tax. Of course, because there is no ceiling for the Medicare portion, this tax is paid on all net earnings from self-employment . . . on top of any compensation from a job.

If a worker in the gig economy has a loss for the year—no net earnings from self-employment—he or she can opt to pay self-employment tax by using an *optional method* on Schedule SE. Doing this helps the worker to build up Social Security credits.

The optional method for nonfarm earnings can be used for 2017 if net nonfarm profits are less than $5,630 and also less than 72.189 percent of gross nonfarm income. The worker must have had net earnings from self-employment of at least $400 in two of the prior three years. This optional method can only be used up to five times.

¶505

Self-employment tax is not deposited with the Treasury Department as are FICA taxes. Self-employment taxes usually are paid through estimated taxes, discussed next.

## Estimated Taxes

Self-employed individuals need to understand and comply with estimated tax rules. Estimated taxes are *not* an additional liability; they are a way to pay other federal or state tax liabilities.

Working as a self-employed individual means that there is no withholding for income tax and Social Security/Medicare taxes such as employees see on their pay stubs. Generally, these tax obligations must be satisfied for the IRS by paying estimated taxes in four instalments, paid April 15, June 15, September 15, and January 15 of the following year—unless April 15 falls on the weekend. Thus, for the 2017 tax year the due dates are April 18, June 15, September 15, and January 16.

In the following situations, estimated taxes do not have to be paid:

- A self-employed individual also has a job. He or she can adjust withholding on wages to cover tax obligations for working in the gig economy;
- A spouse has a job. If agreeable, the spouse can adjust his or her withholding from wages to cover the tax obligations for the other spouse who is working in the gig economy; and
- Projected estimated taxes for the year are less than $1,000. For example, if net income from the gig economy for the year is estimated to be less than $4,000 and the taxpayer is in a tax bracket of 25 percent or less, it may not be necessary to pay estimated taxes; the taxes owed can be paid with the filing of the tax return for the year.

**Determining the Optimal Amount of Estimates.** The big question is how much estimated tax should a self-employed taxpayer pay? It's a Goldilocks situation: A worker doesn't want to overpay, because then he or she has to wait until the return is filed to recover the excess money. Effectively, this is an interest-free loan to the government! And the worker doesn't want to underpay, which can result in underpayment penalties. The aim with estimated tax: get it "just right."

Avoiding underpayment penalties can be done by pegging estimates to either of the following safe harbors. No penalties apply if estimated taxes, plus withholding, are at least:

- 90 percent of the current year's tax liability; or
- 100 percent of the prior year's tax liability (or 110 percent if the taxpayer's adjusted gross income in the prior year exceeded $150,000, or $75,000 if married filing separately).

Estimated tax payments can be adjusted for remaining instalments. This may make sense if there are:

- Income changes (up or down);
- Personal changes (e.g., a change in filing status resulting in a change in tax liability); and
- Law changes.

Estimated taxes should cover not only the regular income tax resulting from gig economy activities, but also any:

- Alternative minimum tax;
- Self-employment tax;

**¶505**

- Employment tax for a domestic employee; and
- Additional Medicare taxes on earned income and investment income (the net investment income tax).

Estimated taxes can be paid by personal check, charged to a credit/debit card, or made via electronic transfer. EFTPS.gov is a free government service that can be used to pay estimated taxes. Individuals can schedule payments up to 365 days in advance. However, there are some timing issues:

- Some lead time is needed to set up an account. This is because registering is step one, but to use the account requires the government to send a PIN number by mail; and
- The payment must be made or scheduled to be made the day before the payment due date to ensure that funds are timely credited to the tax account.

**Discipline Required to Fund Payments.** As a practical matter, the biggest challenge to paying estimated taxes is coming up with the funds to make the payments. For individuals who are used to tax withholding ("W-2 employees"), having to set aside funds to pay estimated taxes may be a new experience.

For some individuals, it is advisable to create a separate bank account in which to place funds that will be needed to pay estimated taxes. For example, if a freelancer receives a payment of $1,000, it may be a good business practice to put 10 percent (or more) into this separate account for estimated tax purposes.

Discipline in creating cash flow for estimated taxes is necessary even if a taxpayer does not have to pay quarterly instalments because he or she is under the $1,000 estimated tax payment threshold. The money nevertheless will be needed to pay taxes when the annual tax return is filed.

For the self-employed individual with net earnings from self-employment of $400 or more in a tax year, he or she must file a federal income tax return. Filing is required even if his or her gross income is below the usual filing threshold.

## STUDY QUESTION

---

**4.** Which of the following statements is **not** correct?

   **a.** Self-employment tax is part of estimated taxes.

   **b.** The deduction for one-half of self-employment tax is a business expense.

   **c.** All net earnings from the gig economy are subject to the Medicare portion of self-employment tax.

   **d.** An optional method can create Social Security benefits.

---

# ¶ 506  THE SHARING ECONOMY

The gig economy includes the sharing economy. The sharing economy is characterized by renting out property on a short-term basis. This action triggers a host of tax rules, including special rules for home rentals, the passive activity loss limitations, and the hobby loss rules.

> **CAUTION:** The following discussions offer only a cursory treatment of some very complex tax rules. The aim here is to alert a prospective taxpayer to the various rules, limitations, and planning opportunities that relate to the sharing economy. Delving deeper before renting out is advised.

## Home Rentals

Special rules apply for home rentals for individuals listing their personal residences or vacation properties with Airbnb or another rental platform.

**Nontax Issues.** There are a number of nontax concerns for the sharing economy:

- Zoning rules, rules in homeowners' associations, or the terms of a lease may restrict the ability of a homeowner to have short-term rentals. Violating the rules may lead to angry neighbors and financial penalties; and

- Insurance is another issue. A homeowner's policy does not cover rentals, so additional coverage is essential; only a few carriers will insure homeowners on Airbnb. Airbnb, for example, offers a host guarantee of up to $1 million for property damage; this does not cover any liability (such as injury on the premises) and has limited protection for jewelry, artwork, and collectibles).

Obviously, the nontax issues need to be addressed along with the tax issues discussed next.

**Tax Issues for Short-Term Rentals.** A taxpayer rents out his or her home, which could be a principal residence, a vacation home, or property used exclusively for rental purposes. This discussion assumes that the taxpayer is renting out his or her home— either the entire home or a room or other part of it.

If the annual rental of the taxpayer's home is fewer than 15 days, a special tax rule, the 14 day/10 percent rule, applies. Rental income during this period is tax free. It does not have to be reported. That means if a taxpayer uses his or her personal residence or vacation home during the year for fewer than 14 days or rents out the home for less than 10 percent of the total days at a fair rental value, the rental income earned is tax free.

However, no rental-related expenses can be deducted, other than deductions allowable as itemized deductions to homeowners, such as mortgage interest, real property taxes, and casualty and theft losses. These itemized deductions are subject to the same limitations that apply to all homeowners, including a cap on mortgage interest, a 10 percent-of-AGI threshold for casualty and theft losses, and a phaseout of itemized deductions for high income taxpayers.

**Tax Issues for Longer-Term Rentals.** Different tax responsibilities apply for longer rentals during the year. A particular rental during the year may be fewer than 15 days, but the total number of days rented is more than 14 days. This triggers a new set of rules used to determine deductible expenses.

First, the taxpayer must distinguish between the rental of a personal residence or vacation home used by the taxpayer during the year for more than 14 days or, if greater, 10 percent of the days rented at a fair rental value and a property that is held exclusively for rental or the taxpayer does not use the property more than the 14 day/10 percent test. In the latter situation, a taxpayer owns a property that is used exclusively for rental purposes, such as a beachfront condo or a mountain ski house. Or the taxpayer rents the home for days, weeks, or months at a time, using it for personal purposes only one week during the year.

Is the rental activity a business? If the homeowner provides substantial services for the benefit of tenants in connection with rentals, the income is treated as business income reported on Schedule C. According to the IRS, substantial services include:

- Regular cleaning;
- Changing linens; and
- Maid service.

Substantial services do not include:

- Trash collection;
- Cleaning common areas; and
- Providing heating/cooling and lighting.

**PLANNING POINTER:** If the rental of a home that is co-owned by spouses is a business, the couple must file a partnership return (Form 1065) with the IRS. However, if both spouses materially participate in the activity (material participation is discussed later) and they file a joint income tax return, they can each complete Schedule C.

If the rental is offered without substantial services, then income is reported on Schedule E, *Supplemental Income and Loss*. This is so whether or not the home is used for personal purposes.

More specifically, Part I of Schedule E is used to list income from rental real estate. The physical addresses of each property must be listed.

If the property is personally used by the taxpayer during the year and is also rented out, he or she determines whether this is treated as a personal residence. If so, then rental expenses are deductible only to the extent of rental income.

Once again, Part I of Schedule E requires a listing of the fair rental days and personal use for each property. It also requires a notation that the type of property is "short-term rental"; number 3 must be indicated in the space provided for the type of property.

If the property is rented for 15 or more days and personal use of the property is more than 14 days or, if greater, 10 percent of the number of days it's rented at a fair rental value, it's a personal residence under the 14 day/10 percent test. If rental income is more than rental expenses, all allowable deductions can be claimed.

If rental expenses exceed rental income—as determined by an allocation explained shortly—a deduction for expenses is limited to rental income in the current year. Excess deductions usually can be carried forward and used to the extent of rental income.

There is a hierarchy for deducting expenses against rental income when personal use of the home exceeds the 14 day/10 percent test and expenses exceed rental income.

Step 1: Offset rental income by:

- Home mortgage interest;
- Real estate taxes;
- Casualty and theft losses; and
- Directly related rental expenses. These are expenses not related to the maintenance of the property. Examples of directly related expenses include: advertising, rental agency fees, and office supplies.

Step 2: If rental income is not fully offset by expenses in step 1, then offset remaining rental income by operating expenses. These include utilities, insurance, and repairs.

Step 3: If there is still any rental income that has not been fully offset, then claim depreciation on the rental portion of the home.

Depreciation is figured only on the rental portion, and only on the building or unit; not on the land. So the taxpayer makes an allocation between land and improvements.

This can be done using county assessor assessments for improvements or an appraisal of the property. An allocation based on the assessor assessments is suggested in IRS Publication 551. It's also the method that was used in a recent case (***Nielsen,*** TC Memo 2017-31).

Then the taxpayer determines the basis of the depreciable portion of the home. This is the lower of adjusted basis or fair market value at the time of the first rental. In other words, if the home has steadily increased in value, depreciation is going to be based on the adjusted basis of the home—generally, the original cost plus capital improvements.

Rental real estate has a 27.5 year recovery period; depreciation is claimed on a straight-line basis. The percentage for depreciation depends on the month in which the property is first used for rental. The percentage is taken from an IRS table for this purpose. Table 2-2, Section D, of IRS Publication 527, *Residential Rental Property,* shows percentages for depreciation of residential rental property.

A special allocation formula is used to determine the portion of expenses that are deductible from rental income for the three steps just outlined. The deductible portion equals total expenses for the year multiplied by this formula:

$$\frac{\text{Days unit is rented for fair market rental price}}{\text{Total days of rental and personal use}}$$

**PLANNING POINTER:** The taxpayer should not count any days that the home is merely available for rental, such as the days that the home is advertised as available but not actually rented. If a day has both personal and rental use, it counts as a rental day.

Homeowners know that they can deduct their mortgage interest and real estate taxes whether or not there's any rental involved. The question is how to allocate these expenses when there is rental of the home.

According to the IRS, the fraction discussed earlier should also be applied to mortgage interest and real estate taxes. For example, if a home is rented for 38 days and used 72 days for personal purposes, then 50 percent of these expenses (38 ÷ 72 of expenses for the days used) would be allocated to rental.

Some courts, however, have said that the allocation of these expenses should be made on a daily basis. In other words, if the home is rented for 38 days during 2017, then the allocation of these expenses to rental would be limited to 10 percent (38 days ÷ 365/days).

Why does it matter? The property owner wants the least amount to be allocated to rental because the balance is then deducted as itemized deductions. This allows a greater amount of other expenses—those that can't otherwise be deducted—to be used.

Deductible expenses typically associated with renting out a home can include:

- Cleaning;
- Commissions;
- Depreciation on the residence;
- Insurance; and
- Repairs.

What about buying linens and other small items? Technically, any item with a useful life of more than one year must be depreciated. First-year expensing (using the Section 179 deduction) does not apply to a rental activity that is not a business. However, under a *de minimis* rule, a taxpayer can elect to treat the item as materials and supplies (i.e., currently deductible). The dollar limit is $2,500 per item or invoice. A taxpayer's own election statement must be attached to the return.

After determining which expenses are deductible and how to apply them, there are certain limitations that may curtail writeoffs.

The passive activity loss (PAL) limitations restrict losses from passive activities— which includes rental real estate—to income from such activities (Code Sec. 469). If the PAL rules apply, unused losses are carried over and can be used to offset passive activity income from any sources in future years. Also, if there is a complete disposition of the property, unused passive losses can be taken in full in the year of the disposition.

There are two exceptions to the PAL rules that could enable losses from renting out a home to be deductible. If the taxpayer "actively participates" in the rental activity, then losses up to $25,000 per year can be claimed if the taxpayer's modified adjusted gross income (MAGI) is no more than $100,000. The $25,000 loss limit phases out for MAGI up to $150,000 (50 percent of the difference between this limit and the taxpayer's MAGI). These dollar limits are halved if a married person files separately.

Active participation is a modest threshold. It means making management decisions regarding rental terms and conditions (not merely approving the decisions of others), or arranging for others to provide services, such as repairs. There is no set number of hours of participation required for this purpose. Doing investment-like activities, such as looking for new rental properties, does not count as active participation.

> **PLANNING POINTER:** A taxpayer eligible for the $25,000 PAL limitation does not have to complete Form 8283, *Passive Activity Losses,* assuming this is the taxpayer's only passive activity.

The second exception to the PAL rules applies to real estate professionals.

If the taxpayer is a "real estate professional," then there is no limit on losses. To be a real estate professional, a taxpayer must pass a two-prong test:

- More than half of all services by the taxpayer for the year are performed in real estate businesses in which he or she materially participates. A real estate business includes renting or leasing out property that the taxpayer owns; and

- The taxpayer must materially participate for more than 750 hours.

Material participation is a higher threshold than active participation described earlier. It means being involved in the real estate business' operations on a regular, continuous, and substantial basis during the year.

> **PLANNING POINTER:** For married couples, participation of a spouse in the activity can count as material participation even if that spouse does not own an interest in the property and/or files a separate return.

## Hobby Loss Rule

Most who participate in the sharing economy do so because they want to make money. However, this doesn't always happen. Another potential limit on deducting losses is the hobby loss rule (Code Sec. 183). If a taxpayer cannot demonstrate a profit motive, income is reported as "other income" directly on Form 1040; Schedule E is not used.

Losses are deductible only to the extent of income from the activity. There is no carryover of unused losses. The deductible losses are claimed as miscellaneous itemized deductions subject to the 2 percent-of-AGI threshold.

One of the big distinctions between those providing services in the gig economy and those renting out their homes is self-employment tax. More specifically, income

**¶506**

from real estate rentals not received in the course of a business is specifically exempt from self-employment tax.

However, if the rental activity is a business, then net income reported on Schedule C or Form 1065 is subject to self-employment tax.

It's important to remember that short-term rentals can be applied to just about anything. As mentioned earlier, there are platforms for renting out tools, airplanes, and more.

As in the case of rental real estate, if no substantial services are provided, the rental income is reported on Schedule E for individuals. If the rental activity is a business, or if an existing business shares its machinery and equipment, rental income is business income reported on the relevant business income tax return.

Tax practitioners should become expert in the tax issues affecting those engaged in the gig economy, as well as the sharing economy, because these alternative work and income arrangements represent growth areas for workers and tax planners alike.

## STUDY QUESTIONS

**5.** Which of the following is *not* treated as a substantial service for purposes of determining whether a rental activity is a business?

    **a.** Trash collection.

    **b.** Regular cleaning.

    **c.** Changing linens.

    **d.** Maid service.

**6.** All of the following tax rules may limit a deduction of rental losses *except:*

    **a.** Hobby loss rule.

    **b.** Passive activity loss rule.

    **c.** 14 day/10 percent rule.

    **d.** Zoning rule.

**CPE NOTE:** When you have completed your study and review of chapters 1-5, which comprise Module 1, you may wish to take the Final Exam for this Module. Go to **cchcpelink.com/printcpe** to take this Final Exam online.

# MODULE 2: SMALL BUSINESS TAXATION—
## Chapter 6: Expense or Capitalize?

### ¶ 601 WELCOME

This chapter covers the general tax rules requiring the capitalization of expenses that create an asset with a useful life that extends substantially beyond the taxable year, the rules for capitalizing transaction costs, and the Code Sec. 263A regulations that apply to manufacturers and producers of tangible property. It also discusses how the change in accounting method rules apply to deducted expenses that should be capitalized.

### ¶ 602 LEARNING OBJECTIVES

Upon completion of this chapter, you will be able to:

- Explain general rules determining when expenses should be capitalized
- Identify rules that require capitalization of transaction costs into basis of acquired assets
- Differentiate how Code Sec. 263A requires capitalization of expenses into cost of goods sold
- Recognize how the new "repair regulations" apply in common scenarios

### ¶ 603 INTRODUCTION

Understanding whether an expense should be capitalized or immediately deducted as an expense is a tax question faced by nearly every business. Taxpayers are often required to capitalize otherwise deductible transactional expenses, such as legal fees and appraisals, and even more complicated rules apply to manufacturers and producers of tangible property in determining cost of goods sold.

### ¶ 604 CAPITALIZATION RULES

Even if an expenditure is deductible as a business expense under Code Sec. 162, it may not be deductible in the year in which it is incurred. "Capitalizing an expense" delays the deduction of the expense. Instead of deducting the expense, the taxpayer records the item as an asset on the balance sheet (in this case the tax balance sheet) rather than deducting it as an expense. Depending on capital cost recovery rules such as depreciation and amortization, the taxpayer may be able to deduct the cost of the asset in later years.

An expenditure must be capitalized when it "creates an asset with a useful life that extends substantially beyond the taxable year." In other words, capitalizing is trying to match expenses with the income that they help to generate. To deduct an expense in the current year, it should be part of the cost of current operations. Timing distortions can give an inaccurate picture of annual income.

Even though an expense creates a benefit that extends beyond the taxable year, it is not "substantially beyond" the taxable year. It is too difficult to allocate expenses that relate to multiple assets (but see Code Sec. 263A), or not worth the administrative cost of dividing expenditures between multiple years. Expenses are of a recurring nature, so they will come up each year. Special statutory rules allow immediate expensing (for example, Code Sec. 179 expensing and bonus depreciation).

The *Zaninovich* case (*Zaninovich v. Commissioner,* 616 F.2d 429 (9th Cir. 1980)) holds that "substantially beyond" the taxable year means not more than 12 months beyond the taxable year. While not clear from the case, most commentators think this means 12 months beyond the end of the taxable year in which the expenditure is made. Note that the *Zaninovich* rule is not a "free 12 months" rule, but rather a rule of convenience so that taxpayers do not have to pro-rate expenses. If an expense extends too far, it must be pro-rated among the applicable taxable years. This applies for cash method and accrual method taxpayers.

**EXAMPLE:** Taxpayer A pays 18 months' worth of insurance premiums in July 2017 for the remainder of 2017 and all of 2018. This is fine under the *Zaninovich* rule. But if the taxpayer pays 18 months' worth of insurance in November 2017 for remainder of 2017, all of 2018, and four months of 2019, this extends too far, according to the rule. Taxpayer A must pro-rate the expense and deduct only the 2017 portion in 2017.

Expenses are not typically capitalized if they relate to multiple assets or if under cost/benefit analysis; it is not worth it to determine how much of the expenditure relates to each year. This is true even if the expenditure does have a benefit that extends substantially beyond the taxable year.

## Expenses of a Recurring Nature

If expenses are "ordinary" expenses that will recur every year, they do not need to be capitalized even if they create a benefit that extends beyond the taxable year. The idea is that they will come up again and again, so it does not really matter if a taxpayer capitalizes and amortizes, or deducts them each year. This makes sense only if the taxpayer would be creating an amortizable "asset." If the expenditure would create or enhance goodwill, for example, the taxpayer would not recover the cost as self-created goodwill is not amortizable.

**EXAMPLE:** A drug company spends millions of dollars each year to advertise a new cholesterol drug. It hopes to drive sales immediately and also to build brand recognition for the future. Advertising is considered a regular, recurring expense, so the drug company may deduct, rather than capitalize, these costs—even though the expenditures may help build a brand or goodwill.

## Code Sec. 179 Expensing

Code Sec. 179 allows a taxpayer to elect to take an immediate expense deduction for the cost of certain tangible personal property placed in service during a taxable year. It provides, in part: "A taxpayer may elect to treat the cost of any Code Sec. 179 property as an expense which is not chargeable to capital account. Any cost so treated shall be allowed as a deduction for the taxable year in which the Code Sec. 179 property is placed in service." This provision started as a simplifying convention, making it easy for taxpayers placing a small amount of property in service. The IRS did not want taxpayers to have to capitalize and depreciate these small amounts; accordingly, the limitation amounts were small. While drafting legislation for the post September 11, 2001, tax cuts, Congress decided that raising the Code Sec. 179 limitation to allow immediate expensing of larger amounts would help jump-start the weak economy. Once taxpayers got used to this provision, it was hard for Congress to eliminate it.

Code Sec. 179 expensing is similar to bonus depreciation allowed by Code Sec. 168(k); it is "super-accelerated" depreciation. Most businesses choose to elect this super-accelerated depreciation because of the time value of money in saving taxes today. The cost of doing so is smaller depreciation deductions; a taxpayer can use up part of future years' depreciation deductions in the current year. In addition, Code Sec.

179 deductions reduce the property's basis and must be "repaid" as ordinary income if the asset is later sold at a gain (Code Sec. 1245 recapture).

> **EXAMPLE:** A group of five doctors operating as an LLC purchases an expensive MRI machine for $200,000 in 2017. They elect to immediately expense its cost. In 2018, they buy a second MRI machine for the same cost, and expense that as well. The purchases are financed with loans that will be repaid later. Each of the five doctors gets a $40,000 Code Sec. 179 deduction on their Schedule K-1 for each year. In 2019, no machinery is purchased. The group earns the same amount in revenue as in prior years, and has similar expenses, but the doctors are surprised they owe more in taxes. This is because they "used up" all the depreciation for the machines in the year purchased rather than spreading it over multiple years.
>
> Now suppose Dr. X leaves the group and sells his LLC interest to a new doctor who will join the group, Dr. Z. The group decides to sell the used machines for $150,000 each (their current value). Because the machines have zero basis, each sale will produce $150,000 of ordinary income due to depreciation recapture. Thus, each doctor, including new Dr. Z, who has not taken any prior depreciation, will report $60,000 of ordinary income pursuant to Code Sec. 1245. Sometimes the parties are sophisticated enough to figure this out when Dr. Z buys Dr. X's LLC interest and reduce the price accordingly, but not always.

The maximum Code Sec. 179 deduction for 2017 is $500,000 per year. The maximum amount of property that may be placed into service and still be allowed a full Code Sec. 179 deduction is $2,000,000. Once more than $2,000,000 of qualifying property is placed in service in a given year, the $500,000 limitation starts to be reduced dollar-for-dollar. For example, if a taxpayer places $2,100,000 of qualifying property in service in 2017, he may elect a $400,000 Code Sec. 179 deduction.

New or used property purchased and placed into service in taxable year qualifies for the Code Sec. 179 deduction. This includes:

- Equipment (machines, etc.) purchased for business use
- Tangible personal property used in a business
- Business vehicles with a gross vehicle weight in excess of 6,000 pounds
- Computers
- Computer "off-the-shelf" software
- Office furniture
- Office equipment
- Property attached to a building that is not a structural component of the building (e.g., a printing press, large manufacturing tools and equipment)

The following do not qualify for the Code Sec. 179 deduction:

- Real property, typically defined as land, buildings, permanent structures, and the components of the permanent structures (including improvements)
- Air-conditioning and heating equipment
- Property used outside the United States
- Property acquired by gift or inheritance, as well as property purchased from related parties
- Any property that is not considered to be personal property

¶604

## Bonus Depreciation

Code Sec. 168(k) bonus depreciation is similar to the Code Sec. 179 deduction in that it allows immediate expensing, but only of 50 percent of the cost of the property placed in service. It only applies to new tangible personal property, not used property. Code Sec. 168(k) bonus depreciation may be used in combination with Code Sec. 179. If using both, a taxpayer should use Code Sec. 179 first, and then Code Sec. 168(k) will automatically apply to 50 percent of the remaining basis of the property. There is no limitation on the amount of property placed in service or the amount of the deduction. Code Sec. 168(k) applies automatically unless the taxpayer elects out. Note that taxpayer must *elect in* to Code Sec. 179.

## Cost Segregation Studies

Cost segregation became common in early 2000s because of the significant depreciation advantage given to tangible personal property over real estate. Accounting firms teamed up with engineers to look at the costs of new buildings. Taxpayers had typically capitalized the full cost of the buildings. The studies had engineers review all of the costs to determine which were really "part of" the building and which might be separate personal property (such as fixtures). Taxpayers then filed amended returns to claim large Code Sec. 179 and bonus depreciation deductions for the year they built the building. Some studies were very aggressive, claiming everything "down to the studs" as tangible personal property rather than real property. However, the Tax Court has limited the scope of these deductions in cases such as *AmeriSouth* (*AmeriSouth XXXII, Ltd. v. Commissioner*, TC Memo 2012-67) and *Pecos Foods* (*Pecos Foods Inc. & Subsidiaries v. Commissioner*, TC Memo 2012-18).

## STUDY QUESTIONS

1.  Which of the following Code Sections allows for the immediate expensing of qualifying equipment purchased during the year?

    **a.** Code Sec. 179

    **b.** Code Sec. 121

    **c.** Code Sec. 368

    **d.** Code Sec. 1031

2.  Which does *not* qualify for a Code Sec. 179 deduction?

    **a.** Equipment purchased for business use

    **b.** Office furniture

    **c.** Property used outside the United States

    **d.** Tangible personal property used in business

3.  Which statement with respect to bonus depreciation is correct?

    **a.** It applies to both new and used property.

    **b.** It may be used in combination with Code Sec. 179.

    **c.** There is a $1,000,000 limitation on the amount of property placed in service.

    **d.** A taxpayer must elect the bonus depreciation.

# ¶ 605 CAPITALIZATION OF TRANSACTION COSTS RELATING TO ACQUISITION OF TANGIBLE AND INTANGIBLE ASSETS

## Costs Related to Acquisitions and Dispositions of Assets

Generally, expenses incurred to acquire or dispose of assets (other than inventory) must be capitalized. Examples include legal fees, professional fees for appraisals and valuations, zoning fees, and sales commissions. Costs that relate to acquiring the asset are capitalized into the basis of the asset, and costs incurred to dispose of an asset reduce the amount realized, thereby reducing the gain on sale. Expenses paid or incurred in defending or perfecting title to property, in recovering property, or in developing or improving property, constitute a part of the cost of the property and are not deductible expenses.

> **EXAMPLE:** Moe owns a restaurant with a patio and an outdoor parking lot. The neighboring restaurant owner repaves his parking lot and builds a wall. Moe discovers that the neighboring wall encroaches on his land, and he hires a lawyer to make the neighbor remove the wall. The legal fees must be capitalized into the basis of the property.

## INDOPCO and Anti-INDOPCO Regulations

For many years, taxpayers only capitalized costs relating to the acquisition of a "separate and distinct asset." This included intangible property, such as stock and other financial instruments, in addition to tangible property. Then in 1992 came the U.S. Supreme Court case of *INDOPCO* (*INDOPCO v. Commissioner*, 503 U.S. 79). In *INDOPCO*, the taxpayer incurred legal and investment banking fees to fend off a hostile takeover attempt. The fees were large amounts, and the taxpayer deducted them in the year incurred. The IRS challenged the deduction and said the fees must be capitalized.

The problem was that there was no "asset" in which to capitalize the fees since the taxpayer had not purchased an asset (the taxpayer was fending off a takeover). Thus, requiring capitalization would essentially deny the deduction, since there was not a good way for the taxpayer to recover those costs. On the other hand, the costs were large, one-time expenses, so deducting them in one year would be distortive.

The Supreme Court held for the IRS, concluding that the taxpayer had to capitalize the fees because they created a "significant future benefit." The Court said no "separate and distinct asset" was necessary to require fee capitalization. Taxpayers and their advisors panicked, worrying that any expense with a significant future benefit might have to be capitalized. The IRS issued regulations to clarify the rules, essentially overriding the Supreme Court decision.

The "anti-*INDOPCO*" regulations generally adopt the separate and distinct asset test, requiring that a separate asset exists to capitalize transaction costs. Costs incurred to acquire stock are added to the stock basis; costs incurred to acquire assets are added to the asset basis. In a multi-asset acquisition of the entire business, the transaction costs are likely added to goodwill, which takes the residual purchase price allocation under Code Sec. 1060. In a nontaxable asset acquisition such as a tax-free reorganization, the fees are capitalized, but they cannot be recovered until the entity is dissolved.

Simplifying conventions provide that employee compensation and overhead does not have to be allocated and capitalized, even if it relates to an acquisition. Costs incurred prior to the acquisition do not have to be capitalized, but they may be deducted. The regulations provide that the costs incurred prior to signing a letter of intent are "investigative" costs that may be deducted. Any costs that are "facilitative" to the acquisition must be capitalized. Contingent fees that are conditioned on a successful acquisition are generally capitalized as facilitative. The burden is on the taxpayer to show what portion of the fees, if any, are investigative, prior to the letter of intent. There is also a safe harbor under which the taxpayer may treat 30 percent of contingent fees as investigative and thus deductible (Rev. Proc. 2011-29).

## STUDY QUESTION

---

**4.** A In which of the following U.S. Supreme Court cases did the court conclude that a taxpayer had to capitalize certain large, one-time fees because they created significant future benefit?

    **a.** *INDOPCO*

    **b.** *AmeriSouth*

    **c.** *Pecos Foods*

    **d.** *Zaninovich*

---

# ¶ 606 CODE SEC. 263A AND CAPITALIZATION OF INVENTORY COSTS

As mentioned earlier, expenses are not capitalized even if they might relate to a future year, if it is too difficult to determine which assets to allocate them to, or it is not worth the administrative cost to do so. However, because a taxpayer is trying to get to the most precise number possible for cost of goods sold, he has to make sure to include every possible expense of producing or acquiring inventory in cost of goods sold.

The cost of goods sold is not really a "deduction"; it is the tax basis of the taxpayer's inventory. The rule typically does not allow taxpayers to recover basis until property is sold. Allowing a taxpayer to deduct costs of producing inventory—even when the costs look like ordinary expenses—prior to selling that inventory would run counter to that general rule. Also, if a taxpayer buys inventory from a manufacturer, he would not deduct this cost until selling the inventory. A taxpayer who produces his own inventory should not be better off from a tax perspective. Code Sec. 263A (sometimes called UNICAP) details the uniform capitalization rules that require certain costs normally expensed to be capitalized as part of inventory for tax purposes. These rules apply to:

- Real or tangible personal property produced by the taxpayer
- Real or personal property acquired by the taxpayer for resale

Exceptions to the rule include (1) producers of property with gross receipts of $10M or less during last three years (this does not apply to resellers), and (2) some farm use property with various requirements.

Code Sec. 263A applies to all tangible real or personal property produced by the taxpayer. The regulations under Code Sec. 263A are very strict and require capitalization of all direct and indirect costs into cost of goods sold (for inventory) or the basis of the property produced. This includes all direct costs of the inventory, plus indirect costs properly allocable to the inventory. Note that this can defer some of the "bonus" depreciation the taxpayer may have been counting on. Costs included under Code Sec. 263A include the following:

- Wages, salaries, employee benefits, and payroll taxes (including an allocable share of executive salaries, to the extent they relate to the manufacture or purchase of inventory)

- Payments to independent contractors

- Direct raw material costs

- Purchasing and storage costs

- Rent, utilities, insurance, taxes, and depreciation

- Engineering and design costs

- Royalty payments and franchise fees

## Code Sec. 263A "Repair Regulations"

The IRS and taxpayers have long disagreed about whether expenditures on tangible property are currently deductible or must be capitalized and recovered through depreciation over time. The distinction between deductible repairs and capital improvements has been determined largely through case law and is based on facts and circumstances.

The "repair regulations," issued in late 2013, clarify this area by explaining the factors to be considered and giving examples. In general, expenditures that restore the property to its operating state are a deductible repair. However, expenditures that provide a permanent improvement in life or value of the property are more likely capital. The regulations apply to anyone who pays or incurs amounts to acquire, produce, or improve tangible real or personal property.

A *de minimis* safe harbor election allows the deduction of amounts paid to acquire or produce tangible property to the extent such amounts are deducted for financial accounting purposes or in keeping books and records. It covers up to $5,000 per invoice or item if the taxpayer has applicable financial statements or $2,500 per invoice or item if he does not. It does not apply to inventory costs. Incidental supplies and materials may be deducted in the year in which they are paid or incurred; other supplies and materials may be deducted when they are used or consumed. The repair regulations do not change the requirement to capitalize inventory-type costs for property produced or acquired for resale by taxpayer.

The rules apply for taxable years beginning in 2014, and simplifying conventions and elections apply for certain taxpayers. If a taxpayer has been treating items differently prior to these regulations, it must file Form 3115, *Change in Accounting Method*, to adopt the new and proper method. The repair regulations synthesize prior case law to give guidelines for the facts-and-circumstances analysis as to when a taxpayer may deduct a "repair" versus when it must capitalize an "improvement."

A unit of property is generally the entire building with respect to real estate; for other property, it is all components that are functionally interdependent or perform a discrete function or operation together. An expense must be capitalized if it betters, restores, or adapts a unit of property. Examples of a "betterment" include a material addition to property, a material increase in strength, or an expense that ameliorates a material defect. Examples of "restoration" include a restoration after a casualty loss or after a property has deteriorated to a state of disrepair, or rebuilding a property to like-new condition. An "adaptation" might be changing a property to a new and different use (e.g., converting a fishing boat to a sightseeing boat, or a manufacturing building to a retail showroom.)

# ¶ 607  CHANGE IN ACCOUNTING METHOD RULES AND CODE SEC. 481 ADJUSTMENTS

## Change in Accounting Method

An accounting method is the treatment of any material item of income or deduction that has been correctly used by the taxpayer once, or incorrectly used twice, *and* does not involve the proper time for the inclusion of the item of income or the taking of a deduction. An accounting method item does not permanently affect the taxpayer's lifetime income. It is very easy to adopt an accounting method, but a taxpayer may not change its accounting method without IRS permission (implicit or explicit). Any "timing questions" are considered accounting methods. If a mistake or improper position is an accounting method, there is no statute of limitations, and the IRS may make an adjustment that goes back to the earliest relevant year pursuant to Code Sec. 481.

> **EXAMPLE:** Neon Co. has deducted legal fees for its acquisitions since 2000. These fees should have been capitalized into the basis of the stock and real estate it acquired. The IRS may make a positive Code Sec. 481 adjustment (income inclusion) that "unwinds" all prior deductions and moves them into the basis of those assets.

> **EXAMPLE:** Corporation MNO built a new building in 2005. It failed to capitalize salaries and employee benefits of employees who worked on the building, supervised construction, and so on. It also claimed bonus depreciation for machines it purchased in 2005 that were used to build the building. All of these costs should have been capitalized. The IRS may make a positive Code Sec. 481 adjustment. (This one is a tougher case, because if the year is closed, it is hard to see how this could come up on audit, and whether the IRS would have this power even if Corporation MNO is not still engaging in this accounting method.)

## STUDY QUESTIONS

5.  The rules outlined by Code Sec. 263A apply to each of the following, *except:*

   a.  Tangible personal property produced by the taxpayer

   b.  Certain farm use property

   c.  Real property acquired by the taxpayer for resale

   d.  Producers of property with gross receipts of $20M or less during last four years

6.  In accordance with the requirements of Code Sec. 263A, which types of costs are deductible in the current period?

   a.  Expenditures that restore property to its operating state

   b.  Direct raw material costs

   c.  Engineering and design costs

   d.  Expenditures that provide permanent improvement in value of property

# MODULE 2: SMALL BUSINESS TAXATION—
# Chapter 7: S Corporation and Shareholder Tax Reporting

## ¶ 701 WELCOME

This chapter examines how a business meets the requirements to become and remain an S corporation entity, which entail both the entity's eligibility and that of the corporate shareholders. A major responsibility for an S corporation is filing its federal tax return using Form 1120S, *U.S. Income Tax Return for an S Corporation,* so the chapter explains how to complete the form and related schedules. Because various elections are available to S corporations, the chapter describes the options available at the entity level. Some issues that pertain to the cancellation of debt are covered. Finally, the text describes the types of distributions that S corporations make and the types of taxes that apply to this form of entity.

## ¶ 702 LEARNING OBJECTIVES

Upon completion of this chapter, you will be able to:

- Identify qualifications for electing and maintaining S corporation status;
- Recognize the steps commonly followed in completing Form 1120S; and
- Recognize the effects on shareholders of S corporation distributions.

## ¶ 703 INTRODUCTION

When a business selects its entity type, the organization tends to treat S corporations and partnerships interchangeably because both are passthrough entities. They're really not interchangeable; they have very different sets of rules. And that's because S corporations, for the most part, follow the same tax rules applied to C corporations, because an S corporation, unlike a partnership, is a separate entity for tax purposes.

Partnerships, on the other hand, for the most part use an aggregate approach, so the entity is disregarded and the government, legal profession, and accountants look to the underlying partners. Well, that creates differences with respect to issues such as allocation of profit and loss, treatment of cancellation of debt income, and treatment of distributions (particularly at the corporate level). There is also the opportunity, in certain cases, to have corporate level taxes that could apply to an S corporation. And those issues don't really apply to partnerships.

This chapter looks at the organization of Form 1120S, and some of its related schedules and the information questions on the 1120S. Some of those simply request background information that the government wants to know. And some of the questions can actually be very difficult to answer. Those target abuses, but in many cases, filers don't necessarily know all of the information to answer the questions. So preliminarily, the discussion clarifies how to complete Form 1120S before proceeding to topics unique to the S corporation, such as cancellation of debt reporting and the types of distributions that the entity can make.

# ¶ 704 ISSUES FOR ELECTION TO BECOME AN S CORPORATION

The practitioner plays a special role as a business elects S corporation status. If the client is a new S corporation, the practitioner should ensure that a valid election was filed using Form 2553, *Election by a Small Business Corporation*. Compliance measures the practitioner applies check that:

- The client met all the tests described in the form's instructions;
- All shareholders are valid;
- All shareholders signed the consent statement;
- An officer signed the form; and
- All information on the form was complete.

An issue that comes up in terms of eligibility relates to whether the client resides in a community property state or a separate property state. So, those in community states are well aware that because of the community ownership form, the practitioner typically has to obtain the spouse's consent for share ownership. Under state law in those states, spouses also own some of the S corporation stock and they have to consent to transactions. So, practitioners have to be careful about that at the entity's formation.

For a new client, the practitioner should review the mechanics of a late or corrective election and, of course, maintain a copy of the election when compliance is met as well as a copy of the IRS acceptance letter for the election. Five, six, or seven years down the line, if a purchaser wants to buy the stock of the client's S corporation, part of the due diligence this buyer ought to be doing is making sure that the organization is actually an S corporation. Part of the due diligence would be to request to see the Form 2553 and the IRS acceptance letter so that it's clear that the IRS actually received this letter. It doesn't necessarily mean that the client is an S corporation; the IRS can't really evaluate whether the organization qualifies.

# ¶ 705 REVIEWING CONTINUED ELIGIBILITY FOR S CORPORATION STATUS

The first action the practitioner takes each year for the client is verifying continued eligibility for the S corporation status by checking:

- Whether any new shareholders were admitted and, if so, whether the shareholders satisfy the eligibility requirements;
- Whether any restricted shares or options were issued and, if so, whether they satisfy the safe harbors of the Code Sec. 1361 regulations;
- Distributions for Second Class of Stock (SCOS) issues (and remediation if there are concerns); and
- New or existing debt for SCOS issues.

The practitioner wants to examine changes in shareholders. As the practitioner prepares Form 1120S, the client needs to list to whom Schedule K-1 should be provided. Issuance of any possible equity equivalents or new debt instruments, as well as existing debt instruments are subject for review. The practitioner wants to make sure that new debt instrument is not going to create a second class of stock, that it really is going to be debt. Or arguably, if the instrument isn't debt, if it might be equity—at least it's not going to be a second class of equity. Then existing debt instruments are reviewed. The S corporation that has a debt instrument being treated as debt for two or three years without having made any payments on the debt, could the client have a second class of stock? At some point it becomes very difficult to continue to call that debt. If that's not debt, is that going to create a second class of stock? Those issues come up in C corporations, too, for a closely held entity that's been carrying some debt for two or three years and not making any payments. But the worst thing that happens in a C corporation is a reclassification as equity, and that situation simply affects the tax treatment of the payments. In an S corporation, it can be a lot worse than that treatment because if the entity has equity, potentially it creates a second class of stock and perhaps disqualifies the S status.

## New Shareholders

The practitioner must check whether any new shareholders were admitted. In case new shareholders are included, new Schedule K-1 records must be created. And are the shareholders eligible? In another scenario, for estate planning purposes a shareholder transferred shares of S corporation stock into a trust. Then the trust must elect to be a shareholder—an eligible shareholder. The practitioner would obtain a copy of the trust instrument, check that the election is eligible, and store the document.

Next the practitioner looks at distributions. The regulations provide some safe harbors to avoid a second class of stock when the client makes unequal distributions. Typically, distributions have to be in proportion to stock ownership. Clients may do something inconsistent with the S corporation requirements; maybe they gave one shareholder some cash that they didn't give to another one.

The practitioner may not be aware of that because the client didn't inform him or her. The client didn't understand that this was an issue. When the information is divulged at the end of the year, the discrepancy in payments is revealed. And there's a way to fix that. The regulations let the preparer fix that.

## Restricted Shares

The practitioner also checks whether any restricted shares or options were issued. There is actually a question on the Form 1120S that inquires whether the filer has done that. If the client doesn't provide the information, at a minimum the preparer must ask about options issued. The reason is that restricted shares, as a general rule, are not treated as being outstanding. So at this point in time, nobody is receiving Schedule K-1 and there is no concern about whether that person is an eligible shareholder.

If shareholders made a Code Sec. 83(b) election to ignore those restrictions and became shareholders, they must be issued a Schedule K-1 and verified as an eligible shareholder.

If options are outstanding, the general rule is that until those options are issued as shares, the preparer doesn't do anything. The holders are not shareholders yet; there is no concern about whether they're eligible shareholders. The only exception to that is if the terms of the option are such that it's basically an economic certainty that the option is going to be exercised. Typically, that means the option is very deep in the money. So, maybe the S corporation stock is worth $100 per share, and the exercise price on these options is $0.50 per share.

In a situation like that, the practitioner makes sure that the options are not going to be treated as outstanding stock. Even though technically they are called options, they are not really options if there's an economic certainty that they'll be exercised. The regulations under Code Sec. 1361 say in those situations, options are a stock equivalent. The person is a current shareholder right now; if not, the practitioner must question whether or not the entity remains an S corporation.

## Distributions

The practitioner should check the distributions, which obviously are reported as part of the Form 1120S return. The practitioner should make sure that a distribution is actually in proportion to the stock ownership. Any distributions with respect to stock must be proportionate, because an S corporation can only have one class of stock. Clients must be reminded that an S corporation must have a single type of stock; distributions must be proportional with ownership.

## Debt

The practitioner review should check any new or existing debt to ensure the client doesn't have a problem. The practitioner can examine a straight debt safe harbor in Subchapter S. It's Code Sec. 1361(c)(5). And Code Sec.1361(c)(5) says if a debt instrument meets all of the listed requirements, the instrument could be reclassified as equity. If under general tax law principles it appears more like equity than debt, the IRS has the authority to reclassify the instrument. But if the instrument is reclassified it, it can't possibly be a second class of stock. So, one of the procedures the practitioner fulfills is to test the arrangement under the straight debt safe harbor. The practitioner wants to come within that safe harbor so that the client doesn't risk losing the S election.

If it turns out that the debt instrument doesn't meet the criteria, the Code Sec. 1361 regulations also provide some safe harbors. There is a statutory safe harbor and then there are some regulatory safe harbors. For example, if the debt is held in proportion to equity, then it can't be treated as a second class of stock. It can get reclassified as equity, but it can't be a second class of stock.

Failing that safe harbor, then the practitioner can look to Code Sec. 385 in the Subchapter C area. Subchapter C provisions do apply to S corporations as long as they're not fundamentally inconsistent. So, if the debt doesn't meet a safe harbor, Code Sec. 385 offers some factors to determine whether an arrangement is really debt or really equity.

Now the difference between Code Sec. 385 and the straight debt safe harbor is that the safe harbor says if the instrument meets all of the following requirements, it can't be a second class of stock, whereas Code Sec. 385 simply says in evaluating whether something is debt or equity, some further considerations may apply. Five factors are listed, but the client doesn't have to meet them all because it's a facts and circumstances determination. The practitioner applies those factors to the client's particular fact pattern, and tries to match the S corporation's situations to the factors. The practitioner should examine whether the client either has new debt issuances or a difference arose in the existing debt instrument—being an issue like the S corporation hasn't been making payments. The consequences of such a change is that the problem is so severe.

# ¶706 FILING DUE DATES FOR FORM 1120S

Generally, the due date for filing the Form 1120S return is the fifteenth day of the third month following the close of the corporation's year. There's an extension period of six months.

The AICPA website pages for taxes provide checklists for different types of tax returns. One way to avoid a preparer penalty is to implement procedures to avoid filing problems; a second way is to follow those procedures. The due date of the final Form 1120S would depend on whether the client has liquidated the S corporation, in which case the due date is the fifteenth day of the third month following the last month of that corporation's life.

## Termination or Liquidation

As just described, if the corporation is liquidated, the due date is the fifteenth day of the third month following the liquidation. So, just like with passthrough entities like partnerships, sometimes people can run afoul of the due date of the return if they terminate the S corporation. If the termination occurs in June, shareholders may think the return is not due until March 15 of the subsequent year.

But the practitioner can hope clients keep him or her apprised of the kind of actions that they're doing. The practitioner can determine the due date of the return. Otherwise, the client will be subject to that $195 per-shareholder-per-month penalty to the extent that it is late filing the S corporation return. In some cases, such as in the case when a spouse's consent has not been obtained, the IRS may abate a penalty for first-time late filings of Form 1120S. A series of Revenue Procedures going back to 1997 grant relief for late S elections. And generally, the requirement in order to get that relief is that the organization has filed consistently; it has filed an 1120S, but then also all the shareholders have filed consistent with that.

## Conversion to a C Corporation

If an S corporation is converted to a C corporation, the due date is based on the C corporation short year. This allows the practitioner to run it out the whole year. So, in other words, two different situations apply. One would entail selling the assets of the S corporation and, for example, adopting a plan of liquidation to distribute all of the assets on June 30. In that case, the return is due September 15, the fifteenth day of the third month following the close of the corporation itself. Then the shareholders have liquidated the corporation.

Now, if on June 30 the shareholders convert from a C corporation to an S corporation, the S corporation's return is not due until March 15 of the subsequent year. The reason for that due date is that, as a general rule with S corporations, a conversion like that uses a prorated, per-share-per-day, calculation to allocate the income during the year.

So, the practitioner doesn't necessarily know how much of the income is going to fall in those first six months until the entity gets to the end of the year. The practitioner needs a full year's income to determine how much goes into the short S corporation year and how much goes into the short C corporation year. So, rather than requiring the S corporation to file a return of September 15, when the client doesn't have the information needed, the client gets to run it out the entire year, and the due date then becomes March 15.

In case a shareholder's interest is terminated—but there is not a liquidation of the entire corporation—the rule calls for allocating the interest on a per-share-per-day basis. The entity may elect to close the books if all of the shareholders consent.

The general rule is that the practitioner uses per-share-per-day allocations to determine how much income the former shareholder picks up and how much income the new shareholder picks up. If both agree, then the practitioner can close the books. Other shareholders do not have to agree to that closing of the books. And the reason is they were shareholders for the entire year and, as a result, they're not really affected by this election. The only folks who are affected are the departing shareholder and the incoming shareholder. The practitioner could use the closing of the books in a situation like that.

If the S corporation actually terminates—an S termination year—shareholders can elect to close the books, allocating the income between the S corporation year and the C corporation year. But all of the S corporation shareholders must consent to that, and all the shareholders of the C corporation must be determined on the first day of the C corporation year.

So, following up on the previous example, the S corporation terminates its S status election as of June 30, and as a calendar year entity, the practitioner would need the consent of all of the S corporation shareholders to close the books and the consent of anybody who owned that stock on July 1 as a C corporation shareholder. In that case, the entity could split the year in half, as opposed to doing a per-share-per-day allocation.

The only situation in which an S corporation has a mandatory closing of the books as opposed to a pro rata allocation is for an S termination year in which there is a transfer of 50 percent or more of the stock within that S termination year. In that situation it's a mandatory close.

# ¶ 707  COMPLETING FORM 1120S

## Page 1 Information

The first page of Form 1120S asks for basic information, but it also asks whether the filer has terminated its S election. Has the entity revoked affirmatively its S status election? The first page has a whole section that deals with corporate tax payment, so if one of the penalty taxes discussed later applies, for which the corporation itself can actually pay a tax, the return actually shows the computation of that tax at the bottom of the first page. That result has implications for what is passed through to the shareholders.

Also requested on the first page is the effective date on which the entity elected S corporation status.

So, the corporation passes through not only, for example, gains that the corporation realized during the year but, to the extent that the corporation has made a payment, say a built-in gains tax, the entity passes that through to the shareholders as separately stated loss. So, the IRS can tie that back to page 1.

## Page 2: Schedule B Other Information

The second page of Form 1120S asks what type of shareholders compose the corporation and the ownership of those shareholders. The form requests any information for restricted stock grants or option grants that the entity has outstanding. Those first two items reveal to the IRS whether the entity is really an S corporation and whether the entity is eligible to be an S corporation.

The information on page 2 thus supplies the IRS with:

- Shareholder type and ownership;

- Information for restricted stock or option grants outstanding;

- Cancellation of debt (COD) items (existence); and

- "Difficult" information reporting, such as

  — Earnings and profits balance

  — Net Unrealized Built-In Gain (NUBIG), minus Net Unrealized Built-In Loss (NUBIL), minus prior Recognized Built-In Gains (RBIGs)

As described later, the AICPA SSTS No. 2 offers as guidance to answering the difficult questions.

The form asks about the existence of any COD items. It is not necessarily asking how the corporation treated those items. But if the entity has cancellation of debt at the

S corporation level, under this entity approach, the corporation actually applies the Code Sec. 108 exclusions at the entity level.

So, for example, insolvencies may have arisen. One of the Code Sec. 108 exclusions covers them. If the S corporation is insolvent, then any cancellation of debt income is not recognized. It becomes nontaxable income. It's not going to be taxable to the shareholders. If the entity is a partnership, it has to pass the income through as COD income and then the partners individually determine whether they qualify for the exception.

> **EXAMPLE:** Fred Campbell is a client who has 30 different entities, most of which are partnerships, and he's got six S corporations. He personally has a fairly significant net worth, but he holds real estate assets in these passthrough entities. Since the economic downturn—New Mexico has not really fully recovered from that—Fred has had a couple COD events in some of these passthrough entities.

> The passthrough entities that are S corporations turn out to be insolvent and so the income goes nowhere. The income never hits his tax return. He's had other COD events in partnerships, and those pass through to him. Fred has plenty of insolvencies, so he ends up having to report that income on his return. In a couple of cases he qualified for the qualified real property debt exception, but for the most part, the COD is applied at the entity level for an S corporation.

So, all Form 1120S asks here is whether the entity has had COD income. Then the entity reports the amount of any earnings and profits. Typically a client had earnings and profits when the entity used to be a C corporation; then it converted to an S corporation. Now, the entity could also acquire COD income in two other ways:

- A nontaxable acquisition of the assets of the C corporation, in which the attributes carry over to the S corporation; or
- The S corporation buys the stock of a C corporation and makes a QSub election.

In the latter case the client either affirmatively liquidates the C corporation, which typically the entity won't do. If the client is buying the stock, it's because he or she has a need for the stock. There's something valuable in connection with that entity itself—intangible assets, licenses, leases, and so on. The client needs that company so the owners really don't want to liquidate it.

But the client also doesn't want to have a C corporation subsidiary, so the best option is to make a QSub election if the client acquires 100 percent of the stock and then pretends that the corporation was liquidated up into the parent S corporation. Then the client gets a carryover basis and a carryover of attributes, including earnings and profits.

So, one of the problems occurs if the entity used to be a C corporation or if it is acquiring the E&YP of the C corporation. C corporations very often don't know what their earnings and profits is. They haven't been keeping a regular record of that. The calculation for figuring the built-in gains tax goes like this:

NUBIG – NUBIL – RBIGs

And the same thing with the net unrealized built-in gain (NUBIG), minus net unrealized built-in loss (NUBIL), minus prior recognized built-in gains (RBIGs). The government wants to know what potential exposure the entity has to the built-in gains tax. The client may never had an appraisal done when the entity converted from a C corporation to an S corporation, so the tax practitioner doesn't really know that number.

In such a case the practitioner can refer to the AICPA Statement on Standards and Tax Services (SSDS) No. 2, which deals with answers to questions on returns. If the client and practitioner cannot answer the questions, SSDS No. 2 goes into more depth and says that in some cases, the client might have to disclose on the return why the question cannot be answered. In other cases, he or she doesn't have to.

With these particular issues, the form doesn't have to separately describe why the client can't answer the question if it doesn't have an immediate tax impact on the current year return. However, the SSDS provides a much more extensive discussion of that issue.

## Schedule K-1 Reporting

Schedule K-1 obviously asks for the filer's stock ownership percentage. It's typically a much easier question than in partnerships, because the S corporation can only have one class of stock. So, it has to be clear as to what the stock ownership is.

Schedule K-1 asks for items affecting basis, tax-exempt income, and expenses associated with tax-exempt income. They all affect the client's basis. Nondeductible expenses affect basis. Distributions affect basis. Repayments and shareholder debt are actually reported on the Schedule K-1 because an S corporation shareholder gets basis. Shareholders get debt basis for loans that they've made to the corporation when there's a direct economic outlay from the shareholder to the corporation. So, the government wants to know what kind of repayments the client has made on that debt, because obviously that's going to reduce his or her debt basis.

## STUDY QUESTION

---

**1.** A condition for an S corporation to maintain S status is having only one class of stock. Which of the following would *not* potentially result in a second class of stock and risk the corporation's S status?

  **a.** Issuance of a new debt instrument

  **b.** A change in capital structure

  **c.** Disproportionate distributions

  **d.** Issuance of restricted stock

---

## Schedule M-2 Analysis of Accumulated Adjustments Account, Other Adjustments Account, and Shareholders' Undistributed Taxable Income Previously Taxed

Schedule M-2 asks for the accumulated adjustments account (AAA), as well as the other adjustments. The AAA is an account that used to determine the tax effect of distributions to the shareholder. And generally, the AAA becomes important only if the client has earnings and profits (E&P). The general rule in an S corporation is if the shareholder gets a distribution, it's tax-free to the extent of basis; if it exceeds the shareholder's basis, it's capital gain. C corporations have a whole different set of rules. They have dividends to the extent of E&P, followed by return of capital, followed by capital gain.

So, what the practitioner needs to learn is whether the S corporation has earnings and profits, whether it is making distributions, and which set of rules these distributions follow. And the tax law says that to the extent that distributions are taken out of AAA, they are drawn out of the S corporation rules. Once the entity has burned off the AAA, distributions now follow the C corporation rules.

¶707

As a general rule, if the S corporation doesn't have earnings and profits, the AAA account has no significance. But it's still a good idea to maintain it, because in later periods the corporation may acquire E&P. For example, if a C corporation is merged into the S corporation, the latter acquires some earnings and profits.

The other situation for maintaining the AAA is that the entity could have a post-termination transition period (PTTP). If the S corporation loses its S election and becomes a C corporation, all distributions from that point forward are dividends to the extent of E&P. They're taken using the C corporation rules.

Shareholders will say, "Well, that's not fair. I've got all this income that I was taxed on that I never distributed when we were an S corporation." And so, the tax law takes kind of a rough justice approach to helping in such a situation: a one-year PTTP time. The corporation now has one year to make distributions of cash to the shareholders and to pull those out tax-free, to the extent of the shareholders' basis. However, the corporation also has to prove that those distributions came out of old S earnings. So, in other words, the entity has to have maintained an AAA.

If for some reason, the client has not computed the AAA because the entity has always been an S corporation and has no E&P, if the entity loses its S status, the client and practitioner must go back and recompute the AAA to figure out what amount can be distributed during that PTTP. The practitioner can inform the client that he or she actually acquired E&P during the time that the entity was an S corporation, but it's going to be in one of these two situations—nontaxable asset acquisition or the acquisition of the stock of a C corporation when the client gets a carryover basis because he or she made a QSub election.

The corporation also has an "other adjustments" account. The AAA, for the most part, at least conceptually, reflects the adjustments to the shareholder's basis during the time that it was an S corporation. The exceptions to that are tax-exempt income and expenses associated with tax-exempt income. Those affect the shareholder's basis, but they don't get run through the AAA account. Those end up in the other adjustments account.

And then to the extent that the corporation is paid any taxes, built-in gains tax, excess passive income, LIFO recapture—all of those taxes get run through the other adjustments account.

## Schedule K Shareholders' Pro Rata Share Items

**Material Participation.** Schedule K, just like with a partnership, is a summary statement of all of the information that is entered on Schedule K-1. However, certain decisions have to be made to complete Schedule K, and the decisions have pros and cons. One major decision is whether to elect Section 179 expensing, which is discussed later. The other decision involves how activities are grouped to deal with the passive activity loss (PAL) rules. These rules say that to avoid passive loss restrictions, the client must have a business or trade activity in which he or she materially participates. The regulations describe some factors for material participation, but they also give the client some flexibility in determining what the activity is (as opposed to one that is disaggregated as a separate activity).

But the S corporation has to report the separate activity also. Even though the S corporation is not subject to the passive loss rules itself, because the shareholders of the S corporation are subject to those rules, the S corporation has to make a decision as to how broadly or how narrowly to define an activity.

Two reasons prompt the decision. Number one is the PAL rules, and number two is the net investment income tax. So, if the client has losses from an activity, the practitioner wants to be able to show that the client materially participates in the trade or business so that those losses can be claimed. So, the goal is to group activities in such a way that it makes it easier to do.

Second, if a high-income client has income from the activity, he or she wants to avoid being subject to the net investment income tax. Thus, the activities should be grouped in such a way that the client can materially participate. The reason is if he or she is materially participating, it is not an investment activity, and so the income from that activity is exempt from the 3.8 percent Medicare surtax. But what the shareholder wants can be upset by what the S corporation does, the way the S corporation groups activities.

**Section 179 Expense Election.** The limitations for currently expensing acquired business or trade items apply to both the corporation and the shareholder. This is an entity type approach. The corporation is treated as if it's a taxpayer, and so the $500,000 limitation applies, the taxable income limitation applies. The dollar limit is reduced if acquisitions exceed $2 million (inflation indexed). If the S corporation has negative taxable income, then it doesn't get any current benefit of a Section 179 expense election.

And then these limitations also apply at the shareholder level. One factor to think about is before the client claims this expense election is whether the shareholders are going to be able to benefit. With a permanent $500,000 limitation, in many cases the practitioner doesn't have to worry about whether the S corporation and/or the shareholders are going to be able to receive the benefit, so the determination is easier.

But the shareholders may have limitations on their ability to use the Section 179 expense election because they've already maxed out at their level or perhaps they don't have taxable income at their level. Another issue is that in order to claim the 179 expense election, the shareholder has to have business income. So, the income in question has to be from the active conduct of a trade or business, and the definition of a trade or business uses the Code Sec. 162 definition. Section 162 says the taxpayer can deduct ordinary and necessary trade or business expenses.

The practitioner computes corporate taxable income before any deduction for shareholder compensation. Basically, because it's a flow-through entity, the aim is to put the shareholders on the same footing as if they were sole proprietors operating this particular business. And how much income are they actually going to report from the business?

Then the shareholder compensation is added back to the taxable income to figure out whether there is a limitation at the corporate level. And then at the shareholder's level because the shareholder's taxable income limitation includes any salary from the S corporation.

A separate issue is that in order for this shareholder to benefit from a Section 179 expense election, he or she has to be involved in the trade or business of the S corporation. First, at the corporate level, is the S corporation involved in a trade or business? If it is, the practitioner can now pass through the 179 expense election to the shareholders. As mentioned earlier, the PAL rules require material participation, and different rules are required for the 179 expense election: participation in a "meaningful way."

If the corporate taxable limit applies, the excess election carries forward at the corporate level to the next tax year. The shareholder's taxable income limit includes salary from the S corporation.

Some other factors of note for the Section 179 election include:

- The Section 179 expense is not allowed for estates and trusts;
- The S corporation can remedy an otherwise unusable allocation to an estate or trust by not claiming the expense election for the portion of property attributable to the ownership of the trust or estate;
- The shareholder's tax basis is reduced by a claimed expense election; and
- If the expense was limited at the shareholder level (e.g., taxable income limitation), the basis reduction is restored immediately before a taxable disposition of the stock.

 **PLANNING POINTER:** Certain types of trusts that can be eligible shareholders in the S corporation, such as grantor trusts, and qualified Subchapter S trusts, and electing small business trusts. Well, those trusts in the estates cannot qualify to get a passthrough of the 179 expense election. So, without any remedy, without any fix to that problem, heirs could be an estate or trust as the shareholder, plus some individuals. Fortunately, the regulations allow the practitioner to make the 179 expense election, applying it only to those shareholders eligible to receive a benefit. So, if the client has estates and trusts as part of the shareholder group, then their portion of the 179 expense election just doesn't apply. Thus the practitioner could, for example, depreciate the portion of the basis attributable to that property.

# ¶ 708 REPORTING PAL ACTIVITIES

The S corporation itself is not subject to the passive loss rules. But what the shareholders need to do is to decide what is an activity. So, the shareholders have certain operations in the S corporation, and they must decide how broadly or narrowly they define an activity. Does the client throw all of these things together and say he or she has one activity, or does he or she try to pull them apart, maybe say there are three activities?

The decision doesn't matter to the S corporation because it is not subject to the passive loss rules, nor does the entity have to pay the net investment income tax. But it does matter to the shareholders. And the reason is the rule is that anything that the S corporation groups as an activity, the shareholder cannot pull apart. The shareholder cannot disaggregate.

The general rule is that the S corporation wants to disaggregate as much as possible. There are a couple of constraints on that. The more shareholders disaggregate, the more reporting they have to do, because the corporation has to attach a statement to the Schedule K-1 showing the income and loss for each of these PAL activities. The regulations also consider facts and circumstances applied in grouping activities. Although disaggregation enables shareholders the greatest flexibility in grouping at their level, corporate groupings must satisfy the appropriate economic unit standard.

Thus, the corporate grouping may affect shareholders in two ways:

- Application of the PAL rules; and
- Application of the Code Sec. 1411 Medicare surtax.

One exception to the PAL rules applies when an S corporation has both rental and nonrental activities, and one type is incidental to the other, they may be reported together. Shareholders must prove the activity is for a trade or business. When that income is passed through to shareholders who are qualified real estate professionals, the PAL rules do not apply.

## STUDY QUESTIONS

---

**2.** When an S corporation claims the Section 179 deduction, the deduction does not benefit the shareholder if:

   **a.** The shareholder has reached the Section 179 dollar limitation as an individual.

   **b.** The shareholder does not have taxable business income, as defined by Code Sec. 162.

   **c.** The shareholder is not actively involved (does not meaningfully participate) in the trade or business for which the S corporation is making the election.

   **d.** All of the above.

**3.** It is beneficial for an S corporation not to aggregate passive activities because:

   **a.** The S corporation's reporting burden is alleviated by keeping the activities separate.

   **b.** It allows shareholder flexibility.

   **c.** Aggregation by the shareholders, rather than at the entity level, will eliminate application of the net investment income tax.

   **d.** It minimizes the S corporation's exposure to the passive activity loss rules.

---

# ¶ 709 REPORTING CANCELLATION OF DEBT

During the economic downturn in 2009 and 2010, there were numerous COD events. Congress responded with Code Sec. 108(i), allowing a special election not to report the forgiven debt as income in those years. Beginning in 2014, the income could be spread evenly over five years.

Thus, if an S corporation made that election and has disposed of the trade or business that created the COD income, the entity has to accelerate all of the incomes. So, every year, if shareholders made this election back in 2009 and 2010, every year the practitioner must ask if the entity has done something that would cause this deferred income to be accelerated. Such an action could be a disposition of substantially all of the assets of the business in which the COD income originated, or perhaps the S corporation stopped running that business. In either case, the client has to accelerate that income.

Otherwise, the S corporation is treated as a taxpayer that triggers the COD income. It's an entity approach. And that means that the client has COD income under Code Sec. 61's general definition of gross income but also has the Code Sec. 108 exclusions. Exclusions apply for discharge in bankruptcy, insolvency, qualified farm debt, qualified real property debt, and purchase money debt. The shareholder receives no basis increase for excluded COD income. At the entity level, those exclusions can be reported on the Form 1120S using Form 982, *Reduction of Tax Attributes Due to Discharge of Indebtedness (and Section 1082 Basis Adjustment.*

# ¶ 710 SHAREHOLDER SCHEDULE K-1 ISSUES

Shareholders' Schedules K-1 obviously show their allocable share of profit and loss, show ownership of stock, and show items affecting basis with codes entered in the form's boxes. The schedule enables tax software to track basis at the shareholder level.

# ¶ 711  DISTRIBUTIONS

## Corporate Effect

S corporations are generally subject to the same rules that govern C corporations. Thus, distributions of property are subject to the same rules:

- Code Sec. 311 for nonliquidating distributions; and
- Code Sec. 336 or 337 for liquidating distributions.

Tax practitioners often say a corporation is like a lobster trap, easy to get into but hard to get out of. Practitioners (and clients) need to be careful in equating S corporations to partnerships for these reasons:

- Partnerships can distribute appreciated property without recognition of gain;
- S corporations are corporations, and therefore are subject to the "normal" rules that apply to corporate distributions of appreciated property; and
- Appreciated property distributions then cause gain to be reported on the Form 1120S; there may be no corporate-level tax, but gain is accelerated to shareholders.

## Nonliquidating Distributions to Shareholders

S corporations are treated under an entity approach, just like C corporations. And what that means is that if an S corporation distributes property to the shareholders, not money but property, something other than money, Code Sec. 311 provides that it is treated as if the corporation sold that property to the shareholder at fair market value.

If shareholders are liquidating the S corporation, it's the same rule except Code Sec. 336 applies. Code Sec. 311 states that if shareholders distribute property and it's not in liquidation of the corporation, they recognize gains but don't recognize losses, whereas Code Sec. 336 applies to a distribution in liquidation and shareholders generally recognize both gains and losses.

But unlike a partnership, if an S corporation distributes a piece of property that has a value of $2 million and a basis of $1 million, the transaction creates $1 million of gain at the S corporation level. Now, the S corporation may not pay any tax, but that $1 million gain passes through to the shareholders. They are getting property and, as a result, they have no cash. And they've got to pay taxes.

> **PLANNING POINTER:** Standwell, an S corporation, pays $2 million in 2015 for a duplex building, and it increases in value to $3.5 million in 2017. Standwell's tax planner warns the shareholders not to distribute (sell) the property because the fair value is more than the shareholders' basis and the sale will trigger income. In 2017 the shareholders sell the property and incur $1.5 in passthrough income. If, instead, Standwell uses the building as rental property, the shareholders are just taxed on the rental income. However, the tax planner advises them not to get out of the ownership until the building is sold or will have to be retitled in the name of the shareholders and treated as a deemed sale.

> **EXAMPLE:** Sarah Newcomb is the sole shareholder of the Newco S corporation, and Newco has got some land with a fair market value $800,000 and basis of $400,000. What happens if Newco distributes this land? Sarah mistakenly thinks nothing, that the ownership is the same as for a partnership. When she distributes the property, Newco has to report a $400,000 gain. Very likely there's no corporate tax or a built-in gains tax. But Newco passes through a $400,000 gain to Sarah on Schedule K-1.

She's received nothing but property; she has no cash. Plus the IRS says she owes the tax on a $400,000 gain through Schedule K-1, plus an $800,000 distribution that may or may not be taxable, in a type of secondary type event. So generally, it's preferable to avoid disturbing appreciated property from an S corporation.

**EXAMPLE:** Assume Sarah's tax planner notes the plight of the S corporation's holding and sets up a limited liability company (LLC), then merges her S corporation into the LLC. Most states allow mergers of corporations and LLCs, even though LLCs are not corporations under state law.

If Sarah is the only owner of the LLC, that building is now sitting in a disregarded entity—a single-member LLC disregarded entity. And so, that's going to be a deemed liquidation of the S corporation and that's going to trigger this $400,000 gain.

**EXAMPLE:** A third possibility may arise. If Sarah is married and she and her husband set up an LLC to be taxed as a partnership, it is a two-person LLC. They live in a community property state, so as husband and wife they own the LLC as community property. They can elect to treat it as a disregarded entity or as a partnership, and they prefer the partnership entity. So, they merge the assets of the S corporation into this two-person LLC. Because they've changed the form of the business from an S corporation to a partnership, again it is considered a deemed liquidation of the S corporation and triggers the $400,000 gain. So, really there's no happy way to get this building out of this S corporation. Even if the couple sells the land for the $400,000, distributing the land triggers that gain. Or if she is deemed to sell the land to the only shareholder of the S corporation—herself—under Code Sec. 1239, the gain is recast as ordinary income, not capital gain.

Setting up the entity as a partnership often does not rectify the problem.

**EXAMPLE:** A partnership has some problems, but at least it's a feasible solution, referred to as a drop and swap. Three owners form a partnership to own a building. First the partnership distributes undivided interest in the building to the three owners, and then the partners sell their fractional interest in the building. Two partners want to do a Code Sec. 1031 transaction, and one doesn't.

If that same situation arises for an S corporation, the problem is the fact that the building is distributed, creating a taxable event. So, the taxable event has already occurred, so now the owners think that they're going to sell the fractional interest and do a Code Sec. 1031 transaction, but a 1031 is now worthless because they've already picked up all of the gain. So, again, that's the entity type concept with an S corporation.

## Shareholder Effect

The tax result of a nonliquidating distribution depends on the existence of earnings and profits (E&P). If there are no earnings and profits at the corporation level, the normal S corporation rules are applied to the distribution; the distribution is tax free to the extent of basis, followed by capital gain. E&P is a C corporation concept, so E&P exists only when:

- The S corporation is a former C corporation;
- The S corporation acquired E&P in a nontaxable acquisition, such as
  - Nontaxable asset acquisition, and
  - Stock acquisition followed by a QSub election.

There are transactions that could occur in an S corporation that has always been an S corporation that cause that S corporation to now have earnings and profits. How do shareholders deal with the E&P? The corporation has to apply a last-in, first-out (LIFO) or a first-in, first-out (FIFO) rule. Do shareholders assume that those distributions come out of the S corporation earnings—meaning tax-free to the extent of basis, followed by capital gain? That would be a LIFO approach. Or do they have to go back and treat the profits as if they come out of the earnings that were first in the life of this corporation, way back when, when it was a C corporation—meaning dividend to the extent of E&P?

**AAA Versus E&P.** The S corporation is allowed to take profits out of the S corporation earnings. Distributions are first pulled under S corporation rules. This is where the AAA enables a tax-free return of capital gain. Once that is depleted and distributions continue, they come from out of the C corporation rules as a dividend to the extent of E&P, followed by a return of basis, followed by capital gain.

Shareholders can choose to bypass the AAA and go straight to depleting the E&P, which would simplify future distributions. However, a more important reason is when corporate level penalty taxes apply, there is a tax on excess passive income in an S corporation. And two results happen:

- A penalty tax, which is bad enough;
- If that tax applies for three years in a row, the corporation loses its S corporation status as of the first day of the fourth year.

People call it the sting tax because the IRS gains shareholders' attention the first three years and in the fourth year, shareholders get stung.

So, shareholders want to get rid of the E&P if they have that problem. And one way to do that is make a distribution and jump right into the E&P layer. Shareholders make an affirmative election to do that on the Form 1120S return, and the election applies year-by-year. So, the corporation makes it for 2017, but it doesn't apply to 2018's return. To apply to 2018, shareholders must make the election again.

The AAA is really close to basis, but is not exactly the same. The biggest differences are items of tax-exempt income and tax-exempt expenses. They affect the basis but they don't affect AAA. They go into the other adjustments account. But there's another difference: basis is an individual account, shareholder-by-shareholder. If the S corporation has four shareholders, each shareholder has his or her own basis. For example, one shareholder acquired some shares by purchase. She got a gift from her parent for some of the shares, and then inherited some of the shares from her parent, so she has three different blocks of stock. And the basis for the one that she bought is whatever she paid for it. The basis for the one received as a gift is a carryover from her parent. The basis for the one that she inherited from their parent is fair market value on date of death. So, the shares have multiple bases.

The AAA account is simply based on these positive and negative adjustments made year-by-year. The AAA account is also a corporate level account. It is not a shareholder level account, so it belongs to the corporation. It's an attribute of the corporation.

Normally shareholders care about AAA when the corporation has E&P. That means that the S corporation had some life as a C corporation prior to becoming an S corporation. So, during the life of the C corporation, it could be that the shareholders have an aggregate basis of $1 million, and now become an S corporation. On that day the AAA is zero; from that date forward, the AAA starts to build up and make adjustments. But it's still a corporate-level account, not a shareholder-level account.

**Nonliquidating Distributions and Compensation.** By now, all practitioners are familiar with the use of low compensation as a payroll tax avoidance strategy. This is particularly a concern with one shareholder. "Reasonable" compensation is fine, but "reasonable" requires some professional judgment to satisfy professional standards of practice. Then the payments recorded as distributions may be considered salary payments by the IRS and subject to payroll taxes.

> **EXAMPLE:** With a one-shareholder S corporation, the incentive is to treat distributions in this way. If the S corporation has multiple shareholders, though, not paying somebody enough for the value of his or her services, the entity could end up with a deemed distribution, a constructive distribution to a shareholder and end up possibly with disproportionate distributions. Under the regulations, it's not going to create a second class of stock. If the shareholders reclassify distributions as compensation so that unequal distributions result, that's not going to create a second class of stock. Code Sec. 1361 regulations protect them, so the entity doesn't have to be concerned about that.

## STUDY QUESTIONS

---

**4.** When would it be unnecessary for an S corporation to have an accumulated adjustments account (AAA)?

   **a.** The S corporation transitions to a C corporation.

   **b.** The S corporation has tax-exempt income and expenses.

   **c.** The S corporation acquires a C corporation and makes a QSub election.

   **d.** The S corporation acquires earnings and profits through the nontaxable asset acquisition of a C corporation.

**5.** Taxation of an S corporation is similar to that of a partnership with respect to:

   **a.** The distribution of appreciated property.

   **b.** The type of entity.

   **c.** Cancellation of debt (COD).

   **d.** The purpose of Schedule K.

---

# ¶712 CORPORATE LEVEL TAXES

Corporate level taxes may apply in three general scenarios:

- Conversion of a C corporation to an S corporation;
- Acquisition by an S corporation of the assets of a C corporation in a carryover basis/tax attribute transaction; and
- Acquisition by an S corporation of 100 percent of the stock of a C corporation followed by a QSub election (carryover basis/attributes).

## Conversion of a C Corporation to an S Corporation

This is the most common scenario in which the corporate-tax issue arises. C corporations have two levels of tax, and the IRS does not permit conversion of two levels of tax to one. So the IRS devised antiabuse penalty taxes that can also apply if an S corporation acquires the assets of a C corporation in a nontaxable transaction (i.e., carryover basis). The taxes can also apply if the S corporation acquires the stock of a C corporation by making a QSub election (not a true liquidation). The election allows a carryover basis from the C corporation, which potentially imposes the penalty tax. In 1986, when the built-in gains tax was enacted, the IRS established a 10-year recognition period within which assets sold were deemed to be subject to the built-in gains tax unless proven otherwise. S corporations had to prove they didn't own the asset at the date of conversion or could show the asset appreciated after the date of conversion so the appreciation was not subject to the penalty.

To avoid discouraging nontax business restructuring during the economic downturn in 2008 and 2009, Congress tweaked this recognition rule, rolling back the 10 year period to:

- 7 years for 2009 and 2010 tax years; and
- 5 years for 2011 and beyond (the change is now permanent).

The shortened period means that entities are more likely to avoid the built-in gains tax. Even if the C corporation possesses appreciated property, it can make an S corporation election now to start the shortened recognition period to avoid built-in gains tax.

## Acquisition of C Corporation Assets in a Carryover Basis/Tax Attribute Transaction

Anytime the entity has a carryover basis transaction, the corporation is going to be subject to these penalty taxes, even if it has always been an S corporation. Basically, on the conversion date, the entity takes a snapshot of the assets of the corporation and determines asset-by-asset the built-in gain amount. The snapshot shows not only built-in gains on that date but also built-in losses. The client should create evidence of both.

Question 6 on Form 1120S Schedule B asks for the excess of the net unrealized built-in gain, which is the built-in gain on assets with fair value in excess of basis, over the net unrealized built-in loss. The client may not know the answer to that question, so the practitioner refers to SSDS No. 2 to figure out what to do about it. The guidance lists the maximum tax due if the client has actual amounts on the conversion date or appraisals of the assets. If the amounts cannot be proven, any gains triggered during the five-year recognition period are considered built-in. Again, the tax is not triggered if the asset was not held on the date of conversion or only the appreciation on the asset, not the full sale price, is built-in gain.

To summarize the rules, there are:

- Section 381 carryovers, including acquisitive reorganizations, most commonly under "A," "C," or acquisitive "D" of Code Sec. 368(a)(1) or the forward triangular merger of Code Sec. 368(a)(2)(D); and
- Section 332 subsidiary liquidation of C corporation, including a QSub election (100 percent owned) or an actual liquidation (greater than or equal to 80 percent owned).

## Involuntary Conversion

What happens to the built-in gains if fixed assets have an involuntary conversion? An involuntary conversion is a nonrecognition event if the owner elects it.

**EXAMPLE:** The warehouse owned by the Shippers S corporation burned down and the insurance company pays Shippers the proceeds, the fair value of the warehouse. The corporation now has either two years or three years, depending on the nature of the asset, to use the insurance proceeds to rebuild that warehouse as similar related in use property.

After the warehouse is rebuilt, it is discovered that the warehouse that burned to the ground had a built-in gain. Code Sec. 1033 allows Shippers to elect to defer that gain into the new warehouse. If it's a built-in gain item, though, the deferred gain on the building that burned to the ground continues to be a built-in gain on the new building during the five-year recognition period, so Shippers must hold the property beyond the five-year recognition period to avoid the built-in gains tax.

The same rules apply to a like-kind exchange. If Shippers had a warehouse and sold it through like-kind exchange, the corporation defers the gain. The new property steps into the shoes of the old property with respect to the built-in gain and the corporation still has to hold the property beyond the five-year recognition period.

**EXAMPLE:**  The Patterson S corporation has a net unrealized built-in gain of $2 million on the date of conversion. The corporation has a recognized built-in gain in 2015 of $500,000. So, the net unrealized built-in gain—that $2 million—is important because that's the maximum amount for which Patterson could be subject to tax on a built-in gain.

Now, the amount that Patterson actually recognized this year was $500,000. Ordinarily, the corporation would have to pay built-in gains tax on $500,000. But there's another limitation: the taxable income for the year as if Patterson had stayed as a C corporation.

The basic idea here is that an entity shouldn't be worse off by becoming an S corporation. Had Patterson stayed as a C corporation, it obviously would have been taxed only on $300,000. So, Patterson is going to pay the built-in gains tax on $300,000, that taxable income number. And the way the law was written, that would have been the end of the story. But then Congress changed the law to say that built-in gain that was not subject to tax because of the taxable income limitation, carries forward to the next year. It'll carry forward to 2016. So, in 2016, the facts say taxable income is still $300,000; nothing else happened in 2016, so the built-in gains tax applies to $300,000, taxable income. The net unrealized built-in gain is reduced from $2 million to $1.7, but Patterson carries forward the $200,000 gain that was not taxed in 2015 because of the taxable income limitation. That carries forward to 2016. The built-in gains tax is at the highest corporate rate, 35 percent. So, Patterson pays a tax of $105,000.

In 2015, the shareholder gets a Schedule K-1, which shows a $500,000 gain. That's the gain for the property that was sold. But it also shows a $105,000 separately stated loss, and the reason is if Patterson had remained a C corporation, technically it doesn't have double taxation, it has 1.65 times taxation. To the extent that the corporation is paying 35 percent of the gain to the government, Patterson can't pay that tax again at the shareholder level. Okay, so what the shareholder gets in 2015 is a $500,000 passthrough gain and a $105,000 passthrough loss.

Now, this is a capital asset, so that loss is a capital loss. It mirrors the treatment of the gain. Now, the problem is in the next year, 2016, the shareholder carried forward the $200,000. The shareholder pays a $70,000 built-in gains tax in 2016, and that shows up as a negative item on the shareholder's Schedule K-1. And in this case, it's a capital loss because that asset was a capital asset.

Now, the shareholder has a $70,000 capital loss in year two and may not be able to do anything with it. So, that taxable income limitation is kind of a neat deal but taxpayers can end up getting burned by it because they carry forward the amount that was limited by the taxable income.

The situation also involves a passive income tax reason for involuntary conversions. C corporations can be classified as personal holding companies and can have to pay a penalty tax. The concern is that a C corporation might avoid this tax by becoming an S corporation. But following the conversion the entity will still be subject to something similar to the tax if it has earnings and profits. That's what triggers it. So, in general, the S corporation has to have been a C corporation at some time during its life.

The IRS knows about this from the return. The passive income has to exceed 25 percent of gross receipts. It's a 35 percent penalty tax and it applies only if the passive investment income exceeds 25 percent of the gross receipts.

And the S corporation can lose its status on the first day of the fourth year, so it's important not to have this income received into a fourth year. One way to do that is to make distributions and bypass the AAA and use up the E&P. And that may even require that the client does an E&P calculation, that the practitioner goes back to the beginning and figures out what E&P is.

The corporation can reduce its passive income. Alternatively, it can increase its gross receipts, because passive income has to exceed 25 percent of the gross receipts. So, what is passive investment income? What creates the problem? What is normally considered passive income includes dividends, interest, rents, and royalties. Now, rents may or may not be included. Very much as for a personal holding company, if the client is in the active conduct of a trade or business, which is defined in a different way than Code Sec. 162, basically the corporation is required to have significant costs or significant services. That means beyond the norm.

> **EXAMPLE:** Allertone, a C corporation, dates back to 1978. If Allertone elects S status, could it get hit with the passive investment income tax? Yes it could. Its rental income could be passive investment income subject to the excess passive income tax.

> Probably the tax would not be incurred if Allertone hadn't already been a personal holding company. That corporation was a personal holding company and never reported that way. So Allertone could have an excess passive income tax, which not only creates a problem with paying the tax, but it means that the entity converted to an S corporation with the idea that it could avoid the built-in gains tax after five years, and in the fourth year it flipped back to being a C corporation because it had the penalty tax.

## STUDY QUESTION

**6.** How can an S corporation avoid having to pay the passive investment income tax?

   **a.** By distributing earnings and profits.

   **b.** By selling stocks and securities that will generate a loss.

   **c.** By making investments that generate interest income.

   **d.** By divesting of rental property that generates income but also has significant costs associated with the property.

# MODULE 2: SMALL BUSINESS TAXATION—
# Chapter 8: Partnership Tax Filing Issues

## ¶ 801 WELCOME

This chapter discusses partnership tax filing issues, including essential reporting issues and obligations in partnership taxation, planning opportunities, and best practices for preparing partnership returns.

## ¶ 802 LEARNING OBJECTIVES

Upon completion of this chapter, you will be able to:

- Describe essential reporting issues and obligations in partnership taxation
- Identify planning opportunities with partnership tax returns
- Apply best practices for preparing partnership returns

## ¶ 803 INTRODUCTION

As more sophisticated taxpayers are using partnerships, the IRS has expanded the types of questions that it asks on Form 1065, *U.S. Return of Partnership Information*. Tax practitioners commonly face a number of technical issues and procedural issues in preparing partnership tax returns.

## ¶ 804 FORMS AND SCHEDULES

Form 1065 contains "simple" questions about the partnership and its partners, as well as questions designed to highlight possible areas of controversy. Preparers need technical knowledge to complete return. For 2016, the due date for a partnership return is the 15th day of the third month following the close of the partnership's year

The extension period remains at six months. For example, the return would be filed on March 15, 2017, with a September 15, 2017 extension.

Page 1 of Form 1065 asks for basic information, such as the partnership's name, employer identification number, and address. It also asks whether the partnership terminated, and if so, whether the return is the final return of the "old" partnership or the initial return of the "new" partnership. Schedule M-3, *Net Income (Loss) Reconciliation for Certain Partnerships*, is used by large partnerships, and Schedule C is for supplemental information for M-3 filers.

Ordinary business income or loss is computed on Page 1 of Form 1065. Anything that would not have a separate impact on any of the partners' tax liability does not have to be separately stated. Partners need separate reporting for anything that might impact their tax reporting. Page 1 of Form 1065 reports those items that are treated the same for all partners.

### Entity Type

Page 2 of Form 1065 asks what type of entity the partnership is. Generally, this is based on the classification ("check-the-box") regulations. Hence it includes general partnerships (GPs), limited partnerships (LPs), limited liability partnerships (LLPs), and limited liability companies (LLCs). A partnership need not be an entity; for example, the "Other" classification can be used if it is a joint venture.

## Schedule K-1

Various separately stated items are reported on Schedule K-1, such as the allocable share of profit and loss, reconciliation of capital account, and share of liabilities (recourse, nonrecourse, and qualified nonrecourse).

Generally, allocations of profit and loss may be made by agreement. However, allocations by agreement must have "substantial economic effect" (SEE); these allocations are governed by Code Sec. 704(b). Allocations that lack SEE, or allocations made in the absence of any specific agreement, must follow the partners' interests in the partnership.

## Schedule K

Form 1054, Schedule K, *Partner's Share of Income, Deductions, Credits, etc.*, summarizes ordinary-separately stated items shown on individual partner Schedule K-1s. Decisions must also be made, such as:

- Code Sec. 179 expense elections
- Grouping of activities for purposes of passive activities. This may also affect the Medicare surtax.

# ¶ 805 TECHNICAL TERMINATION

In a technical termination, the "old" partnership is terminated and a "new" partnership has been formed. The old partnership will file a final tax return with the final return due date measured by reference to the termination. The preparer would check the boxes for both technical termination and final return on Form 1065. Although the new partnership is, in the eyes an outside party, a continuation of the old partnership, the preparer should check both the technical termination and initial return boxes. The new partnership uses same employer identification number (EIN) as the old one.

In a technical termination, the partnership's owners change. If the owners have changed substantially, it is a new partnership. "Substantially" means there was a sale or exchange of 50 percent or more of the capital and profits within a 12-month period. When measuring an ownership change, the following should be ignored:

- Transfers by gift
- Transfers by inheritance
- Redemptions of interests, whether partial or complete
- Contributions to the partnership in exchange for an interest
- Sales of the same interest within a single 12-month period

> **EXAMPLE:** In the ABC partnership, A owns a 60 percent interest, B owns 20 percent, and C owns 20 percent. A wants out of the partnership, and and B and C are going to continue. B and C could purchase A's partnership interest. That transaction that would take place outside of the partnership. If that happens, that is a sale of a 60 percent interest in the capital and profits, and the partnership is terminated.

The old partnership's final return due date is measured by reference to the termination date. The new partnership restarts depreciation using same the basis as the old partnership. However, there is no such restart for amortization. The old partnership gets no bonus or regular depreciation for property placed in service in the termination year, and it accelerates any Code Sec. 481 adjustments.

**OBSERVATION:** Assume a partnership termination occurs on January 15, 2017. The old partnership return due date is April 15, 2017. This is often overlooked; the due date is assumed to be March 15, 2018. The penalty is $195 per partner per month for late filing. Tax elections die, so the Code Sec. 754 election of the old partnership is dead. Keep in mind that although basis of assets and the interests carries over, the holding period of the interests may change. It stays the same for transfers of capital and Code Sec. 1231 assets only. No new Code Sec. 704(c) gains or losses are created.

# ¶ 806 GUARANTEED PAYMENTS

Guaranteed payments are payments made by a partnership to a partner that are determined without regard to the partnership's income. They are deductible by the partnership and are separately reported as ordinary income by the partner. Guaranteed payments can be made for both capital and services. They create their own income and deduction. The recipient of a guarantee has separately stated income, and a partnership has a deduction for guaranteed payments.

It is not always clear how to classify guaranteed payments; they may be for capital or services, which can affect self-employment treatment. The key is that they are not determined by reference to income. A preference return is different; it is a priority that is intended to be matched with an allocation of income. However, some use these terms interchangeably because preferences may mimic guaranteed payments. The intent may not be realized and the preference could carry over. "Target" allocations, discussed later, make it easy to see the link between the preference (distribution) and the allocation of income.

## STUDY QUESTIONS

1. A partner's share of liabilities is reported on the Schedule K-1 to include:

   a. Recourse, nonrecourse, and qualified nonrecourse debt

   b. Recourse and nonrecourse debt.

   c. Only debt that is directly made by a partner to the partnership

   d. All debt other than debt guaranteed by the partner

2. When evaluating the existence of guaranteed payments in a partnership:

   a. It is easy to distinguish distributions from guaranteed payments.

   b. Such payments can be for either capital or services.

   c. There is no distinction between preference returns and guaranteed payments.

   d. Guaranteed payments are reported in the reconciliation of partner capital.

# ¶ 807 FLEXIBILITY IN REPORTING

Rev. Proc. 2002-69 states that if a business is in a community property jurisdiction, the spouses are the only owners, and they own their interest as community property, then they can choose to treat the business as a partnership or as a disregarded entity. However, once they make that choice, they must be consistent.

The same flexibility is afforded to businesses in non–community property states. Code Sec. 761(f) states that if two spouses are running a trade or business together and they both materially participate, they can elect to treat that business as a disregarded entity or as a partnership.

# ¶ 808  CODE SEC. 754 ELECTIONS

Code Sec. 754 is an entity-level election. It affects two transactions:

1. **Sale or exchange of an interest (Code Sec. 743).** This affects the basis of the purchasing partner only, but the partnership must track the adjustment (if notified).

2. **Distributions of money or property from the partnership (Code Sec. 734).** An adjustment may be made to the basis of partnership properties.

Code Sec. 743 adjustments are designed to equate the "inside" and "outside" basis. The outside basis is cost (purchased); it may also be fair market value for inherited interest. Inside basis is a percent share of the partnership's basis. It is allocated among assets using a hypothetical sale of assets. This allocation may need to follow Code Sec. 1060 principles where the partnership is operating a trade or business or where goodwill could reasonably attach to assets. Form 8594, *Asset Acquisition Statement*, is required if Code Sec. 1060 applies.

Code Sec. 734 adjustments are triggered by a distribution to a partner. There are four scenarios when an adjustment occurs:

- A partner usually takes a carryover basis in distributed property.
  - It may be less if the basis of the interest is insufficient to allocate full carryover.
  - It may be more if distribution liquidates the partner's interest.
- Positive adjustments
  - Gain is recognized by the distributee.
  - The distributee's basis in property is less than the carryover.
- Negative adjustments
  - Loss is recognized by the distributee.
  - The distributee's basis in the property is more than the carryover.
- Mandatory adjustments. Generally, Code Sec. 734 and 743 adjustments are not made unless a Code Sec. 754 election is in effect. If not made already, it would not be made for a negative adjustment. But a mandatory adjustment occurs if the adjustment:
  - Is negative, and
  - Exceeds $250,000

# ¶ 809  CODE SEC. 179 REPORTING

The Code Sec. 179 limitations apply to both the partnership and the partner. There is a dollar limit ($500,000, inflation indexed, reduced if acquisitions exceed $2 million, inflation indexed) and a taxable income limit. Thus, partners must be careful of electing where the partner has otherwise reached the limit. This may be less of an issue now that the $500,000/$2 million limits are permanent.

The partnership tax basis is reduced by the claimed expense election. If the expense was limited at the partnership level (e.g., taxable income limitation), the basis reduction is restored immediately before a taxable disposition.

# ¶ 810 REPORTING PASSIVE ACTIVITY LOSS (PAL) ACTIVITIES

A partnership is not subject to the PAL rules. However, a partnership must determine its "activities"—what the partnership aggregates cannot be disaggregated by the partner. The partnership must attach a statement showing the income/loss for each PAL activity or classification. The partnership grouping may affect the partners in two ways:

- Passive loss application
- Code Sec. 1411 Medicare surtax application

It is generally best to disaggregate to allow the partners the greatest flexibility in grouping at their level. However, partnership groupings must satisfy the appropriate economic unit standard.

# ¶ 811 CANCELLATION OF DEBT REPORTING

Cancellation of debt (COD) was a significant issue during the economic recovery. Due to the economic downturn and the frequency of COD reporting events, Code Sec. 108(e) allowed a deferral of COD reporting for 2009–2010 to make it easier for businesses to stay afloat. That election was made by a partnership, if the activity in question was at the partnership level. This deferred income may be accelerated for events occurring at the partnership level, which must be reported. Such events include the disposition of substantially all assets and the cessation of business.

# ¶ 812 CODE SEC. 704(B) SUBSTANTIAL ECONOMIC EFFECT

Under the Code Sec. 704(b) substantial economic effect safe harbor, capital accounts are maintained per the regulations. Liquidating distributions follow the capital accounts with either (1) a deficit restoration obligation or (2) a qualified income offset. To measure substantiality, there is both an overall-effect test and three "insubstantiality" tests.

# ¶ 813 ALLOCATIONS

## Special Allocations of Nonrecourse Deductions

Allocations of nonrecourse deductions are those financed by nonrecourse borrowing. No partner bears a risk for such loans. Allocations of nonrecourse deductions cannot have "economic effect"; they may be allocated by agreement if the agreement satisfies the "deemed in accordance with the partners' interests test," which requires certain language in the agreement.

## Nonrecourse Allocations

Instead of a qualified income offset (QIO) or a deficit restoration obligation (DRO), the partnership agreement must have a "minimum gain chargeback." Partners can be allocated losses in excess of their Code Sec. 704(b) capital if those allocations are nonrecourse allocations. The chargeback ensures they will not exit the partnership with a negative capital account.

A Code Sec. 704(b) safe harbor compliant agreement contains:

- Capital accounts per Reg. § 1.704-1(b)(2)(iv)
- Liquidating distributions that follow ending capital

- One of the following:
  - Deficit restoration obligation, or
  - Qualified income offset
- Minimum gain chargeback

## Target Allocations

Target allocation agreements do not follow the safe harbor language and can be written in different ways. They present more burden on the preparer as no safe harbor is satisfied. However, while a target allocation agreement does not meet the safe harbor (liquidating distributions not based on capital), it generally targets Code Sec. 704(b) capital. It is often characterized by a reference to target capital based on a hypothetical liquidation at book value. The preparer has to decide the target allocation.

To identify a target allocation, the preparer should look to the agreement, which refers to "hypothetical" items such as hypothetical distributions arising from a hypothetical sale of assets (at book value) followed by a hypothetical liquidation of the partnership. Allocations are those that allow one to reach a hypothetical "target" capital equal to the hypothetical distributions.

> **EXAMPLE: Simple target allocation.** Partner A contributes $100,000 and Partner B contributes $50,000 to the AB Partnership. There is a distribution waterfall: A gets 6 percent preference on his capital first, A gets his $100,000 contribution next, B gets his $50,000 capital next, and then A gets 50 percent and B 50 percent of any upside. Year 1 income equals $30,000, and assets after Year 1 equal $180,000 (capital plus income).
>
> **Target allocation.** Find the "target" capital balances. With $180,000 to distribute, A gets $6,000, A gets $100,000, B gets $50,000, A gets $12,000; and B gets $12,000. So target A equals $118,000, and B equals $62,000. The $30,000 profit is allocated so that the capital, based on a hypothetical liquidation, matches the target.
>
> - $100,000 plus $18,000 income = $118,000 target
> - $50,000 plus $12,000 income = $62,000 target

## Other Provisions Governing Allocations

Allocations that relate to pre-contribution gain or loss must be made to take into account the built-in gain or loss at contribution. These allocations are governed by Code Sec. 704(c). If partners' interests change during the year, the "varying interest rule" of Code Sec. 706(d) applies.

## STUDY QUESTIONS

3. Which of the following triggers positive adjustments under Code Sec. 734?
    a. Loss is recognized by the distributee partner.
    b. The distributee's basis in property is more than the carryover from the partnership.
    c. The distributee's basis in property is equal to the partnership's basis.
    d. Gain is recognized by the distributee partner.

¶813

**4.** Allocations of nonrecourse deduction:

    **a.** Refer to deductions financed by nonrecourse borrowing

    **b.** May have "economic effect"

    **c.** May not have economic effect and cannot be allocated by partner agreement

    **d.** Are allocated to match allocations of recourse deductions.

**5.** To properly determine a target allocation, "hypothetical" items or events may include a(n):

    **a.** Sale of assets at tax basis

    **b.** Sale of assets at book value

    **c.** Assumption that value equals tax basis

    **d.** Assumption that all assets are worthless and all debts are due and payable

---

# ¶ 814 VARYING INTERESTS

According to Code Sec. 706(d), if partners' interests change, distributive shares are to be determined using any method prescribed by the Secretary that takes into account the varying interests. The IRS has offered two methods. The interim closing method is the preferred method because it is more accurate, and it is the default rule. The proration method is less accurate but administratively simpler; it must be elected by agreement among the partners.

Partners may agree that interim method is the most accurate but that a particular transaction would, because of its magnitude, be too costly to comply with that method. However, the same partners may decide that another transaction within the same year is not too administratively difficult to use the interim method. In this case, both methods may be used within the same year for different variations.

# ¶ 815 CODE SEC. 704(C) PRE-CONTRIBUTION GAINS OR LOSSES

Partnership allocations relate to items of gain and loss that arise while the owners are in a partnership form. Thus, gains and losses that arose before the owners became partners should not be shared by all owners. Instead, the partner who contributed the property should be allocated the gain or loss that arose outside of the partnership. Code Sec. 704(c) also requires that depreciation or amortization with respect to contributed property consider the difference between FMV and tax basis. Code Sec. 704(c) also applies to unrealized gains and losses of the partnership before a new partner is admitted by contribution.

# ¶ 816 CAPITAL ACCOUNTS

## Capital Account Maintenance

An essential element of SEE is the proper maintenance of capital accounts. The Code Sec. 704(b) regulations have specific rules that are neither traditional "book" or "tax." Schedule K-1 calls it Code Sec. 704(b) book. Special adjustments may be needed for admittance of new partners and distributions of property, including exercise of options and option equivalents.

## Capital Account Reporting

Schedule K-1 asks about the method by which capital accounts are reported—GAAP, Code Sec. 704(b) book, Tax, or Other. To meet the economic effect safe harbor, Code Sec. 704(b) book capital must be maintained, but need not be shown on the Schedule K-1.

# ¶ 817 DISTRIBUTIONS

The partnership recognizes no gain or loss as a result of a distribution. However, a partner may recognize gain or loss, and requires information reporting to assist in determining the tax effect. A partnership Code Sec. 754 election may also lead to a partnership (Code Sec. 734) basis adjustment.

A Code Sec. 743 adjustment happens when somebody buys an interest in the partnership and the adjustment belongs to that person alone. A Code Sec. 734 adjustment is triggered by a distribution, and it belongs to the partnership. It affects the common basis of the assets of the partnership, and it can be a positive or a negative adjustment. Positive adjustments can be triggered when a partner recognize gains. The partner's taxable income goes up, the partner pays more tax, and the partnership gets to increase its basis by the amount of the gain.

The Schedule K-1 capital account reconciliation reports (actual) distributions. Changes in debt shares also create deemed distributions, per Code Sec. 752(b). The Schedule K-1 reporting may or may not permit a user to determine the tax effect of the distribution, depending on the use of tax basis capital or the ability to reconcile to tax basis.

## STUDY QUESTION

6. Distributions from a partnership may lead to which of the following results?

   a. The partnership may recognize gain or loss.

   b. Code Sec. 734 may lead to a partnership basis adjustment.

   c. Partners may not recognize gain or loss.

   d. Basis of distributed property to the partner will always equal the basis to the partnership.

# ¶ 818 LIABILITY SHARES

Increases and decreases in partners' "shares" of entity liabilities affect the basis of the partners' interests. A share of a liability is determined using Reg. §1.752. Recourse liabilities are shared using economic-risk-of-loss principles, and nonrecourse liabilities are shared in a three-step approach, which is somewhat arbitrary. Schedule K-1 requires the reporting of shares of recourse debt, shares of nonrecourse debt, and shares of qualified nonrecourse debt. Qualified nonrecourse debt allows at-risk basis; it applies only to real property activities where the lender is in the business of lending.

# ¶ 819 PARTNER SELF-EMPLOYMENT TAX

The general rule is clear: a partner is subject to self-employment tax on his share of partnership income attributable to the operation of a trade or business (Code Sec. 1402(a)). Income from rents, dividends, interest, capital gains, and so on are not subject to self-employment. The "exception" is less clear. A "limited partner" is subject to self-employment tax only for guaranteed payments for services rendered (Code Sec. 1402(a)(13)). The application of the exception to a LLC member is an issue of great debate.

The limited partner exception was enacted in 1977 to prevent abuses where partners wanted self-employment income. Because LLCs did not exist at that time, Congress did not consider the application of Code Sec. 1402(a)(13) to LLC members.

---

**CPE NOTE:** When you have completed your study and review of chapters 6-8, which comprise Module 2, you may wish to take the Final Exam for this Module. Go to **cchcpelink.com/printcpe** to take this Final Exam online.

---

# MODULE 3: INTERNATIONAL TAXATION— Chapter 9: The Sourcing Rules: The Building Blocks of International Taxation

## ¶ 901 WELCOME

This chapter discusses the sourcing of gross income. Many of the rules governing sourcing are very mechanical, but they are very important to U.S. taxpayers as well as foreign persons regardless of whether a foreign country taxes the income. The chapter explains the foreign tax credit limitation and how the foreign tax credit is claimed, how various types of income are reported, and the allocation and apportionment of deductions.

## ¶ 902 LEARNING OBJECTIVES

Upon completion of this chapter, you will be able to:

- Recognize the importance of the sourcing rules to U.S. and foreign persons;
- Identify how the various types of income are sourced; and
- Recognize how expenses are allocated and apportioned for U.S.- and foreign-source income.

## ¶ 903 INTRODUCTION

The United States taxes the worldwide income of U.S. persons, but alleviates double taxation of foreign-source income with a foreign tax credit. Just because an income is taxed by a foreign country doesn't mean it's foreign-source income under the U.S. sourcing rules. The challenge is to apportion expenses of a taxpayer's U.S.-source income and foreign-source income.

The foreign tax credit is limited by precredit U.S. tax on foreign-source income using this equation:

$$\text{Foreign tax credit limitation} \quad = \quad \text{Precredit U.S. tax} \quad \times \quad \frac{\text{Foreign-source taxable income}}{\text{Worldwide taxable income}}$$

## ¶ 904 TAXING JURISDICTION

An initial hypothetical scenario can set the stage for sourcing rules. Sissie Pluto is an internationally renowned U.S. citizen and tennis player, and a cola company makes a sports promotion contract with her to wear on the sleeve of her tennis dress a patch advertising a cola brand during the finals of the U.S. Open tennis championship. The final women's match of the U.S. Open is televised worldwide. Is this is foreign-source and U.S.-source income? It matters because the taxpayer or tax preparer doesn't know how to characterize it. Is she performing the service of wearing the patch for a cola company? Then it's a service that's sourced by where it's performed. Or is she associating her image, her phase, and her always-stylist tennis dress with the cola patch, in which case, isn't she receiving a royalty for associating her image, which is her intellectual property? These are the types of issues to consider in sourcing income.

First, Sissie's tax preparer or financial planner tries to source where the economic activity occurs. Where is the economic activity that produces the income?

However, the second point is that there seems to be a tension between location of that activity and the residence of the taxpayer, as Figure 9.1 shows.

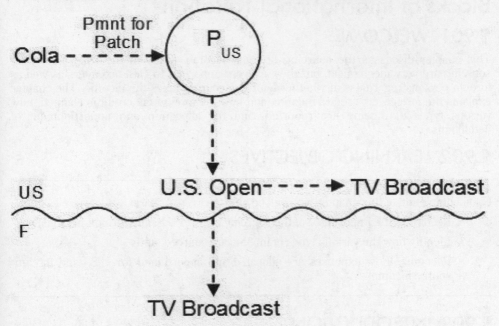

**Figure 9.1. Lines of U.S.- versus foreign-sourced income for market contract**

The U.S. sourcing rules are important to U.S. persons such as players on the world tennis circuit. Now, even though U.S. persons are taxed on their worldwide income wherever derived, the sourcing rules are important because her tax planner can eliminate double taxation in the United States. Presumably she is subject to tax in the United States because she's a U.S. person, but she might have to pay tax to a foreign locale. Under the tax code she can alleviate that double tax with a foreign tax credit. And that foreign tax credit is limited by the amount of precredit U.S. tax on that foreign-source income. So this is a ceiling on the amount of foreign taxes that offset U.S. taxes.

Congress has ceded primary taxing jurisdiction to the foreign country, but the IRS does not want to cede any more taxing jurisdiction to allow the foreign taxes to offset U.S. tax on U.S.-source income. Congress wanted to retain primary taxing jurisdiction. So Congress imposed the foreign tax credit limitation—a precredit U.S. tax on world-wide income times foreign sourcing. Thus, 35 percent of worldwide income is subject to taxation. However, the equation given above is the way the income is actually taxed on Form 1116 (Form 1118 for corporations), as Figure 9.2 shows.

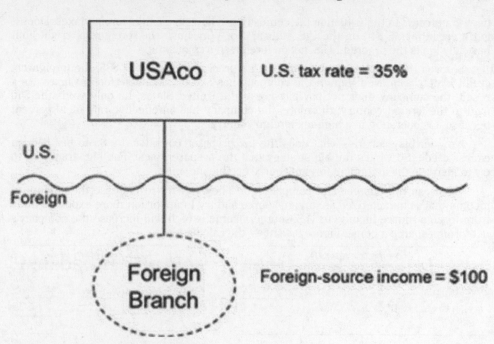

**Figure 9.2. Sourcing to help a company's credit**

With the U.S. tax rate being 35 percent, a lot depends on what the foreign rate is. So this scenario is going to look at two different foreign rates—a low foreign rate of 30 percent and a high foreign rate of 40 percent.

What happens if the foreign rate is 30 percent? Here the $100 of income subject on that foreign branch to a foreign country tax at 30 percent, or $30 of tax. How is that going to look on the U.S. return? The company reports the worldwide income of $100, even though it is foreign-source, on its U.S. return. At the 35 percent rate, the precredit U.S. tax is $35. How much of a credit does the company get? It gets a credit of $30. The company then actually pays a U.S. tax of $5. In effect, the company is paying $35 of tax—$30 to the foreign country and $5 to the United States. Figure 9.3 shows the calculation.

| Foreign tax return | | U.S. tax return | |
|---|---:|---|---:|
| Taxable income.................................. | $100 | Taxable income....................... | $100 |
| Tax rate............................................. | × .30 | Tax rate.................................... | × .35 |
| Foreign tax ........................................ | $ 30 | Pre-credit tax .......................... | $ 35 |
| | | | |
| | | Foreign tax credit .................... | − 30 |
| | | U.S. tax................................... | $ 5 |

**Figure 9.3 Company's taxes for operations in a low-tax country**

In this situation, the foreign taxes are not a tax cost. However, what happens if the company operates in a high-tax foreign country? What happens if the foreign tax rate is now 40 percent? In that situation the company has now paid $40 of foreign taxes. Does it get a credit for all $40 on the U.S. return? No. Why not? The foreign tax credit limit basically limits the precredit U.S. tax on foreign-source income.

So even though the company has paid a precredit U.S. tax of $35, the foreign tax credit is only $35, even though the company has $40 of creditable foreign taxes. As a result, the company does not pay any tax to the United States. Its only tax is the $40 paid to the foreign country; therefore, the company has an effective rate of 40 percent because it is operating in a high-tax foreign country.

Now in this scenario, what does the tax preparer consider the $5 to be? It is an excess credit. So what's the big strategy that the preparer uses? The big strategy is to try to increase the amount of foreign-source taxable income.

What can the planner and company do? They can try to increase the amount of income that's characterized as foreign-source and try to apportion more expenses away from foreign-source income to U.S.-source income, which will increase the company's net foreign-source income. Figure 9.4 shows the calculations.

| Foreign tax return | | U.S. tax return | |
|---|---:|---|---:|
| Taxable income | $100 | Taxable income | $100 |
| Tax rate | × .40 | Tax rate | × .35 |
| Foreign tax | $ 40 | Pre-credit tax | $ 35 |
| | | | |
| | | Foreign tax credit | − 35 |
| | | U.S. tax | $ 0 |

**Figure 9.4. Tax returns for operations in a high-tax country**

Here the company might look at the rules for sale of inventory to adjust foreign- and U.S.-source income.

Now the preparer and client consider the appropriate IRS forms. On Form 1116, *Foreign Tax Credit,* Part I shows $150,000 of foreign-source income (Figure 9.5).

| Form **1116**<br>Department of the Treasury<br>Internal Revenue Service (99) | **Foreign Tax Credit**<br>(Individual, Estate, or Trust)<br>► Attach to Form 1040, 1040NR, 1041, or 990-T.<br>► Information about Form 1116 and its separate instructions is at *www.irs.gov/form1116*. | OMB No. 1545-0121<br>20**16**<br>Attachment<br>Sequence No. **19** |
|---|---|---|
| Name<br>Uncle Sam | | Identifying number as shown on page 1 of your tax return<br>123-45-6789 |

Use a separate Form 1116 for each category of income listed below. See *Categories of Income* in the instructions. Check only one box on each Form 1116. Report all amounts in U.S. dollars except where specified in Part II below.

a ☐ Passive category income     c ☐ Section 901(j) income     e ☐ Lump-sum distributions

b ☑ General category income     d ☐ Certain income re-sourced by treaty

**f** Resident of (name of country) ►

**Note:** If you paid taxes to only one foreign country or U.S. possession, use column A in Part I and line A in Part II. If you paid taxes to more than one foreign country or U.S. possession, use a separate column and line for each country or possession.

**Part I**   Taxable Income or Loss From Sources Outside the United States (for Category Checked Above)

| | | Foreign Country or U.S. Possession | | | Total |
|---|---|---|---|---|---|
| | | **A** | **B** | **C** | (Add cols. A, B, and C.) |
| **g** | Enter the name of the foreign country or U.S. possession . . . . . . . . . . . ► | | | | |
| **1a** | Gross income from sources within country shown above and of the type checked above (see instructions): | | | | |
| | | 150,000 | | | **1a**   150,000 |
| **b** | Check if line 1a is compensation for personal services as an employee, your total compensation from all sources is $250,000 or more, and you used an alternative basis to determine its source (see instructions) . . ► ☐ | | | | |

**Figure 9.5 Part I of Form 1116, Line 1a**

Next, the preparer lists itemized deductions (Figure 9.6) of $12,000 and other deductions of $88,000, for a total of $100,000. The gross income equals $150,000 from foreign sources and $300,000 from U.S. sources. So the preparer proportions income 5/50, and the net foreign-source income is $100,000.

| **Deductions and losses** (Caution: See instructions.): | | | | | |
|---|---|---|---|---|---|
| **2** | Expenses **definitely related** to the income on line 1a (attach statement) . . . . . . . . | | | | |
| **3** | Pro rata share of other deductions **not definitely related:** | | | | |
| **a** | Certain itemized deductions or standard deduction (see instructions) . . . . . . . . . | 12,000 | | | |
| **b** | Other deductions (attach statement) . . . . | 88,000 | | | |
| **c** | Add lines 3a and 3b . . . . . . . . . | 100,000 | | | |
| **d** | Gross foreign source income (see instructions) | 150,000 | | | |
| **e** | Gross income from all sources (see instructions) | 300,000 | | | |
| **f** | Divide line 3d by line 3e (see instructions) . . | .50 | | | |
| **g** | Multiply line 3c by line 3f . . . . . . | 50,000 | | | |
| **4** | Pro rata share of interest expense (see instructions): | | | | |
| **a** | Home mortgage interest (use the Worksheet for Home Mortgage Interest in the instructions) . . | | | | |
| **b** | Other interest expense . . . . . . . . | | | | |
| **5** | Losses from foreign sources . . . . . . | | | | |
| **6** | Add lines 2, 3g, 4a, 4b, and 5 . . . . . . | 50,000 | | **6** | 50,000 |
| **7** | Subtract line 6 from line 1a. Enter the result here and on line 15, page 2 . . . . . . . . . . . ► | | | **7** | 100,000 |

**Part II**   **Foreign Taxes Paid or Accrued** (see instructions)

| Country | Credit is claimed for taxes (you must check one) | | Foreign taxes paid or accrued | | | | | | | | |
|---|---|---|---|---|---|---|---|---|---|---|---|
| | (h) ☑ Paid<br>(i) ☐ Accrued | | In foreign currency | | | | In U.S. dollars | | | | |
| | | | Taxes withheld at source on: | | | (n) Other foreign taxes paid or accrued | Taxes withheld at source on: | | | (r) Other foreign taxes paid or accrued | (s) Total foreign taxes paid or accrued (add cols. (o) through (r)) |
| | (j) Date paid or accrued | | (k) Dividends | (l) Rents and royalties | (m) Interest | | (o) Dividends | (p) Rents and royalties | (q) Interest | | |
| **A** | 12/31/16 | | | | | | | | | 10,000 | 40,000 |
| **B** | | | | | | | | | | | |
| **C** | | | | | | | | | | | |
| **8** | Add lines A through C, column (s). Enter the total here and on line 9, page 2 . . . . . . . . ► | | | | | | | | | **8** | 40,000 |

For Paperwork Reduction Act Notice, see instructions.     Cat. No. 11440U     Form **1116** (2016)

**Figure 9.6. Listing deductions, losses, and source of income**

¶904

And in this case, the total foreign income taxes equal $40,000. The foreign taxes paid comes down to be listed in Part II of the form. There is $200,000 of net income; then the preparer determines that there is $100,000 of net foreign-source income. There is $80,000 of precredit U.S. tax. What is 50 percent of that? It is $40,000 (Figure 9.7), the precredit limit.

| Form 1116 (2016) | | | Page **2** |
|---|---|---|---|
| **Part III  Figuring the Credit** | | | |
| 9 | Enter the amount from line 8. These are your total foreign taxes paid or accrued for the category of income checked above Part I . . | **9**   40,000 | |
| 10 | Carryback or carryover (attach detailed computation) . . . . | **10** | |
| 11 | Add lines 9 and 10 . . . . . . . . . . . . . . | **11**   40,000 | |
| 12 | Reduction in foreign taxes (see instructions) . . . . . . | **12** ( ) | |
| 13 | Taxes reclassified under high tax kickout (see instructions) . . | **13** | |
| 14 | Combine lines 11, 12, and 13. This is the total amount of foreign taxes available for credit . . . | **14** | 40,000 |
| 15 | Enter the amount from line 7. This is your taxable income or (loss) from sources outside the United States (before adjustments) for the category of income checked above Part I (see instructions) . . . . . . | **15**   100,000 | |
| 16 | Adjustments to line 15 (see instructions) . . . . . . . . | **16** | |
| 17 | Combine the amounts on lines 15 and 16. This is your net foreign source taxable income. (If the result is zero or less, you have no foreign tax credit for the category of income you checked above Part I. Skip lines 18 through 22. However, if you are filing more than one Form 1116, you must complete line 20.) . . . . . . . | **17**   100,000 | |
| 18 | **Individuals:** Enter the amount from Form 1040, line 41; or Form 1040NR, line 39. **Estates and trusts:** Enter your taxable income without the deduction for your exemption . . . . . . . . | **18**   200,000 | |
| | **Caution:** If you figured your tax using the lower rates on qualified dividends or capital gains, see instructions. | | |
| 19 | Divide line 17 by line 18. If line 17 is more than line 18, enter "1" . . . . . . . . . . . . . | **19** | .50 |
| 20 | **Individuals:** Enter the amounts from Form 1040, lines 44 and 46. If you are a nonresident alien, enter the amounts from Form 1040NR, lines 42 and 44. **Estates and trusts:** Enter the amount from Form 1041, Schedule G, line 1a; or the total of Form 990-T, lines 36, 37, and 39 . . . . . . | **20** | 80,000 |
| | **Caution:** If you are completing line 20 for separate category e (lump-sum distributions), see instructions. | | |
| 21 | Multiply line 20 by line 19 (maximum amount of credit) . . . . . . . . . . . . . . | **21** | 40,000 |
| 22 | Enter the **smaller** of line 14 or line 21. If this is the only Form 1116 you are filing, skip lines 23 through 27 and enter this amount on line 28. Otherwise, complete the appropriate line in Part IV (see instructions) . . . . . . . . . . . . . . . . . . . . . ▶ | **22** | 40,000 |

**Figure 9.7. Entering the credit in Part III**

To summarize, there is $100,000 of foreign-source income, $200,000 of net income, and $100,000 of net foreign-source income. There is $80,000 of precredit U.S. tax, 50 percent of which is $40,000, the credit limit. It is carried down to Part IV of Form 1116 to the summary (Figure 9.8).

| **Part IV  Summary of Credits From Separate Parts III** (see instructions) | | | |
|---|---|---|---|
| 23 | Credit for taxes on passive category income . . . . . . . | **23** | |
| 24 | Credit for taxes on general category income . . . . . . . | **24**   40,000 | |
| 25 | Credit for taxes on certain income re-sourced by treaty . . . . | **25** | |
| 26 | Credit for taxes on lump-sum distributions . . . . . . . . | **26** | |
| 27 | Add lines 23 through 26 . . . . . . . . . . . . . . . . . . . . . . | **27** | 40,000 |
| 28 | Enter the **smaller** of line 20 or line 27 . . . . . . . . . . . . . . . . . . | **28** | 40,000 |
| 29 | Reduction of credit for international boycott operations. See instructions for line 12 . . . . . | **29** | |
| 30 | Subtract line 29 from line 28. This is your **foreign tax credit.** Enter here and on Form 1040, line 48; Form 1040NR, line 46; Form 1041, Schedule G, line 2a; or Form 990-T, line 41a . . . . . . ▶ | **30** | 40,000 |
| | | | Form **1116** (2016) |

**Figure 9.8. Showing the limit of $40,000 in Part IV**

What if the client and preparer erred in sourcing so that the company showed no foreign-source income but the expenses did not change? Figure 9.9 shows this scenario.

¶904

| Form **1116** | **Foreign Tax Credit** | OMB No. 1545-0121 |
|---|---|---|
| | (Individual, Estate, or Trust) | **2016** |
| Department of the Treasury Internal Revenue Service (99) | ► Attach to Form 1040, 1040NR, 1041, or 990-T. ► Information about Form 1116 and its separate instructions is at *www.irs.gov/form1116*. | Attachment Sequence No. **19** |

| Name | Identifying number as shown on page 1 of your tax return |
|---|---|
| Uncle Sam | 123-45-6789 |

Use a separate Form 1116 for each category of income listed below. See *Categories of Income* in the instructions. Check only one box on each Form 1116. Report all amounts in U.S. dollars except where specified in Part II below.

**a** ☐ Passive category income     **c** ☐ Section 901(j) income     **e** ☐ Lump-sum distributions
**b** ☑ General category income     **d** ☐ Certain income re-sourced by treaty

**f** Resident of (name of country) ►

**Note:** If you paid taxes to only one foreign country or U.S. possession, use column A in Part I and line A in Part II. If you paid taxes to **more than one** foreign country or U.S. possession, use a separate column and line for each country or possession.

**Part I**   Taxable Income or Loss From Sources Outside the United States (for Category Checked Above)

| | | Foreign Country or U.S. Possession A | B | C | Total (Add cols. A, B, and C.) |
|---|---|---|---|---|---|
| **g** | Enter the name of the foreign country or U.S. possession ► | | | | |
| **1a** | Gross income from sources within country shown above and of the type checked above (see instructions): _____ _____ _____ | 0 | | | **1a**   0 |
| **b** | Check if line 1a is compensation for personal services as an employee, your total compensation from all sources is $250,000 or more, and you used an alternative basis to determine its source (see instructions) . . ► ☐ | | | | |

**Figure 9.9. Part I of Form 1116 showing no foreign-source income.**

Figure 9.10 lists the deductions and losses, but with the gross income (Line 3e) coming from just U.S.-source income. Note in Part II that $40,000 was still paid in foreign tax

| Deductions and losses (Caution: See instructions.): | | | | |
|---|---|---|---|---|
| **2** | Expenses **definitely related** to the income on line 1a (attach statement) | | | |
| **3** | Pro rata share of other deductions **not definitely related:** | | | |
| **a** | Certain itemized deductions or standard deduction (see instructions) . . . . . . . . . . | 12,000 | | |
| **b** | Other deductions (attach statement) . . . . . | 88,000 | | |
| **c** | Add lines 3a and 3b . . . . . . . . . | 100,000 | | |
| **d** | Gross foreign source income (see instructions) . | 0 | | |
| **e** | Gross income from all sources (see instructions) . | 300,000 | | |
| **f** | Divide line 3d by line 3e (see instructions) . . . | 0 | | |
| **g** | Multiply line 3c by line 3f . . . . . . . . | 0 | | |
| **4** | Pro rata share of interest expense (see instructions): | | | |
| **a** | Home mortgage interest (use the Worksheet for Home Mortgage Interest in the instructions) . . | | | |
| **b** | Other interest expense . . . . . . . . | | | |
| **5** | Losses from foreign sources . . . . . . . | | | |
| **6** | Add lines 2, 3g, 4a, 4b, and 5 . . . . . . . | 0 | | **6**   0 |
| **7** | Subtract line 6 from line 1a. Enter the result here and on line 15, page 2 . . . . . . . . . ► | | | **7**   0 |

**Part II**   **Foreign Taxes Paid or Accrued**   (see instructions)

| Country | Credit is claimed for taxes (you must check one) **(h)** ☑ Paid **(i)** ☐ Accrued | Foreign taxes paid or accrued | | | | | | | | | |
|---|---|---|---|---|---|---|---|---|---|---|---|
| | | In foreign currency | | | | In U.S. dollars | | | | | |
| | **(j)** Date paid or accrued | Taxes withheld at source on: | | | **(n)** Other foreign taxes paid or accrued | Taxes withheld at source on: | | | **(r)** Other foreign taxes paid or accrued | **(s)** Total foreign taxes paid or accrued (add cols. (o) through (r)) |
| | | **(k)** Dividends | **(l)** Rents and royalties | **(m)** Interest | | **(o)** Dividends | **(p)** Rents and royalties | **(q)** Interest | | |
| **A** | 12/31/16 | | | | | | | | 40,000 | 40,000 |
| **B** | | | | | | | | | | |
| **C** | | | | | | | | | | |
| **8** | Add lines A through C, column (s). Enter the total here and on line 9, page 2 . . . . . . . . . ► | | | | | | | **8** | | 40,000 |

For Paperwork Reduction Act Notice, see instructions.     Cat. No. 11440U     Form **1116** (2016)

**Figure 9.10. Source of income changes but taxes do not**

In this case, the limit is going to be zero; that's the maximum amount of the credit.

## STUDY QUESTIONS

**1.** Even though U.S. persons are taxed on worldwide income, the sourcing rules are still important because:

    **a.** Income sourced in a foreign country is included in the foreign tax credit limitation.

    **b.** The foreign country may have higher tax rates than the United States.

    **c.** Foreign countries do not tax U.S.-source income.

    **d.** The amount of foreign tax paid can be used to offset U.S.-source income.

**2.** The purpose of the foreign tax credit is to alleviate double taxation, but not prevent it. In which of the following situations would double taxation still occur?

    **a.** The taxpayer pays foreign income tax and allocates expenses to where net foreign-source income is zero.

    **b.** The taxpayer pays foreign income tax and is not able to offset foreign-source income with expenses.

    **c.** The taxpayer pays foreign income tax at a rate that exceeds the U.S. tax rate.

    **d.** The taxpayer pays no income tax to the foreign country for foreign-source income.

# ¶ 905 U.S. TAXATION OF FOREIGN PERSONS

The situation is similar for completing Form 1118 for foreign corporations. That may be one of the most wicked of all IRS forms!

Why is this calculation important to foreign persons? It's important to foreign persons because they only pay tax on certain types of U.S.-source income. There are two prongs for taxing the U.S.-source income of foreign persons. One is withholding on fixed, determinable annual or periodic income at a 30 percent flat rate. This is often known as FDAP withholding. And FDAP withholding involves dividends, interest, rents and royalties, and believe it or not, compensation.

The second way by which the IRS taxes the U.S.-source income is the effectively connected income of a foreign person to a U.S. trade or business. So that's why foreign persons are concerned about U.S.-source income.

## Withholding

Also in this fixed determinable annual or periodic income prong when it's withholding at a 30 percent rate, the U.S. payers of the items of income want to know what it is because they need to know whether they have to withhold or not.

In the situation for Figure 9.11, 3W, a U.S. corporation, pays a $100 dividend to Norman Ray Allen (NRA), a nonresident alien, a $100 dividend and in this situation 3W is going to have to withhold $30, a 30 percent rate on the FDAP, dividend paid by a U.S. company. It's all U.S.-source income.

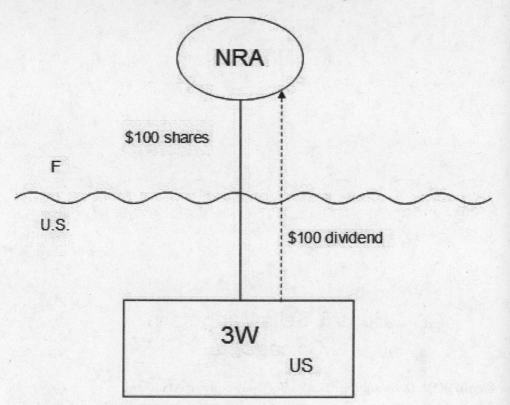

**Figure 9.11. Sourcing of income for withholding**

This time NRA buys and sells widgets in Chicago, Illinois for three months from a hotel room. Those activities would constitute a trade or business in the United States. The net income effectively connected with that U.S. trade or business (Figure 9.12) is going to have to pay U.S. tax at graduated rates. So the tax preparer needs to know what is the source of that income. The preparer needs to look at the sourcing rules to determine the source of the income.

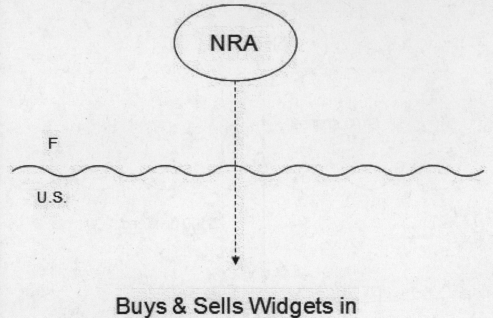

**Figure 9.12. Determining Allen's effectively connected income**

By checking part of the Form 1120-F, the preparer can see that looking at the U.S.-source gross profits and U.S.-source cost of goods sold to get total income, so Allen has compensation and other expenses shown in Figure 9.13, against that amount of U.S.-source income.

Form 1120-F (2016)                                                                                           Page **4**

**SECTION II—Income Effectively Connected With the Conduct of a Trade or Business in the United States** (see instructions)

*Important:* *Fill in all applicable lines and schedules. If you need more space, see **Assembling the Return** in the instructions.*

| | | | | | |
|---|---|---|---|---|---|
| **Income** | 1a | Gross receipts or sales [____]  b Less returns and allowances [____]  c Bal ▶ | 1c | 20,000,000 |
| | 2 | Cost of goods sold (attach Form 1125-A) | 2 | 16,000,000 |
| | 3 | Gross profit (subtract line 2 from line 1c) | 3 | |
| | 4 | Dividends (Schedule C, line 14) | 4 | |
| | 5 | Interest | 5 | |
| | 6 | Gross rents | 6 | |
| | 7 | Gross royalties | 7 | |
| | 8 | Capital gain net income (attach Schedule D (Form 1120)) | 8 | |
| | 9 | Net gain or (loss) from Form 4797, Part II, line 17 (attach Form 4797) | 9 | |
| | 10 | Other income (see instructions—attach statement) | 10 | |
| | 11 | **Total income.** Add lines 3 through 10 ▶ | 11 | 4,000,000 |
| **Deductions (See instructions for limitations on deductions.)** | 12 | Compensation of officers (see instructions—attach Form 1125-E) | 12 | 500,000 |
| | 13 | Salaries and wages (less employment credits) | 13 | 500,000 |
| | 14 | Repairs and maintenance | 14 | |
| | 15 | Bad debts (for bad debts over $500,000, attach a list of debtors and amounts) | 15 | |
| | 16 | Rents | 16 | |
| | 17 | Taxes and licenses | 17 | |
| | 18 | Interest expense from Schedule I, line 25 (see instructions) | 18 | 125,000 |
| | 19 | Charitable contributions | 19 | |
| | 20 | Depreciation from Form 4562 not claimed on Form 1125-A or elsewhere on return (attach Form 4562) | 20 | |
| | 21 | Depletion | 21 | |
| | 22 | Advertising | 22 | 1,000,000 |
| | 23 | Pension, profit-sharing, etc., plans | 23 | |
| | 24 | Employee benefit programs | 24 | |
| | 25 | Domestic production activities deduction (attach Form 8903) | 25 | |
| | 26 | Deductions allocated and apportioned to ECI from Schedule H, line 20 (see instructions) | 26 | |
| | 27 | Other deductions (attach statement) | 27 | |
| | 28 | **Total deductions.** Add lines 12 through 27 ▶ | 28 | 2,125,000 |
| | 29 | Taxable income before NOL deduction and special deductions (subtract line 28 from line 11) ▶ | 29 | 1,875,000 |
| | 30 | **Less:** a Net operating loss deduction (see instructions) .... 30a [____] | | |
| | | b Special deductions (Schedule C, line 15) . . . . . . 30b [____] | | |
| | | c Add lines 30a and 30b | 30c | |
| | 31 | Taxable income or (loss). Subtract line 30c from line 29 | 31 | 1,875,000 |

Form **1120-F** (2016)

**Figure 9.13 Deductions against effectively connected income**

Note that a consideration under the Trump administration is changing how the sourcing rules are applied, so that people will have income taxed within the territory, much like the rest of the world handles sourcing. Paul Ryan (R-WI) has a different blueprint for taxation: the border adjustment tax that affects the cost of goods sold for foreign sales into the United States. Perhaps whichever plan is adopted will use the sourcing rules as a guide to determine which income is on each side of the border.

## Other Income

Interest is sourced by the residence of the debtor. Dividends are sourced by the residence of the paying corporation. Services are sourced by where the services are performed. Rents are the payments for the use of tangible property sourced by where the underlying tangible property is used. Royalties are payments for the use of intangible property and are sourced by where the underlying intangible property is used. Real estate is sourced by where the real estate is located. Sales of personal property are sourced by the residence of the seller. All of these income types are discussed later.

And inventory rules kind of eat up the personal property rules. The inventory rules apply a different standard for purchased inventory than manufactured inventory. Purchased inventory is sourced by where title passes. Manufactured inventory is sourced half by where the manufacturing assets are located and half where the title passes. These types of income are discussed with examples later.

¶905

Sometimes it's hard to try to fit income within a category. For example, if a client has an installment sale, it may involve part gain on sale, part interest income. What about a lease? A lease is going to probably generate rental income. What if it's a lease with the purchase of a property, a lease to own? It's often hard to characterize the income. Figure 9.14 illustrates the characterization of income using the sale of compact discs in the United States and abroad.

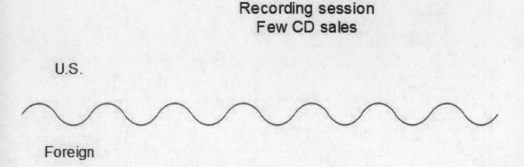

**Figure 9.14. Characterizing income from CD sales**

One big issue is the distinction between personal services and royalty income. For characterizing income from the CD sales, the example features a foreign orchestra conductor and a U.S. recording company for which the conductor records the music tracks in the United States. The conductor's income is based on the percentage of the recording sales, and the recording is owned by the record company.

Now most of the sales occur outside of the United States, so personal services are sourced by where the services are performed. Royalty income is sourced on the basis where the intangible is used. What is it? Is it personal services income, or is it foreign-source income?

The weight of authority is that it's more royalty income, but there isn't any really great guidance on the issue. So once the tax preparer determines the category of income the item is in, the source rule applies. Again, the source is where the underlying economic activity occurs.

## Interest

Interest is sourced by the residence of the debtor, regardless of where the debt was incurred or paid, regardless of the currency in which the payment is denominated.

> **EXAMPLE:** Mary Walden's brother, Rupert, who is German, borrows $100 from Mary's husband Bob during Rupert's visit to Dayton. He gambles and loses the money. Bob insists that Rupert will pay him back with 10 percent interest. Rupert repays Bob $110 in $10 bills the next week. What is the source? It's foreign-source income to Bob because of the rule that income is sourced by the residence of the debtor—in this case, Rupert from Germany. It doesn't matter that Rupert got the money in Dayton from a U.S. branch of the Deutsche Bank.

In addition, interest from a foreign branch of a U.S. bank is foreign-source income. So if Bob had visited Rupert in Germany and got money to lose to Rupert that was repaid with 10 percent interest from a Munich branch of Bob's Bank of America account, it would be foreign-source income. However, U.S. branch interest is U.S.-

source income. A final rule is that interest paid to a U.S. shareholder of a controlled foreign corporation is foreign-source income.

**Loans.** Figure 9.15 shows the sourcing of interest and principal payments by a U.S. company with a foreign branch that receives a loan from a bank in the United Kingdom.

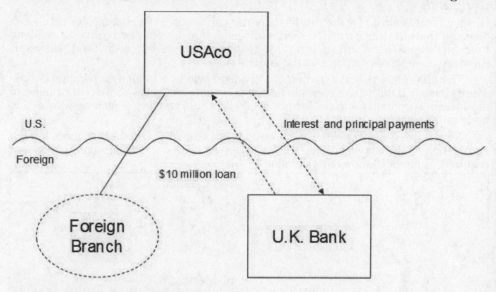

**Figure 9.15 Sourcing interest payments**

In this case, a U.S. company sells women apparel. Five years ago, the company opened a retail outlet in London structured as an unincorporated branch and financed that U.K. store with a $10 million loan from a U.S. bank. The loan paid out of the profits of the U.K. branch, and so the acquisition, the use, and the repayment all occurred abroad. But who is the debtor? The debtor is the U.S. company. What's the residence— the residence of the U.S. company? It is U.S.-source income.

Now there are a couple of exceptions. First, interest earned on deposits made with a foreign branch of a U.S. bank is treated as foreign-source income. The policy here is that Congress would rather have companies put their money abroad with a foreign branch of a U.S. bank than with a foreign bank. And if that's treated as U.S.-source income because it's a U.S. bank, people won't want to put their money there because they can get foreign-source income by depositing with a foreign bank.

Another exception applies if a foreign corporation pays interest to a 10 percent-or-more U.S. shareholder, and the corporation is at least 50 percent owned by U.S. persons. Basically, the rule is that paying interest to a 10 percent shareholder of a CFC, that interest is U.S.-source to the extent it's derived from U.S. sources. This only applies for purpose of the foreign tax credit limitation.

The government doesn't want U.S. people forming foreign corporations to monkey around with the foreign tax credit limitation.

The final exception is that U.S. branch interest is U.S.-source income. This is part of the branch tax regime that's designed to equate the tax treatment of a U.S. branch and U.S. subsidiary of foreign corporations. Essentially, if a U.S. branch pays the interest, it's treated as if it's a U.S. subsidiary so that the debtor is the U.S. subsidiary, not the foreign corporation that operates the branch.

**Bank Deposit Interest.** U.S. bank deposit interest is exempt from withholding when the interest is paid to foreign persons. So if a U.S. bank pays a non-U.S. person interest on savings, the bank won't withhold. The interest is still U.S.-source income, but the bank won't withhold.

## Dividends

Dividends are sourced by the residence of the corporation. If a shareholder receives a dividend from IBM, that's a U.S.-source dividend. If a shareholder receives a dividend from Siemens AG, a German company, that is a foreign-source dividend. However, there are a couple of exceptions to the general rules.

The first rule says that a portion of a dividend paid by a foreign corporation is U.S.-source income if during the current and the preceding two years 25 percent or more of the foreign corporation's gross income was effectively connected income with a U.S. trade or business.

Now that is a slippery cliff. If a company is considered a 25 percent or more foreign corporation, it has to apportion. Under a 25 percent ownership, apportion is not required. Figure 9.16 shows this situation.

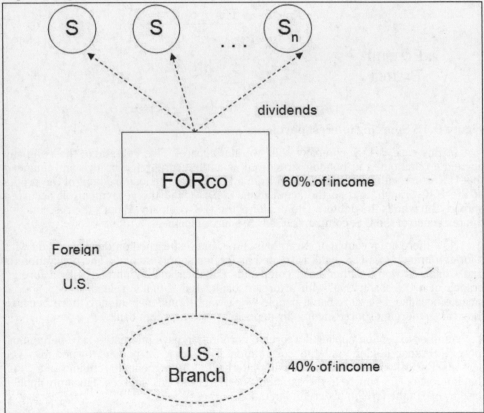

**Figure 9.16. Dividend income of a U.S. branch**

It's a foreign corporation. It earns 60 percent of its income in country F, and it earns 40 percent of its income in the United States, the U.S. branch. When FORco pays a dividend to the shareholders, 40 percent of every dividend is U.S.-source income. And actually, if any of these shareholders is a foreign person, he or she should be withholding. It's actually a big compliance problem because the foreign persons typically don't withhold.

This is where 40 percent of the income is U.S.-source. What happens if 25 percent of the income is foreign-source? FORco is still going to have to apportion between foreign and U.S. sources. Now what happens if only 24 percent of the income earned by FORco is U.S.-sourced, and 76 percent is foreign-source? The entire dividend is foreign-source. The U.S. source has to reach the 25 percent.

Similarly to the rule on interest, dividends paid by a foreign corporation, by a controlled foreign corporation to U.S. owners are considered U.S.-source income to the extent that foreign corporation earned U.S.-source income. But that only applies to a controlled foreign corporation owned by a 10 percent U.S. shareholder, and only for purposes of the foreign tax credit limitation.

## STUDY QUESTIONS

**3.** Which of the following would require a 30 percent U.S. tax withholding on the income paid to a foreign person?

    **a.** A U.S. company paying dividends to a foreign person.

    **b.** A foreign person earning income by conducting business in the United States for the majority of the year.

    **c.** A foreign person residing in the United States for the past month, receiving rental income from property located in a foreign country.

    **d.** A foreign person receiving $1,500 for performing services for another foreign person while residing in the United States for the past month.

**4.** Which of the following is an exception to the U.S. sourcing rules for interest income?

    **a.** Interest paid by a foreign corporation is U.S. source income if 25 percent or more of the foreign corporation's gross income was effectively connected with a U.S. trade or business.

    **b.** Interest paid by the branch of a U.S. bank located in a foreign country is U.S. source income.

    **c.** Interest paid to a foreign person by a U.S. branch of a foreign corporation is U.S.-source income.

    **d.** Interest paid to a U.S. person by a foreign person, when the debt was incurred in the United States, is foreign-source income.

# ¶ 906 SOURCING OF SERVICES

**Taxpayers source services where the services are performed.** If services are performed in the United States, the resulting income is U.S.-source income. Performed abroad, it's foreign-source income, whether wages, fees, salaries, commissions, or emoluments. There is a *de minimus* rule stating that if a foreign person is in the United States for fewer than 90 days, earns less than $3,000, and works for either a foreign person or a foreign person who is not engaged in a U.S. trade or business, the income is exempt from taxation. This basically allows foreign businesspeople to make short business trips to the United States and not have to pay U.S. taxes. Most tax treaties have a stronger standard, and they say that if a foreign person is in the United States fewer than 183 days, no salary threshold applies.

What happens when an individual receives payment for services performed both within and outside of the United States? Rules in that situation normally are based on the number of days of service and apportionment standards apply.

In Figure 9.17, a taxpayer (T) is a U.S. resident, and in a 250-day work year, spends 225 days in the United States and 25 days abroad. The taxpayer earns $60,000. Because 10 percent of the working days is spent abroad, 10 percent of that $60,000 or $6,000 is foreign-source income. The remaining income is U.S.-source.

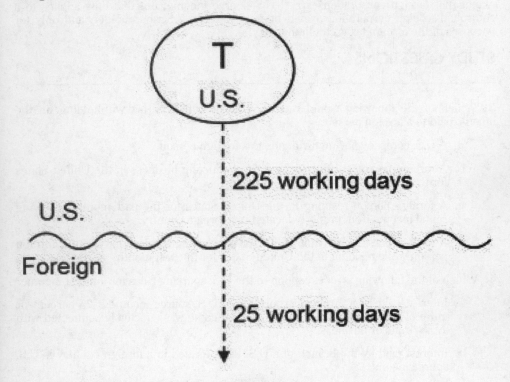

**Figure 9.17. Splitting income from services**

How did the regulations come up with 250 work days? First, they assume that there are 52 working weeks of 5 days per week in the year and everybody gets 2 weeks of vacation. So 50 weeks × 5 is 250 days, considered to be the work year.

However, other methods can be used to reasonably reflect the situation.

**EXAMPLE:** A Dutch painter is hired to come to the United States to paint a portrait. He is to be paid $40,000 to spend 10 days completing the painting. He spends 6 days in the United States, then takes the canvas back to the Netherlands, where he spends 4 days finishing it up. In that situation, 60 percent, the 6 out of 10 days he spends on the art, out of that $40,000 ($24,000) is U.S.-source income. The remainder is foreign-source income because services are sourced where they are performed.

## Fringe Benefits

**Pensions.** Dividing pensions between U.S. and foreign sources is a major issue. Defined benefit pension plans have a compensation component and an earnings component. The compensation component should be based on where the services were performed. So if a taxpayer performed some services in the United States and some abroad, some of that compensation-based component is going to be U.S.-source, and some is foreign-source.

In Figure 9.18, a pensioner receives an annual pension of $15,000, $5,000 of which is attributable to the pension plan earnings, and the remaining $10,000 is attributable to contributions by the taxpayer's employer, who contributed $100,000 to the pension contribution.

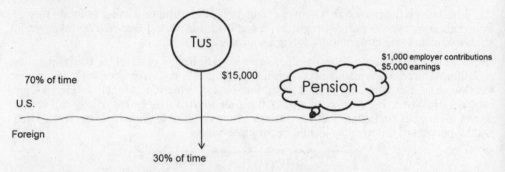

**Figure 9.18. U.S.- and foreign-source pension income**

Of the employer's total of $100,000 to the pension plan contributed on the taxpayer's behalf, $20,000 of which (20 percent) was contributed while he was on foreign assignments. The remaining 80 percent was contributed while the taxpayer was in the United States. Assuming the $5,000 of interest income is U.S. source, the foreign-source portion of the taxpayer's annual pension is $2,000 [$10,000 × ($20,000 ÷ $100,000)].

Now what happens if it's now 70 percent? If it's 70 percent contributed while the taxpayer was stateside, of that $10,000, $3,000 is foreign-source and $7,000 U.S.-source.

**Stock Options.** Nonqualified stock options are allocated between U.S.-source and foreign-source based on the amount of time worked in the respective locales.

So in Figure 9.19, a taxpayer (T) is granted a stock option on January 1 of year 1. He exercises the option on January 3 of year 2 after 18 months, when he recognizes $30,000 of compensation. So he worked all throughout the United States in that entire 12 months of year 1, but the first 6 months of year 2 in which he worked, he was on foreign assignment. So the foreign-source component of the $30,000 of stock option income is going to be $10,000, $30,000 times a third. It's the third 6 months abroad over 18 in the United States.

| January 1, Year 1: | Stock option granted |
|---|---|
| Year 1: | U.S. assignment |
| Year 2: | Foreign assignment |
| June 30, Year 2: | Stock option exercised |

**Figure 9.19 Stock option allocation**

# ¶ 907 Sourcing of Royalties and Rents

*Rentals* are payments for the use of tangible properties, such as a house or rented car. *Royalties* are payments for the use of intangible property. Where does a tax preparer source these payments? They are sourced by where the payments are performed (where the property, tangible or intangible, is used). Sometimes the tax preparer, or even the client, doesn't know, because the person the property is licensed or leased to might be in the United States, but might use the property abroad.

Similarly, if the person to whom the taxpayer is licensing or leasing property to is in a foreign country, the person might be using it in the United States. The taxpayer in such a situation would want more foreign-source income.

Figure 9.20 examines how royalties are sourced. In this case a U.S. taxpayer starts a California production company to produce a film. The taxpayer licenses it for use in London, and the royalties from use in the United Kingdom are all foreign-source income. However, he licenses showing the film to 20 theaters owned by a Toronto movie chain, but that chain has one theater show the film in Buffalo, New York. Then just 95 percent of the royalties would be foreign-source.

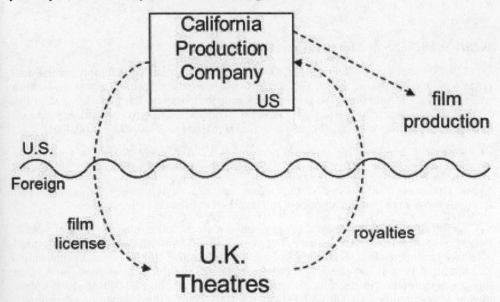

**Figure 9.20. Sourcing royalty income based on location or use**

There is not definitive guidance on distinguishing services and royalty income. Sissie Pluto, that U.S. tennis player who was going to play in the U.S. Open, received payments from a cola company to wear a patch on her tennis dress. The income could either be services or royalty income. If the income is considered compensation for services, all of the income would be U.S.-source. If royalty income, perhaps the income would be based on the percentage of TV sets tuned to the Open.

For rents or leases, the place of use of personal property may be both within and without the United States, in which case the taxpayer must apportion the rental income between U.S. and foreign sources. This apportionment may be done on the basis of time, mileage, or some other appropriate base.

In Figure 9.21, a taxpayer (TP) leases testing equipment to a manufacturer for a flat fee. The lessee uses the equipment at manufacturing plants located both in the United

States and abroad. Therefore, the lessor must apportion its rental income between U.S. and foreign sources, probably on the basis of the relative amount of time the lessee uses the equipment at its U.S. and foreign plants.

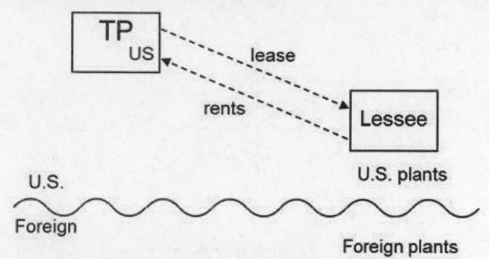

**Figure 9.21. Apportioning rental income based on time of use**

# ¶ 908 SOURCING OF GAINS ON REAL ESTATE

For real estate, gains are sourced by the location of the real estate. Gains on a sale or exchange of U.S. real estate interests are U.S.-source income, whereas gains on a sale or exchange of real estate located abroad constitutes foreign-source income.

> **EXAMPLE:** The gains on a sale of a New York office building to foreign investors is U.S.-source income, even when all of the related sale activities take place in Paris.

In Figure 9.22, Norman Ray Allen (NRA) is a nonresident alien who owns Blackacre Estate, which is located in Music City, USA. Several years later, NRA sells Blackacre for a gain. Because Blackacre is located in the United States, the gain on NRA's sale is U.S.-source income.

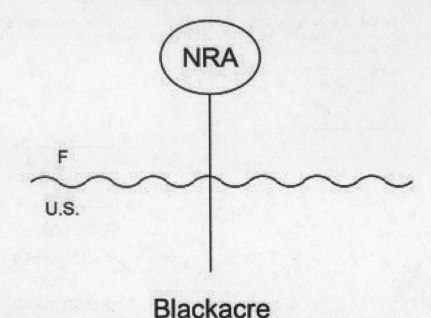

## Blackacre

**Figure 9.22. Real estate sale of U.S. property by a nonresident**

This location rule applies for sales of any U.S. real property interest. It's any real estate located in the United States or the U.S. Virgin Islands. The rule also includes selling shares of a U.S. real property holding company. Those shares are considered real estate interests and not personal property. A U.S. real property holding corporation is any U.S. corporation that during the last five years held more than 50 percent of its fair market value in U.S. real estate. The purpose is to prevent someone from incorporating and claiming to be selling shares as foreign-source when real estate would be U.S.-source.

# ¶ 909 SOURCING GAIN ON SALES OF PERSONAL PROPERTY

Personal property is sourced by the residence of the seller. If property such as a collection is sold by a U.S. resident to a purchaser in Scotland, the income is U.S.-source. Residence is basically where a person's tax home is for his or her principal place of business.

## Sales by Nonresidents

Assets considered to be personal property include inventories, machinery and equipment, and intangibles such as patents and copyrights. Stock shares are also considered personal property. For Figure 9.23, a taxpayer (T) is a nonresident alien. A nonresident is any person other than a U.S. resident (residents broadly including domestic corporations, a person who does not have a tax home abroad, and a trust or estate whose situs is in the United States). T, however resides in Ireland. It's his principal place of business. He's a citizen of Ireland and he sells 100 shares of USAco, a U.S. utility company with shares listed on the New York Stock Exchange. What is the source of the income? It's foreign-source income. Even though USAco is a domestic corporation that conducts business operations only within the United States, T's gain is nevertheless treated as foreign-source income because T is a nonresident.

¶909

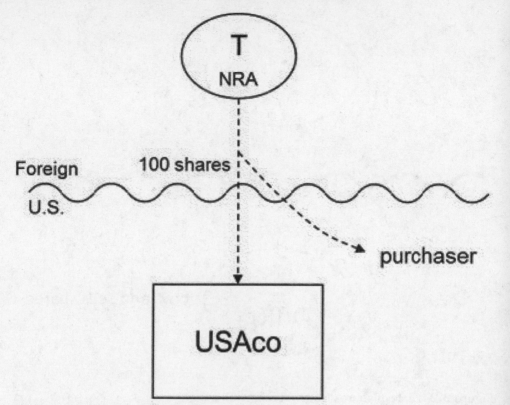

**Figure 9.23. Gains of a nonresident selling U.S. stock**

There are numerous exceptions to this residence-of-seller rule, including special source rules for depreciable property, intangibles, inventories, and stock of a foreign affiliate. So the residence-of-seller source rule applies primarily to security sales.

## Sales Through a Foreign Office

What about gains on sales by a U.S. citizen who has an office in a European country where shares of stock are bought and sold? He earns $100,000 from the sale of shares. If the transaction incurs tax of $10,000 ($10,000 ÷ $100,000 = 10 percent), it is foreign-source. If it's less than 10 percent, the gain from sales is U.S.-source income under a special rule for sales by U.S. citizens through a foreign office. Figure 9.24 shows this exception.

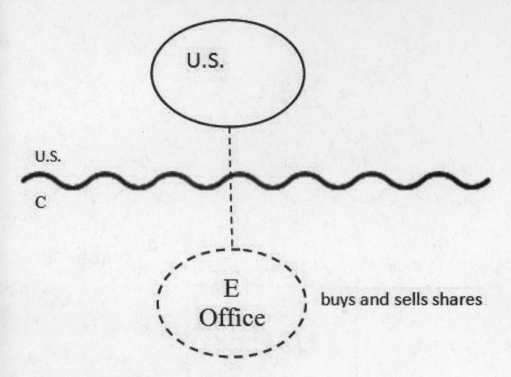

**Figure 9.24. Sale of shares from a foreign office**

## Sales of Inventory

For sourcing income, inventory includes personal property (and not real property) held by the taxpayer primarily for sale to customers in the ordinary course of business. Inventory rules are another exception of sourcing personal property sales by the seller's residence. There is no perfect way to source sales of inventory, and there are basically two different inventory rules.

**Purchased Inventory.** There is a rule for sales of purchased inventory, for example, by a distributor. There is a different rule for manufactured inventory that's sold abroad. With sales of purchased inventory, gain on the sale is sourced by where title passes. It's a very mechanical rule, an all-or-nothing rule that ignores all other functions.

In Figure 9.25, USAco, a domestic corporation, is an independent broker that purchases used commercial aircraft from U.S. airlines for resale abroad. During the current year, USAco purchased 20 planes from a regional airline based in Texas and then resold the planes to a Spanish airline. The Spanish airline first learned about USAco's services at a trade show held in Las Vegas. The sales agreement between USAco and the Spanish airline was negotiated and signed in Florida. Title to the airplanes passed in Spain upon delivery at the Madrid airport. Even though all of the selling activities, including solicitation, negotiation, and closing, took place within the United States, the entire profit from the sale of the airplanes is foreign-source income because title passed abroad.

¶909

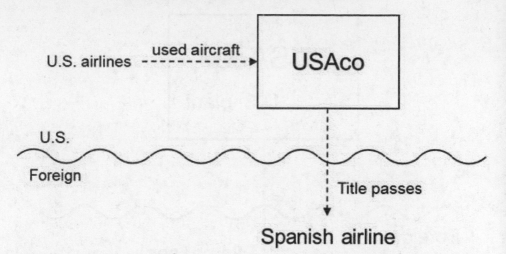

**Figure 9.25. Sourcing purchased inventory profits when title passes abroad**

**Manufactured Inventory.** A 50/50 rule applies to manufactured inventory. The 50/50 rule means that half of the gross income from the sale of manufactured inventory is sourced by where the manufacturing assets are located, and half by where the title passes. For a U.S. manufacturer, the best outcome is to get 50 percent to be foreign-source. What happens if the U.S. manufacturer has the title pass in the United States? None of the income is foreign-source income. The manufacturing asset's half is U.S.-source. The title passage happens through a U.S. source. No foreign-source income results, so no foreign tax credits are available.

In Figure 9.26, USAco manufactures computers in the United States with a cost of goods sold of $1,200 a computer. The company sells its computers through a Mexican branch office with title passing in Mexico. The company sells a thousand computers at a price of $2,000 a computer. The gross income is $800,000 ($800 × 1,000 units = $800,000).

All USAco production assets are in the United States with the average value beginning of the year and the end of the year, of $5 million. So what is the source of the income?

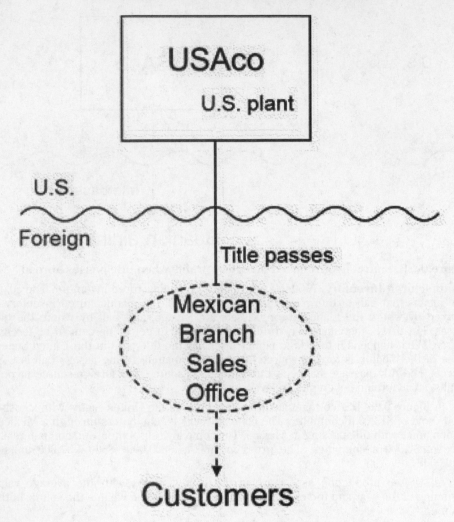

**Figure 9.26. The 50/50 method for manufactured inventory sales**

The taxpayer has to use the 50/50 method. First, the calculation is going to source the sales activity factor, and 50 percent of the $800,000, or $400,000, is all foreign-source because on all sales title passes abroad. What about that production activity factor? Under that production activity factor, none of that half, $400,000 being half of $800,000, is foreign-source income because all the factors of production are in the United States. Again, this is the best outcome possible.

A rarely used strategy is the independent factory price method. It says that if a U.S. taxpayer sells to an independent distributor in the United States, the taxpayer can use that as a basis, and any incremental amount sold to a foreign customer is foreign-source income. This rarely produces more income that is foreign-source income than the 50/50 method, so it's rarely used.

There is also a special books-and-records method that requires advanced permission from the IRS.

¶909

Despite any other sourcing rule, if a foreign person has an office or fixed place of business in the United States, any sale of personal property—including inventory—attributable to that U.S. office is U.S.-source income.

However, this rule doesn't apply if the property is sold for use outside the United States and an office or other fixed place of business in a foreign country materially participates in the sale.

Figure 9.27 shows FORco, a foreign company that manufactures and sells widgets with a U.S. branch to sell and warehouse it in the United States. A Canadian customer purchases a widget at the U.S. branch office and it ships from its U.S. warehouse.

If FORco materially participates in the sale, it's foreign-source income. If a foreign office does not materially participate in the sale, it's U.S.-source income.

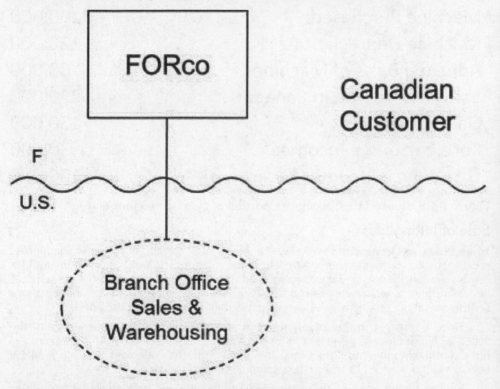

**Figure 9.27. Sale of inventory through a branch office**

# ¶ 910 OTHER SOURCING RULES

## Depreciation Recapture

A few additional rules apply to personal property and other types of income. To the extent that a taxpayer has depreciation deductions that reduce basis, they are going to increase the gain computed when he or she sells the property, and the portion of the gain on the disposition of depreciable personal property attributable to prior depreciation deductions is treated as having the same source as the related deduction.

So if the taxpayer has prior deductions offsetting both U.S.-source and foreignsource income, when the income is recaptured, it's going to be recaptured as U.S.-

source and foreign-source. When any gain over the depreciation deduction is recaptured, the tax preparer is going to use the source rules for inventory.

Figure 9.28 lists amounts for depreciation recapture. During the current year, USAco (a domestic corporation) sold a machine to a Canadian company for $230,000, with title passing to the buyer upon delivery in Canada. USAco purchased the machine several years ago for $200,000 and took $120,000 of depreciation deductions on the machine, all of which was apportioned to U.S.-source income. Therefore, USAco's adjusted basis in the machine is $80,000 ($200,000 original cost – $120,000 of accumulated depreciation) and the total gain on the sale of the machine is $150,000 ($230,000 sales price – $80,000 adjusted basis). The $120,000 depreciation recapture portion of the gain is U.S.-source income, whereas the $30,000 of appreciation is foreign-source income.

| | |
|---|---:|
| Machine Purchased: | $200,000 |
| Machine Depreciation: | 120,000 |
| Adjusted Basis of Machine: | 80,000 |
| Sale Passing Title in Canada: | 230,000 |
| Gain on Sale: | 150,000 |
| Foreign-Source Income: | 30,000 |
| U.S.-Source Income (Recapture): | $120,000 |

**Figure 9.28. Depreciation recapture portion of gain on machine sale**

## Sale of Intangibles

**Intangibles as Personal Property.** As mentioned earlier, licenses of intangibles receive royalty payments sourced by where the intangible is used. Sales of intangibles involve personal property. Those are sourced the locale of the residence of the seller. A key issue here is what happens if a taxpayer sells the intangible for an amount that's contingent on the productivity—how profitable that intangible is in the future.

Does a taxpayer in this situation get to source it for where the residence of the seller is? No. If the intangible is sold for any amount that's based on the contingency—on a contingent amount, like an installment sale, the tax code says the sale is like a royalty, so it is sourced by where the intangible property is used.

Similar to the use of sale of tangible equipment, any gain attributable to prior amortization deductions is also treated as having the same source as the related deduction. Any gain attributable to appreciation in the value of the intangible is sourced using the residence-of-seller rule, assuming the intangible is sold for a price that is not contingent on its productivity, use, or disposition. Gain on the disposition of goodwill is treated as arising from sources within the country in which the goodwill was generated.

**Sale of Stock in a Foreign Affiliate.** Under the general rule, a domestic corporation treats a gain on the sale of stock as U.S.-source income. However, if certain requirements are met, a domestic corporation can treat a gain on the sale of the stock of a foreign affiliate as foreign-source income, which has the beneficial side effect of increasing the taxpayer's foreign tax credit limitation (albeit in the passive basket).

However, it would really mess up the foreign tax credit calculation of many U.S.-based multinationals if every time they sold shares of a foreign company, the result was

U.S.-source income. So if three requirements are met, a U.S. company can actually source the gain on a sale of a foreign subsidiary as foreign-source income:

- The domestic corporation sells stock in an 80 percent-or-more-owned affiliate that is a foreign corporation;

- The sale occurs in a foreign country in which the affiliate is engaged in the active conduct of a trade or business; and

- The affiliate derived more than 50 percent of its gross income during the preceding three taxable years from the active conduct of a trade or business in such foreign country.

In Figure 9.29, USAco, a domestic corporation, owns all the stock of ForCo, a foreign subsidiary corporation. During the past three years, ForCo has earned approximately 60 percent of its gross income from the active conduct of a trade or business in a foreign country (F). USAco personnel travel to foreign country F where they offer to sell all the USAco-owned shares of ForCo to a foreign purchaser. The deal is negotiated and closed in foreign country F. As a result, the gain on the sale of the ForCo shares is foreign-source income.

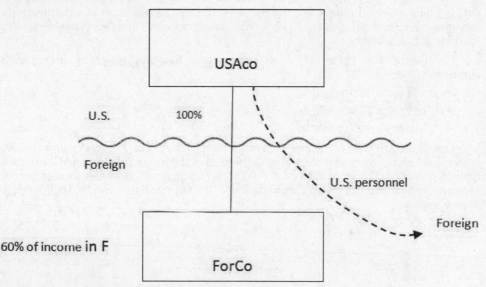

**Figure 9.29. Gain from sale of stock of a trade or business in a foreign country**

**Insurance Underwriting Income.** Underwriting income is sourced by where the insured risk is located. If the insured risk is in the United States, it's U.S.-source. If the insured risk is abroad, it's foreign-source. There is also an antiabuse rule that says such income is U.S.-source if the income comes from insuring risk located outside of the United States that results from some kind of arrangement, and another corporation receives a substantially equal amount of premium for insuring the risk located in the United States. Any other type of underwriting income is treated as foreign-source income.

**International Communications Income.** Basically, this income includes income that starts in the United States and goes abroad or starts abroad and comes into the United States. And the rules depend on whether the taxpayer is a U.S. or foreign person. For U.S. persons, 50 percent of income is foreign-source and 50 percent is U.S.-source. For foreign persons, this income is foreign-source unless they have a fixed place of business in the United States.

**Scholarships and Fellowships.** If services are performed for the scholarship or fellowship, income is sourced where the services are performed. What if services aren't required to be performed? Then income is based on where the payor is located. If the payor is a foreign payor, the income foreign-source. If it's a U.S. payor, it's U.S.-source. Social Security benefits are U.S.-source.

**Space and Ocean Activities.** The general rule for space and ocean activities is to source income by the residence of the recipient.

**Transportation Income.** If the transportation both begins and ends in the United States, income from the activity is U.S.-source income. If it begins in the United States and ends abroad, or begins abroad and ends in the United States, it's 50 percent U.S.-source and 50 percent foreign-source.

# ¶ 911  Sourcing Income of a Flow-Through Entity

For income earned by a flow-through entity, the source flows through to the owners of the flow-through entity, unless, of course, it's for sale of personal property. So income is simply going to flow through. For the partners, the distributed share of a partnership's foreign-source dividend is going to be foreign-source income. And this rule also applies to trusts and beneficiaries.

For Figure 9.30, there are three owners of a flow-through entity (here, an S corporation):

- Leslie owns 25 percent;
- Cindy owns 25 percent; and
- Miranda owns 50 percent.

Out of the $100,000 of income the S corp earns, $20,000 is U.S.-source and $80,000 is foreign-source. So because they have 25 percent of the income, Leslie and Cindy each have 5 percent U.S.-source income ($5,000) and 20 percent ($20,000) foreign-source income. As a 50 percent owner, Miranda has $10,000 U.S.-source and $40,000 foreign-source income.

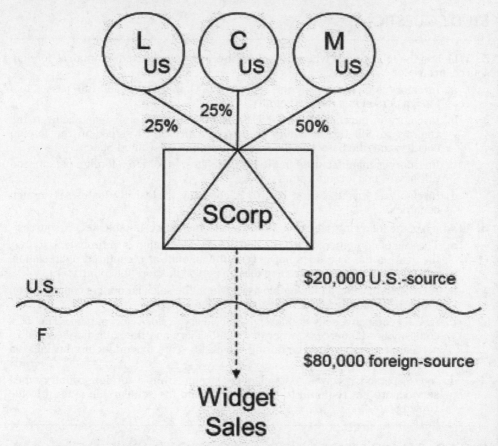

**Figure 9.30. Sourcing income from a flow-through entity**

An exception applies to the sale of personal property by a partnership, in which case the applicable source rule is applied at the partner level rather than the partnership level.

To summarize the general rules for sourcing gross income:

- Interest is sourced by the residence of the debtor;
- Dividends are sourced by the residence of the paying corporation;
- Services are sourced by where the services are performed;
- Rents and royalties are sourced by where the underlying property is used;
- Real estate is sourced by where the real estate is located;
- Sales of personal property are sourced by the residence of the seller;
- Inventory is sourced by
  - Where the title passes for purchased inventory, and
  - The 50/50 rule for manufactured inventory.

## STUDY QUESTIONS

**5.** Which of the following is when the sale of inventory is reported, in total, as foreign-source income for U.S. tax purposes?

    **a.** Inventory is purchased by the seller in the United States and title passes to a foreign person in a foreign country.

    **b.** Inventory is purchased by the U.S. seller from a foreign manufacturer, the contract to sell the inventory to a foreign person is signed in the foreign country, and title passes to the foreign person in the United States.

    **c.** Inventory is manufactured in the United States, is sold to a foreign person, and title passes in a foreign country.

    **d.** Inventory is manufactured by a U.S. company exclusively for use in foreign countries.

**6.** In which of the following scenarios would all income be attributable to U.S. sources?

    **a.** The sale of equipment when the depreciation deduction is entirely U.S.-source, the gain on the sale does not exceed the amount of recaptured depreciation, and title for the sales passes to a foreign person in a foreign country.

    **b.** A U.S. person sells an intangible asset where the sales amount is contingent on productivity and the asset is used in a foreign country.

    **c.** A U.S. company sells its foreign subsidiary's stock for a gain. The U.S. company is a 90 percent owner of the subsidiary and the subsidiary earned 75 percent of its gross income during the past 5 years by conducting business in the foreign country.

    **d.** A U.S. person receives a scholarship income from a foreign country when services are not required to be performed and the scholarship is used in the United States.

---

# ¶ 912 ALLOCATION AND APPORTIONMENT OF DEDUCTIONS

Sourcing a taxpayer's gross income will be sufficient in some situations. For example, there is no need to source the deductions of a foreign person whose only connection to the United States is as a passive investor deriving U.S.-source investment-type income, because such income is taxed on a gross basis through a flat rate withholding tax. In all other cases, however, the operative tax attribute is net taxable income, which necessitates the sourcing of items of both gross income and deductions. For example, a foreign corporation with a branch office in the United States is taxed on the net amount of income effectively connected with the conduct of that U.S. trade or business. Similarly, a U.S. person's foreign tax credit limitation is based on the ratio of net taxable income from foreign sources to net taxable income from all sources.

## Allocation and Apportionment Choices

In computing taxable income from sources within (or outside) the United States, the taxpayer is allowed deductions for expenses and losses directly related to either U.S.- or foreign-source gross income, as well as a ratable portion of expenses and losses that are not definitely related to any specific item of gross income. The taxpayer makes these determinations through a two-step process: allocation and apportionment. First, the taxpayer allocates deductions to a class of gross income. Then he or she apportions the deductions between U.S. and foreign services regarding the one of the many methods listed in Figure 9.31 for step two.

Deductions are allocated basically on a pro rata aspect between the various items of gross income. Once again, this is dependent on how the taxpayer characterizes the item of income.

As noted earlier, the service component must be distinguished from the royalty component for athletes and entertainers. So the taxpayer basically has to go through all these categories to look for a factual relationship between a deduction and an item of gross income.

Figure 9.31 details the process.

| **Step 1:** Allocate deductions to a class of gross income | **Step 2:** Apportion deductions between U.S. and foreign sources |
|---|---|
| • Compensation for services | • Gross income |
| • Gross income from business | • Gross sales |
| • Gains from dealings in property | • Units sold |
| • Interest | • Cost of goods sold |
| • Rents | • Profit contributions |
| • Royalties | • Expenses incurred |
| • Dividends | • Assets used |
| | • Salaries paid |
| | • Space utilized |
| | • Time spent |

**Figure 9.31 Allocation and apportionment process for deductions**

Figure 9.32 illustrates the allocation process. USAco earns $800,000 from the sale of services and $200,000 from the sale of product sales. The company makes $1 million in gross income. What are its expenses? USAco pays $500,000 to the service technicians, $130,000 to salespersons, and $100,000 of rent. Obviously expenses of the service technicians are allocable for the services. Clearly, the salespersons' expenses are allocable to the sales. How is the rent determined?

| Gross Income | | Expenses |
|---|---|---|
| $800,000 services<br>$200,000 sales | **USAco** | $500,000 service technicians<br>$130,000 salespersons<br>$100,000 rent |

**Figure 9.32. Allocation of gross income and expenses**

Rent is one of those expenses that should be allocated to both, most likely allocating $80,000 of rent to the services and $20,000 to the sale. There might be another way to do it that's more reasonable. It's not always easy to determine. But, for example, an exporter is going to have some portion of marketing expenses, including U.S. and foreign sources, based on the resources that it uses. And often it's unclear what the correct basis is.

The second step in sourcing a deduction is to apportion the deduction between U.S.-source and foreign-source gross income. Figure 9.33 shows a U.S. distributor that sells its products in the United States and abroad. The company has $10 million of sales—$6 million abroad, $4 million in the United States. However, the foreign sales aren't quite as profitable as the U.S. sales, so the U.S. sales produce $2.5 million of gross profit, the same as the foreign sales on foreign gross profit, which is based on more sales.

Also the exporter incurs $1 million of selling, general, and administrative (SG&A) expenses. How can the taxpayer apportion those SG&A expenses between foreign sources and U.S. sources? The company can do it either based on sales or gross profit.

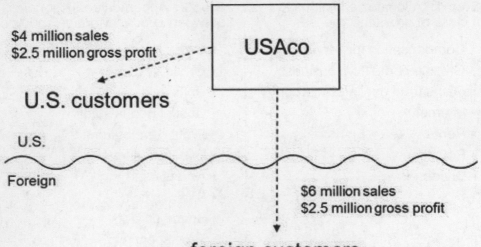

**Figure 9.33. Apportionment based on gross profit or sales**

What if the company apportions expenses based on gross profit? Based on gross profit, 50 percent of the administrative SG&A expenses, $500,000, is going to be apportioned to foreign-source income because 50 percent of the gross profit is abroad.

Alternatively, what happens if the apportionment is based on sales? Based on sales, 60 percent of the SG&A expenses, or $600,000, is going to be apportioned to foreign-source income. In this situation, the gross profit approach is preferable. But next year's sales might produce a better result, and for that tax year the company can change methods, as long as it records a contemporaneous memo in the apportionment files.

Also it also depends on what kind of records the taxpayer maintains. What happens if the company keeps track of time? The same facts apply as above, except that of the $1 million of SG&A, $350,000 of it is compensation. That's $250,000 of the president's salary, and she spends 30 percent of her time abroad, and the $100,000 of that $350,000 is the sales manager's salary, and that sales manager spends 40 percent of her time abroad. Figure 9.34 shows the breakdown.

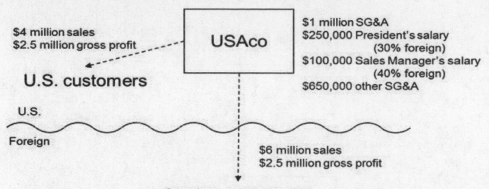

**foreign customers**

**Figure 9.34 Apportionment using time with gross profit or sales**

The figure shows gross profit on the left and sales on the right. Now after listing the $350,000 of salaries, the calculation shows $650,000 of residual expenses. Under the gross profit method, out of that $650,000 of other SG&A, half of it gets allocated, so .325 gets apportioned to foreign-source income.

For the president, 30 percent of her .25 is $75,000 to be apportioned to foreign-source income, and 40 percent of her .04 million of the sales manager's salary gets apportioned. Thus, .354, is going to be apportioned using gross profit and time to foreign-source income.

What about under sales? Here 60 percent of the $650,000 is going to be $325,000. Then for the sales manager's salary, once again it's going to be .04. And for the president it's .075. If the company uses sales, the result will be $440,000. So by using time and gross profit gives the company the best result.

The time calculation need not be recorded in increments like attorneys do but just rough estimates of the breakdown.

## Interest Expense Apportionment

Interest expense is apportioned based on the basis of the assets producing the income. But it's not a worldwide apportionment. In Figure 9.35, USP, a domestic corporation, owns all the stock of FSub, a foreign corporation. USP has a basis of $1,000 in its U.S. operating assets and a basis of $500 in its shares of FSub. FSub has foreign operating assets with a basis of $600 as well as $200 of debt, on which FSub pays $20 of interest expense that is apportioned against income earned by the subsidiary, and any dividends are going to be reduced by that $20 because earnings and profits (E&P) are reduced. It's a de facto deduction against foreign-source income.

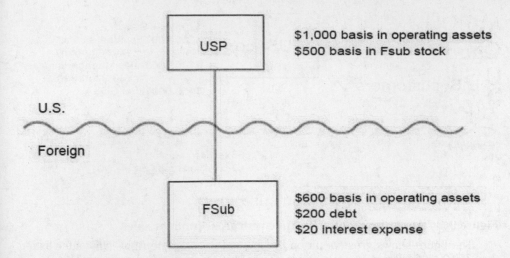

**Figure 9.35. Interest expense apportionment**

On the other hand, if you look at the $30 of interest expense that the U.S. parent incurs in Figure 9.36, the company has $1,000 operating assets in the United States. It has a primary basis in foreign shares, not the basis of the foreign subsidiary in its operating assets, but it's the shares that produce dividend income. One-third of the $30 gets apportioned to foreign-source income, and two-thirds of the interest, hence $20, get apportioned to U.S.-source income.

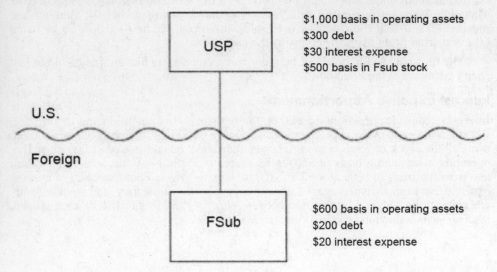

**Figure 9.36. Apportioning interest expense**

# MODULE 3: INTERNATIONAL TAXATION—
## Chapter 10: Check-the-Box Entity Elections: U.S. and Foreign Tax Implications

## ¶ 1001 WELCOME

This chapter provide detailed guidance on how to successfully make a check-the-box election, both on a timely and delinquent basis, and the practical tax planning implications for both domestic and international entities.

## ¶ 1002 LEARNING OBJECTIVES

Upon completion of this chapter, you will be able to:
- Understand the tax law, requirements, and procedures for making check-the-box elections
- Identify opportunities where making a check-the-box election will save taxes

## ¶ 1003 INTRODUCTION

Tax practitioners can provide their business clients with significant tax benefits by understanding the right circumstances to file a timely check-the-box election on Form 8832, *Entity Classification Election*. For example, a company may use foreign taxes paid as a credit to eliminate double taxation. Although Form 8832 looks simple, an improper understanding of the filing process can have an undesirable tax effect.

## ¶ 1004 HOW TO CHECK THE BOX

Choice of entity planning comes into play when a U.S. entity and, in particular, a flow-through entity (an LLC, an S corporation, a partnership, etc.) does business in a foreign country. A foreign branch results in current U.S. taxation of the income, while offering the opportunity for a foreign tax credit, which may reduce double taxation.

**EXAMPLE 1:** USCo, an S corporation, operates a branch sales office in foreign country F. All the income earned in foreign country F gets reported on its U.S. return. In addition, if the foreign branch has to pay country F income taxes, USCo may get a foreign tax credit on its U.S. return (Figure 10.1).

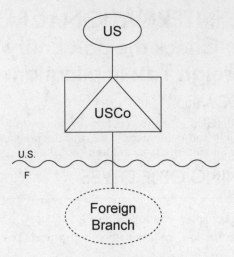

**Figure 10.1. Reporting of income earned in foreign country**

Incorporating a foreign subsidiary provides deferral from U.S. taxation until repatriated (typically in the form of a dividend) but may result in double taxation.

    **EXAMPLE 2:** USCo, an S corporation, operates in foreign country F through ForSub. ForSub pays tax in foreign country F. Furthermore, when ForSub distributes a dividend, that dividend will flow through USCo to its individual owners, who will also pay U.S. tax (Figure 10.2).

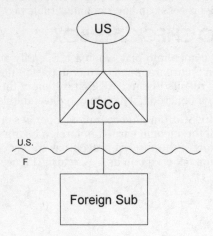

**Figure 10.2. Distribution of dividend**

A nontax advantage of incorporating a foreign entity is to limit the liability of any potential claimants against the U.S. assets of the business.

## Application to Foreign Entities—Simplification of Entity Classification Rules

Treas. Reg. § 301.7701-1(a)(1) provides that whether an organization is an entity separate from its owners for federal tax purposes is a matter of federal tax law and does not depend on whether the organization is recognized as an entity under local law. Treas. Reg. § 301.7701-1(d) provides that an entity is a domestic entity if it is created in the United States or under the law of any state or the District of Columbia; an entity is foreign if it is not domestic.

> **EXAMPLE 3:** USCo is an S corporation incorporated in Delaware. USCo owns PRCo, a company incorporated in Puerto Rico. Because USCo's state of incorporation is Delaware, it is a U.S. corporation. Because PRCo is not incorporated in any U.S. state or the District of Columbia, it is a foreign corporation (Figure 10.3).

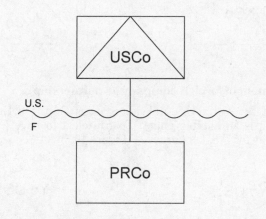

**Figure 10.3. Foreign versus domestic corporation**

A taxpayer can "check the box" by filing Form 8832, *Entity Classification Election*, within 12 months before the desired effective date or 75 days after the desired effective date. Although it is a relatively short form to complete, the impact of filing Form 8832 is large. It the wrong box is checked, the tax implications will be different. Those preparing the form should double-, triple-, and even quadruple-check their work.

# ¶ 1005 ENTITIES TO BE CHECKED

## Eligible Entity

Treas. Reg. § 301.7701-3(a) provides that any business entity that is not classified as a corporation (referred to in the regulations as an *eligible entity*) may elect its classification for federal tax purposes.

An eligible entity with at least two members can elect to be classified as a corporation or a partnership. So, if the entity is domestic, it would have to file either Form 1120 or Form 1065. If the entity is foreign, it would have to file either Form 5471 for a corporation or Form 8865 for a partnership.

An eligible entity with a single owner can elect to be classified as a corporation or to be disregarded as an entity separate from its owner.

**EXAMPLE 4:** Two U.S. individuals, Prince and Ryan, incorporate UKCo, a private limited company organized in the United Kingdom, which is an eligible entity. Prince and Ryan can elect to have UKCo treated as a partnership for U.S. tax purposes only (Figure 10.4).

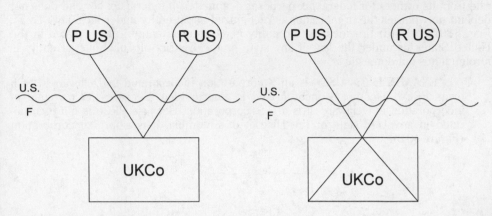

**Figure 10.4. Treatment of foreign company as partnership**

**EXAMPLE 5:** Yo, a U.S. individual, owns GerCo, a GmbH organized in Germany, which is an eligible entity. Yo can elect to have GerCo treated as a disregarded entity for U.S. tax purposes (Figure 10.5).

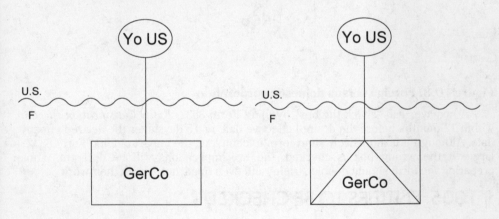

**Figure 10.5. Treatment of foreign company as disregarded entity**

## Default Rules

Treas. Reg. § 301.7701-3(b)(2)(i) provides that a foreign eligible entity, unless the entity elects otherwise, is a partnership if it has two or more members and at least one member does not have limited liability; a corporation if all members have limited liability; or disregarded as an entity separate from its owner if it has a single owner that does not have limited liability.

A member of a foreign entity has limited liability if the member has no personal liability for the debts of or claims against the entity by reason of being a member. This is based solely on the statute or law pursuant to which the entity is organized. A member has personal liability if the creditors of the entity may seek satisfaction of all or *any* portion of the debts or claims against the entity from the member as such. If protection from personal liability is optional under the applicable statute or law, the entity's organizational document will be determinative.

> **EXAMPLE 6:**   Ernie and Bernie are U.S. individuals that own ForCo, an entity organized in country F and for which they have never filed Form 8832. Pursuant to country F laws, both Ernie and Bernie have limited liability. As a result, their default status is that of a corporation for U.S. tax purposes. However, if either Ernie or Bernie had unlimited liability under foreign law, the default status of ForCo would be a partnership for U.S. tax purposes (Figure 10.6).

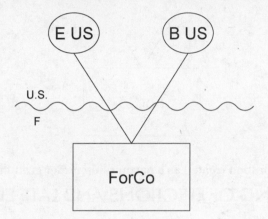

**Figure 10.6. Default status as a corporation**

## Grandfather Provisions

A foreign business entity described in Treas. Reg. § 301.7701-2(b)(8)(i) as a *per se* corporation that qualified as a partnership under the prior rules may retain its partnership status if it meets the following conditions:

- The entity was in existence on May 8, 1996.
- The entity's classification was relevant on May 8, 1996.
- No person for whom the entity's classification was relevant on May 8, 1996, treats the entity as a corporation.
    - A foreign eligible entity's classification is relevant when its classification affects the liability of any person for federal tax or information purposes.
    - The date of relevance is the date an event occurs that creates an obligation to file a federal tax return, information return, or statement for which the classification of the entity must be determined.
- Any change in the entity's classification within the 60 months prior to May 8, 1996, occurred solely as a result of a change in the organizational documents, and the federal tax consequences of the change were recognized by all members.
- A reasonable basis existed on May 8, 1996, for treating the entity as other than a corporation.
- The entity's classification was not under examination by the IRS on or prior to May 8, 1996.

**EXAMPLE 7:** Ernie and Bernie are U.S. individuals that have owned ForCo, an entity organized in country F in 1977. Pursuant to country F laws, both Ernie and Bernie have limited liability despite ForCo's income flowing through to them. Because Ernie and Bernie have treated ForCo as a partnership for U.S. tax purposes on every return filed since 1977, ForCo was treated as a partnership for U.S. tax purposes under the grandfather rule (Figure 10.7).

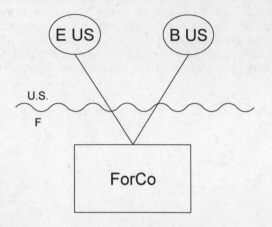

**Figure 10.7. Corporation treated as a partnership under grandfather rule**

# ¶ 1006 TIMING OF ELECTIONS AND LATE ELECTION PROCEDURE

## General Timing of Election

An election will be effective on the date specified in Form 8832 as long as the date specified is not more than 75 days prior to the date the election is filed and not more than 12 months after the date the election is filed (Treas. Reg. § 301.7701-3(c)(1)(iii)). Thus, an entity wishing to make an election effective on the first day of a taxable year should file the election no later than the 76th day of that taxable year. If the election specifies a date earlier than 75 days, then the election will be effective 75 days before the date it was filed.

**EXAMPLE 8:** USCo files a check-the-box election for ForSub on March 17, 2015. The election may be effective as of January 1, 2015. However, because 2016 is a leap year, if USCo formed ForSub on January 1, 2016, it must file a check the box election by March 16, 2016 to have it apply as of January 1, 2016.

The IRS must consent to any late election, and there are two general methods to obtain such consent: simplified procedures (Rev. Proc. 2009-41 and Rev. Proc. 2010-32) and full private letter ruling (§ § 301.9100-1 and -3).

## Simplified Procedures

The IRS has provided relief for an eligible entity that requests a late classification election filed within three years and 75 days of the requested effective date of the election (Rev. Proc. 2009-41).

To be eligible for relief under Revenue Procedure 2009-41, the taxpayer must meet the following requirements.

- The entity must show that either:
  - The entity failed to obtain its requested classification as of the date of its formation or (upon the entity's classification becoming relevant) "solely" because Form 8832 was not filed timely, or
  - The entity failed to obtain its requested change in classification "solely" because Form 8832 was not filed timely.

**EXAMPLE 9:** USCo requested its tax advisor to file a check-the-box election effective January 1, 2015. USCo's tax advisor mailed the form on March 17, 2015, but failed to include the proper postage. The U.S. Postal Service returned the form to the tax advisor for failing to include proper postage. In this case, the election was not made solely because Form 8832 was not timely filed, and the taxpayer should be eligible for relief under Rev. Proc. 2009-41 (assuming the other requirements are satisfied).

**EXAMPLE 10:** USCo forms ForSub on January 1, 2014, with the assistance of its tax advisor. USCo relies on the tax advisor to inform it of the eligibility and advantages of making a check-the-box election, but the tax advisor does not so inform USCo until March 10, 2016. If USCo had known of the advantages of making a check-the-box election when it formed ForCo, it would have done so. Is USCo eligible for the simplified procedure? Did it fail to obtain its requested classification "solely" because Form 8832 was not filed timely?

- The entity must show it either:
  - Has not filed a federal tax or information return for the first year in which the election was intended because the due date has not passed for that year's tax or information return, or
  - Timely filed all required federal tax returns and information returns consistent with its requested classification for all of the years it intended the requested election to be effective, and no inconsistent tax or information returns have been filed by or with respect to it during any of the taxable years.
- The eligible entity must demonstrate that it has reasonable cause for its failure to timely make the entity classification election, and that three years and 75 days from the requested effective date of the eligible entity's classification election have not passed.

To obtain relief under Revenue Procedure 2009-41, the eligible entity must file a completed Form 8832 with the applicable IRS Service Center within three years and 75 days from the requested effective date of the eligible entity's classification election.

The IRS has provided additional relief to taxpayers that have a concern about the validity of elections made by certain foreign eligible entities to be classified for federal tax purposes as a partnership or a disregarded entity (Rev. Proc. 2010-32, 2010-36 IRB 320). This procedure is designed to provide relief when a foreign entity makes an election to be a partnership (under the reasonable assumption that it has more than one owner) but then determines it only had one owner. If certain requirements are satisfied, the original election will be treated as an election to be a disregarded entity. The procedure also applies to a foreign entity that elected to be a disregarded entity (under the reasonable assumption that it has only one owner) but then determines it had more than one owner.

The IRS promulgated a similar procedure for late S corporation, Qsub, ESBT, and QSST elections (Rev. Proc. 2013-50; effective for late elections made after September 3, 2013). This Revenue Procedure also covers late entity classification elections that are intended to be effective at the same time as the S election.

## Private Letter Ruling

Filing a private letter ruling is a long and expensive procedure (see Treas. Reg. § § 301.91001 and 3. The IRS filing fee is high—$10,000—making this option quite cost ineffective. Taxpayers must make a detailed submission similar to a brief. The submission must include all relevant documents and affidavits.

Under Treas. Reg. § 301.9100-1(c), the IRS may grant a reasonable extension of time to make a regulatory election—or a statutory election under all subtitles of the Code except E, G, H, and I—if certain conditions are satisfied. The term *regulatory election* includes an election whose deadline is prescribed by a regulation published in the *Federal Register* (§ 301.9100-1(b)). This includes check-the-box elections, but not certain other elections such as Code Sec. 83(b) elections.

Treas. Reg. § 301.9100-2 provides automatic extensions of time for making certain elections, and § 301.9100-3 provides extensions of time for making elections that do not meet the requirements of § 301.9100-2. The IRS will grant requests for relief under § 301.9100-3 when the taxpayer provides evidence to establish that the taxpayer acted reasonably and in good faith, and that granting relief will not prejudice the interests of the government.

## Signing the Election

Form 8832 must be signed by each member of the electing entity who is an owner at the time the election is filed or any officer, manager, or member of the electing entity who is authorized to make the election (Treas. Reg. § 301.7701-3(c)(2)(i)). In the latter case, this authorization can be based on local law or the entity's organizational documents. In addition, the electing official must represent under penalties of perjury to possess such authorization.

In the case of retroactive elections, additional owners are required to sign the election. If the election is to be effective for any period prior to the time that it is filed, each additional person who was an owner between the date the election is to be effective and the date the election is filed must also sign the election (Treas. Reg. § 301.7701-3(c)(2)(ii)).

Additional rules are provided concerning who must sign an election in the case of an entity that elects to change its classification from a prior classification (Treas. Reg. § 301.7701-3(c)(2)(iii)). Because certain transactions are deemed to occur at the end of the day prior to the day the election is to be effective, the owners on that prior day must also sign the election.

Another issue is whether USCo can obtain the required signatures to file the form. There are two routes to obtaining the proper signatures. First, all the foreign owners of ForCo could sign the election. However, it might be difficult to obtain signatures of the foreign owners. Second, an authorized officer of each foreign entity could sign the election if they have the necessary authority under UK law. If the second route is chosen, USCo would probably need a board or shareholder meeting to approve the election. It may also need the opinion of foreign counsel in this regard because it involves the interpretation of foreign law. As a practical matter, USCo might want to take the first approach so that it can confirm that no foreign owner of ForCo will have any negative tax consequences from the election. The real question under the first alternative is whether USCo can obtain consents and signatures from the foreign owners before the extended due date of its tax return.

## STUDY QUESTIONS

**1.** Each of the following represents a default rule with respect to a foreign entity election, *except:*

    **a.** It is a partnership if it has one or more members.

    **b.** It is a partnership if it has two or more members and at least one member does not have limited liability.

    **c.** It is an association if all members have limited liability.

    **d.** It is disregarded as an entity separate from its owner if it has a single owner that does not have limited liability.

**2.** Which of the following identifies the first general requirement when making a late election through Rev. Proc. 2009-41?

    **a.** The entity must show that it has not filed a return for the first year in which the election was intended because the due date has not passed for that year's return.

    **b.** The entity must show that either it failed to obtain its requested classification as of the date of its formation or (upon the entity's classification becoming relevant) "solely" because Form 8832 was not filed timely, or it failed to obtain its requested change in classification "solely" because Form 8832 was not filed timely.

    **c.** The entity must show that it timely filed all required returns consistent with its requested classification for all the years it intended the requested election to be effective and no inconsistent returns have been filed by or with respect to it during any of the taxable years.

    **d.** The eligible entity must demonstrate that it has reasonable cause for its failure to timely make the entity classification election, and that three years and 75 days from the requested effective date of the eligible entity's classification election have not passed.

## ¶ 1007 DOMESTIC CHECK-THE-BOX PLANNING OPPORTUNITIES

Domestic check-the-box planning includes both the filing of Form 8832 for a U.S. entity and, more commonly, entity conversions. Planning ideas include the following:

- File an S election for an LLC taxed as a partnership to minimize self-employment tax and new "Medicare tax" risk.

- Compensation must be "reasonable" (i.e., not too low). Beware of owner salaries too far below the SSI wage base.

- The benefit is clearer for a service business, but the reasonable compensation risk is higher. It is more appropriate when the business has non-owner revenue generators.

- Advise clients of all implications of the S election (e.g., no inside basis step-up on death, limited ability to remove assets without triggering gain, limited flexibility in allocating gains and losses, etc.).

- There are no BIG tax, LIFO recapture, or AAA distribution issues.

- Consider keeping "personal goodwill" outside the business, if possible. This is likely not possible if owners have existing noncompete agreements.

- Beware of liabilities in excess of basis (which triggers gain).

- Convert an S corporation to an LLC taxed as a partnership to cause a liquidation after an asset sale.

- After an asset sale, an S corporation may need to "liquidate" to trigger a capital loss for shareholders.

**EXAMPLE 11:** S corp shareholder has basis of $10 in stock, and S corp has capital asset X worth $20 with a basis of $0. Upon sale of asset X, $20 of gain flows through to shareholder, increasing basis to $30. If S corp liquidates in year of sale, shareholder will receive $20 in proceeds and recognize a $10 loss ($20 – $30), which will offset flow through gain from sale of asset X (resulting in a net $10 of gain).

Shareholder loss on liquidation should occur in the year of sale to offset the gain on the asset sale. In an actual liquidation, this might not trigger a loss until all the assets are distributed. One way to do this is to convert to an LLC to cause a deemed liquidation. However, some issues should be considered

Retained depreciable assets can trigger ordinary income under Code Sec. 1239. This could be a big issue if there was significant bonus depreciation or Code Sec. 179 expensing in recent years. There might be state tax implications. The consequences of deferred payments should be analyzed. The entity may need to distribute all cash before the conversion. It might be possible to "undo" the tax consequences of the conversion by making an S election within 2.5 months and treating the transaction as an F reorganization.

In an S corporation acquisition, use an F reorganization/LLC conversion transaction to avoid the pitfalls of Code Sec. 338(h)(10), allow for tax-free retention of certain assets, and allow certain buyers to have flow-through treatment going forward.

Consider a buyer's acquisition of Target (illustrated in Figure 10.8). Target forms a new corporation (Holdco). Target's shareholders transfer their Target stock to Holdco in exchange for all of Holdco's common stock in the same proportion and in the same classes as they previously owned in Target. Holdco makes a qualified subchapter S subsidiary (Qsub) election with respect to Target by filing Form 8869 (and any applicable state law filings) with the IRS. The form now contemplates this transaction. As shown in Step 2 of Figure 10.8, Target converts to an LLC. Buyer acquires 100 percent of the ownership interest of Target LLC.

**Income tax treatment.** Taken together, the formation of a holding company structure (including the conversion to an LLC) for Target should qualify as a tax-free F reorganization. Target would be "disregarded" as a taxable entity that is separate from Holdco for income tax purposes only. In other words, Target would be treated as a division of Holdco. Holdco would be treated for tax purposes as occupying the same position that Target occupied prior to the holding company formation. Buyer's purchase of 100 percent of Target LLC should be treated for tax purposes as a purchase of 100 percent of the individual assets (and an assumption of 100 percent of the liabilities) of Target.

**Post-closing federal income tax reporting.** Holdco is treated for federal income tax purposes as the continuation of Target. Holdco's fiscal year does not close on the closing date, but rather continues until the end of Target's historic fiscal year or, if sooner, the date Holdco is liquidated. While Holdco is required to obtain a new FEIN, it files its federal tax return for the year of sale as if it was Target, albeit with a new name and FEIN.

**Employment tax reporting.** Target retains its historic FEIN following the transaction. While Target will include its activity under the FEIN of Buyer for income tax purposes, it will report its employment tax activity separately under its own FEIN. As such, Target should continue to report employment taxes on IRS Forms 940, 941, and W-2 as if

Target simply changed its name. Employees should only receive one IRS Form W-2 for the acquisition year, and Target's historic Form 940 and 941 reporting should continue uninterrupted for the acquisition year.

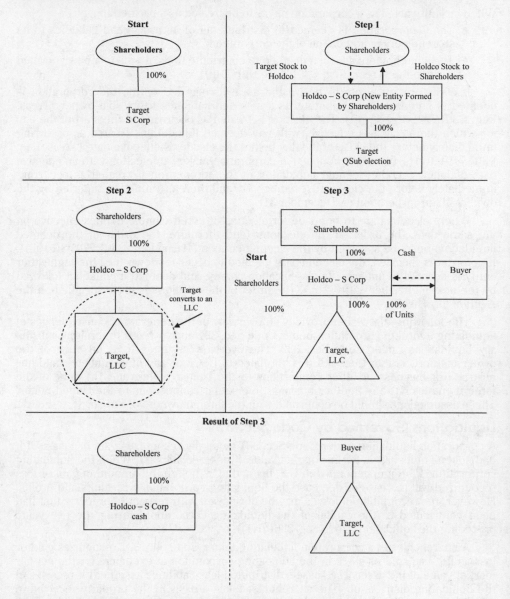

**Figure 10.8. Buyer's acquisition of corporation (Target)**

# ¶ 1008 TAX CONSEQUENCES

## Tax Consequences of Elections

When an entity taxed as a corporation elects to be treated as a partnership:

- The C corporation is deemed to distribute all of its assets and liabilities to its shareholders in liquidation of the corporation.
- The shareholders are then deemed to contribute those assets to a newly formed partnership (Treas. Reg. § 301.7701-3(g)(1)(ii)).

If a corporation elects to be treated as a disregarded entity, the corporation is deemed to liquidate by distributing its assets and liabilities to its sole owner (Treas. Reg. § 301.7701-3(g)(1)(iii)). The election is treated as occurring at the start of the day for which the election is effective, with any deemed liquidations treated as occurring immediately before the close of the day before the election's effective date (Treas. Reg. § 301.7701-3(g)(3)(i)). For example, if a corporation makes an election with an effective date of January 1, the deemed liquidation of the corporation is treated as occurring immediately before the close of December 31 (and therefore must be reported by the owners of the corporation on December 31).

Where elections are to be made for a series of tiered eligible entities effective on the same date, the order of the elections (and therefore, the order of the deemed liquidations) may be specified by the electing entities (Treas. Reg. § 301.7701-3(g)(iii)). If no order is specified, the elections are deemed to occur topdown (i.e., the highesttier entity is deemed to undergo its classification change and deemed liquidation, followed by the next highesttier entity, etc.). The order of the elections is to be specified on the election form itself.

The following discussion provides an overview of the general tax consequences of liquidating a foreign corporation under Code Sec. 331 and "foreign to foreign" subsidiary liquidations under Code Sec. 332. The overview assumes that: (a) each of the owners of ForCo other than USCo is unrelated to USCo or any of its affiliates, and has no trade or business or other connections to the United States, and (b) none of the foreign entities has any trade or business in or other connections to the United States. These assumptions should be confirmed with the foreign owners of ForCo.

## Liquidations Governed by Code Sec. 331

A corporation liquidating under Code Sec. 331 generally recognizes gain or loss as if it had sold all of its assets for fair market value (Code Sec. 336(a)). When the liquidating corporation is foreign, generally no U.S. tax is due, although the amount of gain or loss recognized will increase or decrease the liquidating corporation's earnings and profits. However, the recognition of losses may be disallowed with respect to property that had been contributed to the capital of the liquidating corporation during the five years preceding the liquidation (Code Sec. 336(d)(1)).

A shareholder of a corporation liquidating under Code Sec. 331 recognizes gain or loss as if it had sold its stock in the liquidating corporation in exchange for the net fair market value of the assets (i.e., assets distributed less liabilities assumed) it receives in the liquidating distribution. The shareholder takes a basis in the property received in the liquidating distribution equal to its net fair market value at the time of the distribution (Code Secs. 331(a) and 334(a)).

**EXAMPLE 12:** Two U.S. individuals, Prince and Ryan, have owned UKCo, a private limited company organized in the United Kingdom, which is an eligible entity. By checking the box on Form 8832 for partnership status, Prince and Ryan have liquidated UKCo pursuant to Code Sec. 331. They recognize gain to the extent of the fair market value of the assets over their basis in their shares and recontribute the assets to a partnership (Figure 10.9).

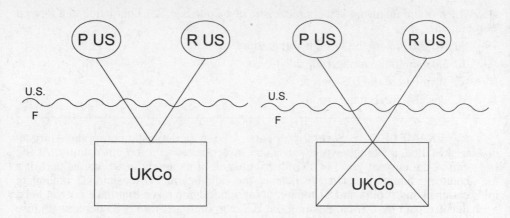

Figure 10.9. Corporation liquidating Under Code Sec. 331

## Foreign-to-Foreign Subsidiary Liquidations Governed by Code Sec. 332

By contrast, foreign-to-foreign liquidations governed by Code Sec. 332 (e.g., the liquidation of a foreign subsidiary into a foreign parent holding 80 percent or more of its stock) generally should not result in either the subsidiary or the parent recognizing gain or loss (Code Secs. 332 and 337; Treas. Reg. § 1.367(e)-2(c)(1)).

As a result of the liquidation, the foreign parent takes a carryover basis in the assets it receives and the earnings and profits and foreign income taxes of the subsidiary carryover to the foreign parent, subject to certain limitations, such as limits on the offsetting of pre-liquidation deficits against pre-liquidation earnings and profits, and so on (Treas. Reg. §§1.367(e)-2(c)(3); 1.367(b)-7).

Code Sec. 332 will not apply, however, unless the fair market value of the assets of the subsidiary (including goodwill and going concern value) exceed its liabilities at the time of the election (Treas. Reg. §1.332-2(b)). If the subsidiary's assets do not exceed its liabilities, the foreign parent may be able to take a worthless security deduction under Code Sec. 165(g), and, if the foreign parent is also a creditor of the subsidiary, possibly also a bad debt deduction under Code Sec. 166(a) (Rev. Rul. 2003-125; CCA 200706011).

## STUDY QUESTIONS

**3.** Which of the following statements is correct when an entity taxed as a corporation elects to be treated as a partnership?

**a.** The shareholders are deemed to contribute those assets to a newly formed corporation.

**b.** Where elections are to be made for a series of tiered eligible entities effective on the same date, the order of the elections may not be specified by the electing entities.

**c.** The C corporation is deemed to distribute all of its assets and liabilities to its shareholders in liquidation of the corporation.

**d.** The C corporation is deemed to distribute only its assets to its shareholders during the election.

**4.** Which of the following is a characteristic of a Code Sec. 331 liquidation of a foreign corporation?

    **a.** No U.S. tax on the foreign corporation

    **b.** No gain to the foreign subsidiary

    **c.** Dividend to the U.S. parent

    **d.** Possible foreign tax credit

---

**EXAMPLE 13:** Several years ago, USAco (a domestic corporation) organized FORco, a wholly owned subsidiary incorporated in a foreign country. At the end of the current year, FORco distributes all of its assets to USAco as part of a complete liquidation. On the date of the liquidation, FORco had $3 million of earnings and profits and $1 million of foreign income taxes that have not yet been deemed paid by USAco. Assume the U.S. corporate tax rate is 35 percent (Figure 10.10).

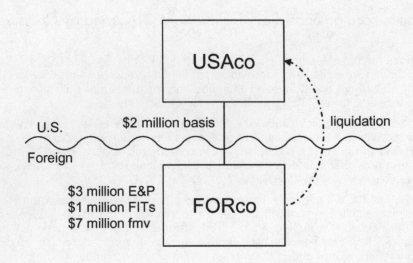

**Figure 10.10. Complete liquidation**

Pursuant to Code Sec. 367(b), USAco recognizes a dividend equal to FORco's earnings and profits of $3 million. Moreover, the $3 million dividend income will carry with it $1 million of deemed paid foreign taxes. Therefore, the pre-credit U.S. tax on the liquidation is $1.4 million [35% U.S. tax rate × ($3 million deemed dividend plus $1 million gross-up)], the deemed paid credit is $1 million, and it will reduce USAco's pre-credit U.S. tax of $1.4 million to $400,000. USAco will take a carryover basis in the assets distributed.

## Miscellaneous Tax Issues

The net operating losses of a liquidating foreign corporation that was not engaged in a U.S. trade or business should not carry over to its shareholders because the liquidating foreign corporation would not have had any deductions for U.S. tax purposes on which to base the net operating loss (see Rev. Rul. 72-421). Therefore, a foreign entity could not use any pre-election net operating losses (NOLs) to offset future income, if any, for U.S. tax purposes. If a foreign entity desires to change its U.S. tax classification back to a foreign corporation, the U.S. owners may be required to recapture any losses they deducted while they were treated as a foreign partnership or disregarded entity (see Code Sec. 367(a)(3)(C)).

The calculated tax loss of ForCo and affiliates may be less than anticipated following the check-the-box election. If the check-the-box election results in a step-down in tax basis of the assets due to the loss realized on liquidation, then there may be less depreciation deductions that generate tax loss. Furthermore, the operations would be calculated and allocated to the members under partnership tax rules, and there may be special accounting requirements that will change the current calculated tax loss.

# ¶ 1009 INTERNATIONAL TAX IMPLICATIONS OF CHECK-THE-BOX PLANNING

## Use Foreign Tax Credits to Avoid Double Taxation

The decision to check the box involves weighing deferral versus the overall effective tax rate. The tax planner must evaluate the interaction between foreign tax credits, withholding taxes, and the tax rate on dividends. The U.S. individual tax rate on dividends from a treaty country (e.g., most of Europe and North America) is 20 percent. Dividends received from non-treaty countries (e.g., tax havens, Hong Kong) are taxed at ordinary rates.

The deemed paid foreign tax credit occurs where a domestic C corporation owns 10 percent or more of the voting stock of a foreign corporation from which it receives a dividend (Code Sec. 902). The foreign tax credit is only available to C corporations; it is not available to S corporations, LLCs, partnerships or their owners.

## Converting a Code Sec. 902 Credit to a Code Sec. 901 Credit

The deemed paid credit regime is not available to individuals. Typically, the only creditable taxes as a U.S. shareholder of a foreign corporation is withholding on the dividend distribution. Therefore, the recipient individual U.S. shareholder is subject to double taxation—first, when the distributed earnings were taxed in the foreign jurisdiction, and second, when such earnings are distributed without a corresponding deemed paid credit. By checking the box for the distributing foreign corporation, an individual U.S. owner may take a foreign tax credit, as the earnings of the foreign entity pass-through and are taxed at the owner level.

Consider the following hypothetical scenario (Figures 10.11 and 10.12). USCo is a single-member limited liability company (a disregarded entity for U.S. tax purposes) in Chicago that manufactures and sells widgets. The owner considers expanding the operations to the Netherlands, where *both manufacturing and sales* will occur. As a result, the owner considers forming a BV in the Netherlands (a checkable entity under the U.S. check-the-box rules). The operations are expected to earn $1 million of taxable income.

The Netherlands imposes a corporate tax rate of approximately 25 percent and has a tax treaty with the United States that imposes a 5 percent withholding tax on dividends. The tax planner should consider both repatriation and deferral options. The tax implications of USCo forming a BV in the Netherlands and not checking the box are shown in Table 10.1.

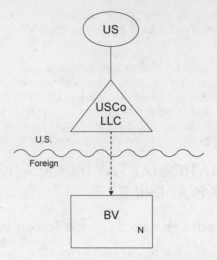

**Figure 10.11. Expansion of single-member LLC without checking the box**

| Table 10.1. Tax Implications of Forming a BV and Not Checking the Box | | |
|---|---|---|
| | **Repatriation** | **Deferral** |
| Foreign taxable income | $1,000,000 | $1,000,000 |
| Foreign income tax | 250,000 | 250,000 |
| Foreign E&P | 750,000 | 750,000 |
| Dividend | 750,000 | 0 |
| Withholding tax on dividend | 37,500 | 0 |
| Pre-credit U.S. tax at 20% | 150,000 | 0 |
| Foreign tax credit on withholding tax | 37,500 | 0 |
| U.S. tax | 112,500 | 0 |
| **Total tax** | **400,000** | **250,000** |

The deferral results do not change because there is not any taxable income in the United States subject to higher rates. The tax implications of USCo forming a BV in the Netherlands and checking the box are shown in Table 10.2.

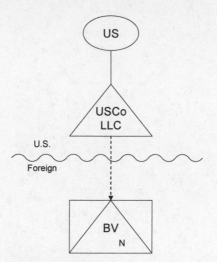

**Figure 10.12. Expansion of single-member LLC with checking the box**

| Table 10.2. Tax Implications of Forming a BV and Checking the Box | | |
|---|---|---|
| | **Repatriation** | **Deferral** |
| Foreign taxable income | $1,000,000 | $1,000,000 |
| Foreign income tax | 250,000 | 250,000 |
| Withholding tax on $750,000 | 37,500 | 0 |
| Operating income to U.S. | 1,000,000 | 1,000,000 |
| Pre-credit U.S. tax at 40% | 400,000 | 400,000 |
| Foreign tax credit | 287,500 | 250,000 |
| U.S. tax | 112,500 | 150,000 |
| **Total tax** | **400,000** | **400,000** |

What is the repatriation goal of the U.S. owner? If the goal is further investment abroad, deferral may be preferable regardless of the immediate tax impact. When purchasing a foreign entity for which flow-through treatment is desired, the purchase agreement should require a signed Form 8832, designating the appropriate effective date, to be presented at close.

## Planning to Take Foreign Losses

**EXAMPLE 14:**  On January 1 of the taxable year, ForSub anticipates losses. By February 28, the projections for ForSub look even worse than anticipated. The losses incurred by ForSub with respect to the taxable year are trapped and cannot be used to offset any income of USCo (Figure 10.13).

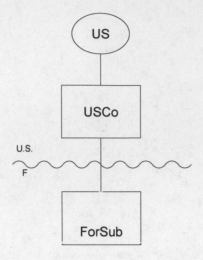

**Figure 10.13. Losses of foreign subsidiaries**

In general, the earnings of foreign subsidiaries are not subject to U.S. tax until distributed or otherwise repatriated. Accordingly, any losses incurred will not passthrough to offset other U.S. taxable income. By checking the box for the loss foreign corporation, the loss may be utilized to shelter other U.S. taxable income.

> **EXAMPLE 15:** On January 1 of the taxable year, ForSub anticipates losses. By February 28, the projections for ForSub look even worse than anticipated. Until March 15, USCo can check the box of ForSub effective to January 1, creating a flow-through entity whose losses for the entire year can reduce U.S. tax liabilities (Figure 10.14).

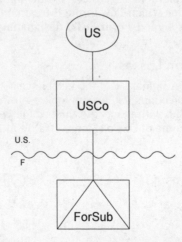

**Figure 10.14. Creating a flow-through entity whose losses can reduce U.S. tax liabilities**

## Domestic Reverse Hybrid Entities

Domestic reverse hybrid entities have been a popular vehicle for "double-dip" financing structures, whereby the interest is deductible against the income of both the U.S. subsidiary and the foreign parent. Domestic reverse hybrid entities are treated as corporations by the United States, but as passthrough entities by the foreign countries.

A domestic reverse hybrid entity would be useful to a foreign corporation that wants passthrough treatment in its country while avoiding any U.S. repatriation costs in the form of either a withholding tax or a branch tax. A popular form of domestic reverse hybrid entity is a limited partnership for which the foreign owner has filed a Form 8832 that checks-the-box for U.S. corporate tax status.

> **EXAMPLE 16:** FORco, a corporation incorporated in country F, operates in the United States through a U.S. subsidiary, USAco. FORco contributes USAco to a domestic reverse hybrid entity (USDRH), which is a passthrough entity for country F tax purposes and a corporation for U.S. tax purposes. USDRH borrows money from a U.S. bank to which USDRH must pay interest. For U.S. tax purposes, USDRH and USAco file a consolidated return, which permits a deduction for the interest payment against the income of USAco. A double-dip occurs because the passthrough nature of USDRH for country F tax purposes permits FORco to also deduct the interest expense on FORco's country F return (Figure 10.15).

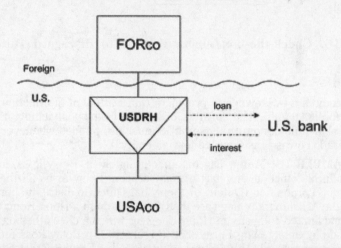

**Figure 10.15. Domestic reverse hybrid entity and "double-dip" financing**

U.S. partnerships are preferable to U.S. LLCs, which are often treated by foreign countries as corporations and not as pass-throughs. Practitioners should watch for debt-to-equity ratios in excess of 1.5 to 1. The lender may be foreign or domestic but cannot be related in any way to FORco.

# ¶ 1010 FLOW-THROUGH FOREIGN OPERATIONS OF U.S. OWNERS

This discussion on flow-through entities and Forms 8858 (*Information Return of U.S. Persons With Respect to Foreign Disregarded Entities*) and 8865 (*Return of U.S. Persons With Respect to Certain Foreign Partnerships*) begins with an example.

**EXAMPLE 17:** A new flag manufacturing client, Betsy Ross, meets her tax preparer in his office at the start of busy season. Betsy owns all the shares of a Netherlands corporation (DutchCo), but is interested in changing accountants. Betsy's previous accountant had filed a check the box election (Form 8832) to disregard DutchCo as a corporation for U.S. tax purposes because the accountant did not want to be bothered with filing Form 5471 (Figure 10.16). Betsy Ross wants the preparer's confirmation that she must no longer file Form 5471.

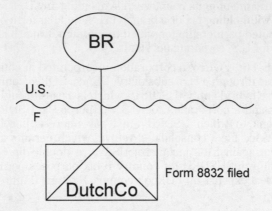

**Figure 10.16. Check-the-box election made to disregard DutchCo as a corporation**

## Form 8858

Form 8858 requires a U.S. owner to provide a wide variety of information regarding a disregarded foreign entity. The form is ordinarily filed by attaching it to the U.S. owner's federal income tax return. Form 8858 must also be filed whenever a controlled foreign corporation owns a disregarded foreign entity.

**EXAMPLE 18:** A new flag manufacturing client, Betsy Ross, meets her tax preparer in his office at the start of busy season. Betsy owns all the shares of a Netherlands corporation (DutchCo). Betsy has DutchCo distribute her flags, but to capture the Asian market, flags are distributed through a Hong Kong office, which is a private limited company in Hong Kong for which a check-the-box election has been made by timely filing Form 8832 (Figure 10.17). Betsy Ross must file Form 8858 with respect to this Hong Kong entity as well as Form 5471 for DutchCo.

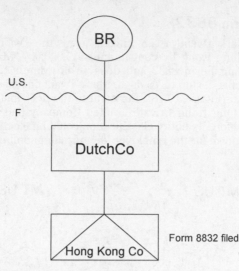

**Figure 10.17. Controlled foreign corporation owning a disregarded foreign entity**

Audit issues with respect to Form 8858 include the following:

- Whether the Form 8858 filed for a tax year for which a Form 8832 check-the-box election has been filed and is effective
- The losses of any foreign disregarded entity
- The proof of foreign tax credits

## Form 8865

Form 8865 requires a U.S. owner to provide a wide variety of information regarding foreign partnerships of U.S. owners. The information on Form 8865 is the first place the IRS looks when conducting examinations of transfer pricing. Form 8865 ordinarily is filed by attaching it to the U.S. owner's federal income tax return.

As with Form 5471, determining the appropriate filing category is critical to determining the schedules to file:

- **Category 1 filer.** A U.S. person who controls a foreign partnership for any time during the partnership's tax year. Control means owning more than 50 percent of the capital, profits, deductions, or losses.
- **Category 2 filer.** A U.S. person who owns at least 10 percent of the foreign partnership at any time during the year while the aggregate of 10 percent U.S. owners exceeds 50 percent.
- **Category 3 filer.** A U.S. person who has directly, constructively, or via attribution contributed property to a foreign partnership and either acquired a 10 percent interest in the foreign partnership or, when added to the value of any other property contributed to the partnership, exceeds $100,000.
- **Category 4 filer.** Anyone who directly:
  - Acquires a 10 percent interest in a foreign partnership,
  - Disposes a 10 percent interest in a foreign partnership, or
  - Changes ownership by 10 percentage points.

## Check the Box (Form 8832)

On January 1, 2015, Mark Twain, a U.S. citizen, forms the Twain Hong Kong Private Limited Company in Hong Kong by contributing $15,000,000. Mark Twain decides to "check the box" by filing Form 8832 and does so on March 15, 2015. Because the election may be retroactive for up to 75 days, Mark Twain chooses to have the election effective January 1, 2015 (Figure 10.18). Pursuant to the IRs's instructions with respect to Form 8832, Twain Hong Kong Private Limited Company had to have an employer identification number before its entity classification could be elected. It is insufficient to put "applied for" on the form for the employer identification number.

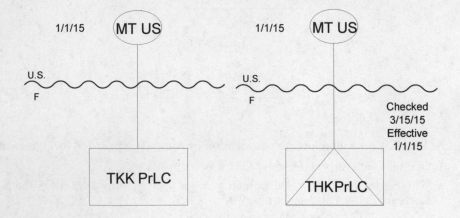

**Figure 10.18. Twain Hong Kong Private Limited Company scenario**

The chartered accountant in Hong Kong provides the following account information in Hong Kong dollars for the year ended December 31, 2015.

| | |
|---|---|
| Sales | HKD 25,000,000 |
| Cost of goods sold | HKD 15,000,000 |
| Compensation | HKD 2,000,000 |
| Cash: | HKD 31,400,000 |
| Accounts payable | HKD 15,000,000 |

The average exchange rate is $.5 U.S. to $1 HK. Twain must prepare Form 8858 for this foreign disregarded entity. See the following filled-in forms.

| Form **8832**<br>(Rev. December 2013)<br><br>Department of the Treasury<br>Internal Revenue Service | **Entity Classification Election**<br><br>▶ Information about Form 8832 and its instructions is at *www.irs.gov/form8832.* | OMB No. 1545-1516 |
|---|---|---|

| **Type<br>or<br>Print** | Name of eligible entity making election<br>**Twain Hong Kong Private Limited Company** | **Employer identification number**<br>88-8888888 |
|---|---|---|

Number, street, and room or suite no. If a P.O. box, see instructions.

City or town, state, and ZIP code. If a foreign address, enter city, province or state, postal code and country. Follow the country's practice for entering the postal code.

▶ Check if: ☐ Address change ☐ Late classification relief sought under Revenue Procedure 2009-41
        ☐ Relief for a late change of entity classification election sought under Revenue Procedure 2010-32

**Part I**    **Election Information**

**1**    **Type of election** (see instructions):

**a** ☑ Initial classification by a newly-formed entity. Skip lines 2a and 2b and go to line 3.
**b** ☐ Change in current classification. Go to line 2a.

**2a** Has the eligible entity previously filed an entity election that had an effective date within the last 60 months?

    ☐ **Yes.** Go to line 2b.
    ☑ **No.** Skip line 2b and go to line 3.

**2b** Was the eligible entity's prior election an initial classification election by a newly formed entity that was effective on the date of formation?

    ☐ **Yes.** Go to line 3.
    ☐ **No.** Stop here. You generally are not currently eligible to make the election (see instructions).

**3**    Does the eligible entity have more than one owner?

    ☐ **Yes.** You can elect to be classified as a partnership or an association taxable as a corporation. Skip line 4 and go to line 5.
    ☑ **No.** You can elect to be classified as an association taxable as a corporation or to be disregarded as a separate entity. Go to line 4.

**4**    If the eligible entity has only one owner, provide the following information:

**a** Name of owner ▶   Mark Twain
**b** Identifying number of owner ▶   123-45-6789

**5**    If the eligible entity is owned by one or more affiliated corporations that file a consolidated return, provide the name and employer identification number of the parent corporation:

**a** Name of parent corporation ▶
**b** Employer identification number ▶

For Paperwork Reduction Act Notice, see instructions.      Cat. No. 22598R      Form **8832** (Rev. 12-2013)

¶1010

Form 8832 (Rev. 12-2013)     Page **2**

**Part I**    **Election Information** (Continued)

**6**   **Type of entity** (see instructions):

a   ☐ A domestic eligible entity electing to be classified as an association taxable as a corporation.
b   ☐ A domestic eligible entity electing to be classified as a partnership.
c   ☐ A domestic eligible entity with a single owner electing to be disregarded as a separate entity.
d   ☐ A foreign eligible entity electing to be classified as an association taxable as a corporation.
e   ☐ A foreign eligible entity electing to be classified as a partnership.
f   ☑ A foreign eligible entity with a single owner electing to be disregarded as a separate entity.

**7**   If the eligible entity is created or organized in a foreign jurisdiction, provide the foreign country of organization ▶   **Hong Kong**

**8**   Election is to be effective beginning (month, day, year) (see instructions) . . . . . . . . . . . . ▶   **1/1/14**

**9**   Name and title of contact person whom the IRS may call for more information    **10**   Contact person's telephone number

   **Mark Twain**       **573-555-8765**

**Consent Statement and Signature(s) (see instructions)**

Under penalties of perjury, I (we) declare that I (we) consent to the election of the above-named entity to be classified as indicated above, and that I (we) have examined this election and consent statement, and to the best of my (our) knowledge and belief, this election and consent statement are true, correct, and complete. If I am an officer, manager, or member signing for the entity, I further declare under penalties of perjury that I am authorized to make the election on its behalf.

| Signature(s) | Date | Title |
|---|---|---|
| | | |

Form **8832** (Rev. 12-2013)

---

Form 8832 (Rev. 12-2013)     Page **3**

**Part II**   **Late Election Relief**

**11**   Provide the explanation as to why the entity classification election was not filed on time (see instructions).

Under penalties of perjury, I (we) declare that I (we) have examined this election, including accompanying documents, and, to the best of my (our) knowledge and belief, the election contains all the relevant facts relating to the election, and such facts are true, correct, and complete. I (we) further declare that I (we) have personal knowledge of the facts and circumstances related to the election. I (we) further declare that the elements required for relief in Section 4.01 of Revenue Procedure 2009-41 have been satisfied.

| Signature(s) | Date | Title |
|---|---|---|
| | | |
| | | |
| | | |
| | | |

Form **8832** (Rev. 12-2013)

**Figure 10.19. Filled-in Form 8832**

| Form **8858** | **Information Return of U.S. Persons With Respect To Foreign Disregarded Entities** | OMB No. 1545-1910 |
|---|---|---|
| (Rev. December 2012) | ▶ Information about Form 8858 and its separate instructions is at *www.irs.gov/form8858.* | |
| Department of the Treasury Internal Revenue Service | Information furnished for the foreign disregarded entity's annual accounting period (see instructions) beginning   January 1  , 20 **14** , and ending   December 31  , 20 **14** | Attachment Sequence No. **140** |

| Name of person filing this return | Filer's identifying number |
|---|---|
| Mark Twain | 123-45-6789 |

Number, street, and room or suite no. (or P.O. box number if mail is not delivered to street address)

City or town, state, and ZIP code

Hannibal, MO

| Filer's tax year beginning | , 20 | , and ending | , 20 |
|---|---|---|---|

**Important:** *Fill in all applicable lines and schedules. All information **must** be in English. All amounts **must** be stated in U.S. dollars unless otherwise indicated.*

| **1a** Name and address of foreign disregarded entity | **b(1)** U.S. identifying number, if any |
|---|---|
| | 88-8888888 |
| Twain Hong Kong Private Limited Company | **b(2)** Reference ID number (see instructions) |

| **c** Country(ies) under whose laws organized and entity type under local tax law | **d** Date(s) of organization | **e** Effective date as foreign disregarded entity |
|---|---|---|
| Hong Kong | | |

| **f** If benefits under a U.S. tax treaty were claimed with respect to income of the foreign disregarded entity, enter the treaty and article number | **g** Country in which principal business activity is conducted | **h** Principal business activity | **i** Functional currency |
|---|---|---|---|
| | Hong Kong | | Hong Kong Dollars |

**2** Provide the following information for the foreign disregarded entity's accounting period stated above.

| **a** Name, address, and identifying number of branch office or agent (if any) in the United States | **b** Name and address (including corporate department, if applicable) of person(s) with custody of the books and records of the foreign disregarded entity, and the location of such books and records, if different |
|---|---|
| | |

**3** For the **tax owner** of the foreign disregarded entity (if different from the filer) provide the following:

| **a** Name and address | **b** Annual accounting period covered by the return (see instructions) |
|---|---|
| | **c(1)** U.S. identifying number, if any |
| | **c(2)** Reference ID number (see instructions) |
| | **d** Country under whose laws organized / **e** Functional currency |

**4** For the **direct owner** of the foreign disregarded entity (if different from the tax owner) provide the following:

| **a** Name and address | **b** Country under whose laws organized |
|---|---|
| | **c** U.S. identifying number, if any / **d** Functional currency |

**5** Attach an organizational chart that identifies the name, placement, percentage of ownership, tax classification, and country of organization of all entities in the chain of ownership between the tax owner and the foreign disregarded entity, and the chain of ownership between the foreign disregarded entity and each entity in which the foreign disregarded entity has a 10% or more direct or indirect interest. See instructions.

| For Paperwork Reduction Act Notice, see the separate instructions. | Cat. No. 21457L | Form **8858** (Rev. 12-2012) |
|---|---|---|

**¶1010**

Form 8858 (Rev. 12-2012)                                                                 Page **2**

## Schedule C    Income Statement (see instructions)

**Important:** *Report all information in functional currency in accordance with U.S. GAAP. Also, report each amount in U.S. dollars translated from functional currency (using GAAP translation rules or the average exchange rate determined under section 989(b)). If the functional currency is the U.S. dollar, complete only the U.S. Dollars column. See instructions for special rules for foreign disregarded entities that use DASTM.*

*If you are using the average exchange rate (determined under section 989(b)), check the following box* . . . . . . ☑

| | | | Functional Currency | U.S. Dollars |
|---|---|---|---|---|
| 1 | Gross receipts or sales (net of returns and allowances) . . . . . . . . . . | 1 | 25,000,000 | 37,500,000 |
| 2 | Cost of goods sold . . . . . . . . . . . . . . . . . . . . . | 2 | 15,000,000 | 22,500,000 |
| 3 | Gross profit (subtract line 2 from line 1) . . . . . . . . . . . . . . | 3 | 10,000,000 | 15,000,000 |
| 4 | Other income. . . . . . . . . . . . . . . . . . . . . . . | 4 | | |
| 5 | Total income (add lines 3 and 4) . . . . . . . . . . . . . . . | 5 | 10,000,000 | 15,000,000 |
| 6 | Total deductions . . . . . . . . . . . . . . . . . . . . | 6 | 2,000,000 | 3,000,000 |
| 7 | Other adjustments . . . . . . . . . . . . . . . . . . . . | 7 | | |
| 8 | Net income (loss) per books . . . . . . . . . . . . . . . . . | 8 | 8,000,000 | 12,000,000 |

## Schedule C-1    Section 987 Gain or Loss Information

| | | | (a) Amount stated in functional currency of foreign disregarded entity | (b) Amount stated in functional currency of recipient |
|---|---|---|---|---|
| 1 | Remittances from the foreign disregarded entity . . . . . . . . . . . | 1 | 0 | |
| 2 | Section 987 gain (loss) of recipient . . . . . . . . . . . . . | 2 | | |

| | | Yes | No |
|---|---|---|---|
| 3 | Were all remittances from the foreign disregarded entity treated as made to the direct owner? . . . . . | | |
| 4 | Did the tax owner change its method of accounting for section 987 gain or loss with respect to remittances from the foreign disregarded entity during the tax year? . . . . . . . . . . . . . . . . . | | |

## Schedule F    Balance Sheet

**Important:** *Report all amounts in U.S. dollars computed in functional currency and translated into U.S. dollars in accordance with U.S. GAAP. See instructions for an exception for foreign disregarded entities that use DASTM.*

| Assets | | (a) Beginning of annual accounting period | (b) End of annual accounting period |
|---|---|---|---|
| 1  Cash and other current assets . . . . . . . . . . . . . . . . | 1 | | 47,100,000 |
| 2  Other assets . . . . . . . . . . . . . . . . . . . . . | 2 | | |
| 3  Total assets . . . . . . . . . . . . . . . . . . . . . | 3 | | 47,100,000 |
| **Liabilities and Owner's Equity** | | | |
| 4  Liabilities . . . . . . . . . . . . . . . . . . . . . . | 4 | | 22,500,000 |
| 5  Owner's equity . . . . . . . . . . . . . . . . . . . . | 5 | | 24,600,000 |
| 6  Total liabilities and owner's equity . . . . . . . . . . . . . . | 6 | | 47,100,000 |

## Schedule G    Other Information

| | | Yes | No |
|---|---|---|---|
| 1 | During the tax year, did the foreign disregarded entity own an interest in any trust? . . . . . . . . . | | ✓ |
| 2 | During the tax year, did the foreign disregarded entity own at least a 10% interest, directly or indirectly, in any foreign partnership? . . . . . . . . . . . . . . . . . . | | ✓ |
| 3 | *Answer the following question only if the foreign disregarded entity made its election to be treated as disregarded from its owner during the tax year:* Did the tax owner claim a loss with respect to stock or debt of the foreign disregarded entity as a result of the election? . . . . . . . . . . . . . . | | ✓ |
| 4 | If the interest in the foreign disregarded entity is a separate unit under Reg. 1.1503(d)-1(b)(4) or part of a combined separate unit under Reg. 1.1503(d)-1(b)(4)(ii) does the separate unit or combined separate unit have a dual consolidated loss as defined in Reg. 1.1503(d)-1(b)(5)(ii)? . . . . . . . . . . . . . If "Yes," enter the amount of the dual consolidated loss ▶ $          Answer question 5a. | | |

Form **8858** (Rev. 12-2012)

Form 8858 (Rev. 12-2012)  Page 3

| | | Yes | No |
|---|---|---|---|
| **Schedule G** | **Other Information** *(continued)* | | |
| 5a | Was any portion of the dual consolidated loss in question 4 taken into account in computing consolidated taxable income for the year? If "Yes," go to 5b. If "No," skip 5b and 5c . . . . . . . . . . . | | |
| b | Was this a permitted domestic use of the dual consolidated loss under Reg. 1.1503(d)-6? If "Yes," see instructions and skip 5c. If "No," go to 5c . . . . . . . . . . . . . . . . . . . . . . . | | |
| c | If this was not a permitted domestic use, was the dual consolidated loss used to compute consolidated taxable income as provided under Reg. 1.1503(d)-4? . . . . . . . . . . . . . . . . . . | | |
| | If "Yes," enter the separate unit's contribution to the cumulative consolidated taxable income ("cumulative register") as of the beginning of the tax year ▶ $ _____ See instructions. | | |
| 6 | During the tax year, did the foreign disregarded entity pay or accrue any foreign tax that was disqualified for credit under section 901(m)? . . . . . . . . . . . . . . . . . . . . . . . . | | |
| 7 | During the tax year, did the foreign disregarded entity pay or accrue foreign taxes to which section 909 applies, or treat foreign taxes that were previously suspended under section 909 as no longer suspended? | | |
| 8 | *Answer the following question only if the tax owner of the foreign disregarded entity is a controlled foreign corporation (CFC):* Were there any intracompany transactions between the foreign disregarded entity and the CFC or any other branch of the CFC during the tax year, in which the foreign disregarded entity acted as a manufacturing, selling, or purchasing branch? . . . . . . . . . . . . . . . . . . | | |

| **Schedule H** | **Current Earnings and Profits or Taxable Income** (see instructions) | | |
|---|---|---|---|

**Important:** *Enter the amounts on lines 1 through 6 in functional currency.*

| | | | |
|---|---|---|---|
| 1 | Current year net income or (loss) per foreign books of account . . . . . . . . . . . . . | 1 | 8,000,000 |
| 2 | Total net additions . . . . . . . . . . . . . . . . . . . . . . . . . . . . | 2 | |
| 3 | Total net subtractions . . . . . . . . . . . . . . . . . . . . . . . . . . . | 3 | |
| 4 | Current earnings and profits (or taxable income—see instructions) (line 1 plus line 2 minus line 3) . . | 4 | 8,000,000 |
| 5 | DASTM gain or loss (if applicable) . . . . . . . . . . . . . . . . . . . . . . | 5 | |
| 6 | Combine lines 4 and 5. . . . . . . . . . . . . . . . . . . . . . . . . . . | 6 | |
| 7 | Current earnings and profits (or taxable income) in U.S. dollars (line 6 translated at the average exchange rate determined under section 989(b) and the related regulations (see instructions)) . . . Enter exchange rate used for line 7 ▶ | 7 | 8,000,000 |

Form **8858** (Rev. 12-2012)

## Figure 10.20. Filled-in Form 8858

# STUDY QUESTIONS

5. Foreign tax credits are available to which of the following types of organizations?

   a. C corporations

   b. S corporations

   c. LLCs

   d. Partnerships

6. Which of the following forms is used for transfer pricing audits and includes four filing categories?

   a. Form 8832

   b. Form 1065

   c. Form 1042

   d. Form 8865

**CPE NOTE:** When you have completed your study and review of chapters 9-10, which comprise Module 3, you may wish to take the Final Exam for this Module. Go to **cchcpelink.com/printcpe** to take this Final Exam online.

¶1010

# ¶ 10,100 Answers to Study Questions
## ¶ 10,101 MODULE 1—CHAPTER 1

**1. a.** *Incorrect.* In 1997, the median home price was $146,000.

**b.** *Incorrect.* The earlier version of Section 121 allowed for a one-time gain exclusion of $125,000.

**c.** *Incorrect.* The average gain on sale of a principal residence in the U.S. could not be $500,000 in 1997 as the median home price was only $146,000.

**d.** *Correct.* **No reason was specified in the** *Taxpayer Relief Act of 1997* **for the exclusion dollar amount.**

**2. a.** *Incorrect.* Sleeping space is not enough; it must also have cooking and toilet facilities.

**b.** *Incorrect.* It must have at least sleeping, cooking and toilet facilities.

**c.** *Incorrect.* Cooking and bathroom facilities are not enough; it must also have sleeping facilities.

**d.** *Correct.* **The boat or structure must have eating, sleeping, and toilet facilities.**

**3. a.** *Incorrect.* There is no rule that allows Henry to treat his father's use of the home as Henry's use of the home.

**b.** *Correct.* **Looking back five years from the date of sale, Henry only used the home for 18 months, not 24.**

**c.** *Incorrect.* A taxpayer may elect not to use Section 121, but there is no election to allow Henry to use the Section 121 exclusion and he does not meet the 24 months use in the prior 5 years requirement.

**d.** *Incorrect.* Henry's father may not claim the gain exclusion because he does not own the home. The gain from sale is taxable to Henry, the owner.

**4. a.** *Incorrect.* If the portion of the home used for business is not a separate structure; no allocation is needed.

**b.** *Correct.* **No allocation of the basis and selling price is needed, but Jane may not exclude the portion of the gain equal to the depreciation claimed on the home.**

**c.** *Incorrect.* The portion of the gain representing depreciation claimed is not excluded under Section 121.

**d.** *Incorrect.* Use of a portion of the home for a home office is not considered nonqualified use under Section 121.

**5. a.** *Incorrect.* 15 months abroad is not a temporary absence per Reg. Section 1.121-1(c)(2)(i).

**b.** *Correct.* **The 24 months of use need not be consecutive.**

**c.** *Incorrect.* The 18 months of prior use counts towards the 24 months of ownership and use needed to qualify for the Section 121 gain exclusion.

**d.** *Incorrect.* There is not special exception to the 24 months use requirement for travel abroad.

**6. a.** *Incorrect.* Although this meets the Section 121(c) exception to the 24-month ownership and use requirement, it is not only possible answer from the list of answers.

**b.** *Incorrect.* Although this meets the Section 121(c) exception to the 24-month ownership and use requirement, it is not only possible answer from the list of answers.

**c.** *Incorrect.* Although this meets the Section 121(c) exception to the 24-month ownership and use requirement, it is not only possible answer from the list of answers.

**d.** *Incorrect.* Although this meets the Section 121(c) exception to the 24-month ownership and use requirement, it is not only possible answer from the list of answers.

**e.** *Incorrect.* Although these fact patterns meet the Section 121(c) exception to the 24-month ownership and use requirement, they are the not only possible answers from the list of answers.

**f.** *Correct.* **All of these fact patterns meet the Section 121(c) and Reg. Section 1.121-3(b) exception to the 24-month ownership and use requirement.**

# ¶ 10,102 MODULE 1—CHAPTER 2

**1. a.** *Correct.* **A separate tax identification number must be obtained for the estate by filing Form SS-4 with the IRS. This form is used to apply for an employer identification number (EIN). An EIN is a nine-digit number assigned to employers, sole proprietors, corporations, partnerships, estates, trusts, certain individuals, and other entities for tax filing and reporting purposes.**

**b.** *Incorrect.* A form SS-5 is not submitted to the Internal Revenue Service in order to obtain a separate tax identification number for an estate. Instead, this form is used to apply for a Social Security card.

**c.** *Incorrect.* A form SS-8 is not submitted to the IRS in order to obtain a separate tax identification number for an estate. Instead, this form relates to the determination of worker status for purposes of federal employment taxes and income tax withholding.

**d.** *Incorrect.* A form W-7 is not submitted to the IRS in order to obtain a separate tax identification number for an estate. Instead, this form is used by an individual taxpayer to obtain a federal identification number.

**2. a.** *Incorrect.* Form 1041 is due on the fifteenth day of the fourth month following the close of the tax year. An estate may obtain an automatic extension of time to file Form 1041 by using Form 7004; however, the extension is not for three months. The extension is for a longer period of time.

**b.** *Correct.* **The due date of Form 1041 is the fifteenth day of the fourth month following the close of the tax year. An estate may obtain an automatic five-and-a-half-month extension of time to file Form 1041 by using Form 7004.**

**c.** *Incorrect.* Form 1041 is due on the fifteenth day of the fourth month following the close of the tax year. However, an estate may obtain an automatic extension of time to file Form 1041 by using Form 7004. However, the extension is not for six months but is instead for a different period of time.

**d.** *Incorrect.* An estate may obtain an automatic extension of time to file Form 1041 by using Form 7004. Form 1041 is due on the fifteenth day of the fourth month following the close of the tax year. The automatic extension of time granted based on Form 7004 is not nine months, but is instead a shorter period of time.

**3. a. *Incorrect.*** A complex trust is not another term for a grantor trust. The terms of a complex trust allow the trustee in its discretion to either pay or to withhold or accumulate current trust income so that it is not required to pay income currently to the beneficiary.

**b. *Incorrect.*** A simple trust is not another term for a grantor trust. The terms of a simple trust require that all income to be distributed currently and the trustee may not withhold or accumulate the trust income.

**c. *Incorrect.*** A revocable trust is not another term for a grantor trust. A revocable trust is a trust whereby provisions can be altered or canceled dependent on the grantor. During the life of the trust, income earned is distributed to the grantor, and only after death does property transfer to the beneficiaries.

**d. *Correct.* A grantor trust is also commonly referred to as a living trust. This type of trust is also referred to as *inter vivos* trusts, created by a person for his or her own use and benefit. For these types of trusts, the grantor will be taxed on the trust income, and the trust is disregarded as a separate taxable entity for federal income tax purposes.**

**4. a. *Incorrect.*** Once the Section 645 election has been made, an electing trust may select a fiscal year rather than a calendar year.

**b. *Incorrect.*** An electing trust may claim a $600 (not $1,000) annual exemption and be entitled to deduct up to $25,000 (not $15,000) in real estate passive losses.

**c. *Correct.* The electing trust may hold S corporation stock in accordance with the broader rules allowing estates generally, but not all trusts, to be S corporation shareholders.**

**d. *Incorrect.*** Once the qualified revocable trust election is made, only one Form 1041 need be filed, rather than separate returns for the trust and the estate.

**5. a. *Correct.* This is the exemption amount for complex trusts. The exemption amount for simple trusts and estates is $300 and $600, respectively.**

**b. *Incorrect.*** This is not the exemption amount for complex trusts. Instead, this is the exemption amount for simple trusts.

**c. *Incorrect.*** This is not the exemption amount for complex trusts. Instead, this is the exemption amount for an estate.

**d. *Incorrect.*** This is not the exemption amount for complex trusts. This figure represents the annual net capital loss deduction limitation against ordinary income.

**6. a. *Incorrect.*** This is not the maximum amount of charitable donations that can be deducted against gross income for a trust or estate. This amount represents the threshold for AGI of an estate when special rules apply with respect to estimated tax payments.

**b. *Incorrect.*** This is not the maximum amount of charitable donations that can be deducted against gross income for a trust or estate. This amount is used in the analysis of the maximum tax rate applied to long-term capital gains and qualified dividends.

**c. *Incorrect.*** This is not the maximum amount of charitable donations that can be deducted against gross income for a trust or estate. This amount relates to estimated tax payments. No estimated tax payments are required from a trust if the balance of tax due is less than $1,000 or the trust had no tax liability for the preceding tax year.

**d. *Correct.* Trusts and estates may claim an unlimited charitable deduction against their gross income. The governing instrument (will or trust) must provide specifically for the charitable contribution in order for the deduction to be available.**

# ¶ 10,103 MODULE 1—CHAPTER 3

**1. a.** *Correct.* **When your client dies, you should apply for a federal identification number for the estate as soon as possible using Form SS-4. This form is referred to as the Application for Employer Identification Number and is available on the IRS website.**

**b.** *Incorrect.* Form 56 is not the form that is used to apply for a federal tax identification number for an estate. Instead, Form 56 relates to the notice concerning the fiduciary relationship.

Form 1040.

**c.** *Incorrect.* Form 1040 is not the form that is used to apply for a federal tax identification number for an estate. Instead, Form 1040 is one of three IRS tax forms used for personal (individual) federal income tax returns filed with the IRS by United States residents for tax purposes.

**d.** *Incorrect.* Form 706 is not the form that is used to apply for a federal tax identification number for an estate. Instead, Form 706 is the *United States Estate (and Generation-Skipping Transfer) Tax Return.*

**2. a.** *Incorrect.* Income through the date of the death should be included in the return. It's important to note that the final income tax return is due on April 15th of the year following the death.

**b.** *Correct.* **Deductible expenses include state and local income tax. Additionally, property taxes as well as certain business expenditures are considered deductible as well.**

**c.** *Incorrect.* Deductions appropriate through date of death include those that are both actually and constructively received. Additionally, it's also important to note that the final tax year ends with the date of the death.

**d.** *Incorrect.* A court appointed executor, administrator or personal representative is responsible for filing the decedent's final income tax return, and signs for the decedent. A surviving spouse which has not remarried and if no personal representative has been appointed by the due date for filing the decedent's income tax return should file a joint return.

**3. a.** *Incorrect.* Payments for wages and salaries received after death are not included on the final 1040. Instead, these are included on Form 1041. Only payments received prior to death are included on the final 1040.

**b.** *Incorrect.* Payments of retirement plan distributions received after death are not included on the final 1040. Instead, these are included on Form 1041. Only payments received prior to death are included on the final 1040.

**c.** *Incorrect.* It's important to note that death is not a disposition of an installment obligation. As a result, unrealized gains related to installment sales should not be included on the final 1040.

**d.** *Correct.* **There are special rules as it relates to trust income received by a decedent. Only actual distributions of trust income received by the decedent through the date of death are included in the final 1040.**

**4. a.** *Correct.* This election is made by completing Form 1041-T and filing within 65 days after the end of the trust's taxable year. This election applies to estimated taxes paid by the trust for any tax year and by the estate only in its final year.

**b.** *Incorrect.* An estate has the option of choosing to report its income on a fiscal reporting year, so long as the year ends on the last (not first) day of a month.

**c.** *Incorrect.* If no estate tax return is filed for the decedent's estate, this election applies for two (not three) years from the date of the decedent's death.

**d.** *Incorrect.* Estates and trusts may elect to treat all or part of distributions made to beneficiaries within the first 65 days (not 45 days) of the taxable year as if they were paid on the last day of the preceding taxable year.

**5. a.** *Incorrect.* In order for a disclaimer to be a qualified disclaimer, it must be in writing. Additionally, Code Sec. 2518 also requires that the disclaimer be signed as well.

Must identify the interest disclaimed.

**b.** *Incorrect.* In order for a disclaimer to be a qualified disclaimer, it must identify the interest disclaimed. It's also important to note that the nine-month period with respect to a qualified disclaimer commences with the transfer creating the interest.

**c.** *Correct.* **In order for a disclaimer to be a qualified disclaimer, it must be, in addition to several other requirements, both unqualified and irrevocable. Additionally, it must be in writing, signed, and must identify the interest disclaimed.**

**d.** *Incorrect.* In order for a disclaimer to be a qualified disclaimer, it must be delivered to the personal representative of the estate or to the transferor of the property or to the holder of legal title to the property within nine months after the creation of the instrument

**6. a.** *Correct.* **The alternate valuation date election is irrevocable once made. It's also important to note that for assets sold or distributed after the decedent's date of death and before the six-month alternate date, the value used is the value of the asset on the date of sale or distribution.**

**b.** *Incorrect.* An estate has the option to report the value of the decedent's assets as of the date of death or as of the date that is six months (not nine months) after the decedent's date of death.

**c.** *Incorrect.* In order for the alternate valuation date election to be used, the gross estate must decrease (not increase) in value and the combined estate and generation-skipping tax liability must decrease (not increase) as the result of making the election.

**d.** *Incorrect.* The alternative valuation date election must be made by checking a box on Form 706 (not Form 1040) and completing the Form indicating the alternate valuation information where appropriate.

# ¶ 10,104 MODULE 1—CHAPTER 4

**1. a.** *Correct.* **Closely held C corporations, not closely held S corporations, are included within the scope of the passive activity loss rules. For a closely held C corporation, when it becomes a non-closely held corporation, the suspended losses cannot shelter portfolio income but may offset active income in non-closely held corporation years.**

**b.** *Incorrect.* Individuals are included within the scope of the passive activity loss rules. An additional example of a taxpayer that is included within the scope of these rules are personal service corporations.

**c. *Incorrect.*** Trusts are included within the scope of the passive activity loss rules. A trust is a fiduciary relationship in which one party, known as a trustor, gives another party, the trustee, the right to hold title to property or assets for the benefit of a third party, the beneficiary.

**d. *Incorrect.*** Estates are included within the scope of the passive activity loss rules. An additional example of a taxpayer that is included within the scope of these rules are closely held C corporations.

**2. a. *Incorrect.*** The test of material participation with respect to substantially all participation is not difficult to satisfy. This test is based on hours worked and is generally an affirmative test that a taxpayer attempts to satisfy.

**b. *Correct.* Regular, continuous, substantial involvement is one of the seven tests with respect to material participation. This test is based on statute and is very difficult to satisfy.**

**c. *Incorrect.*** The test of material participation with respect to material participation in any three preceding years is a type of test based on prior participation and is an anti-abuse rule. It is not difficult to satisfy.

**d. *Incorrect.*** The test of material participation with respect to more than 100 hours and not less than anyone else is not difficult to satisfy. This test is based on hours worked and is generally an affirmative test that a taxpayer attempts to satisfy.

**3. a. *Correct.* The more than 100 hours and not less than anyone else test of material participation is not used by limited partners. Instead, the three tests used by limited partners include the 500 hour test (test 1), the 5 of 10 years test (test 5), and the any three years test (test 6).**

**b. *Incorrect.*** The more than 500 hours test can be used by a limited partner to establish material participation. This test is based on hours worked and is generally an affirmative test a taxpayer attempts to satisfy.

**c. *Incorrect.*** The material participation in 5 of the preceding 10 years test can be used by a limited partner to establish material participation. This is a type of test based on prior participation and is an antiabuse rule.

**d. *Incorrect.*** The material participation in any three preceding years test can be used by a limited partner to establish material participation. This is a type of test based on prior participation and is an antiabuse rule.

**4. a. *Incorrect.*** This is a case in which the taxpayer prevailed, not the IRS. While the taxpayer claimed more than 1,200 hours based on a description of activities and time estimates, the tax court did not accept all of his time estimates but believed he spent greater than 500 hours.

**b. *Incorrect.*** This is a case in which the taxpayer prevailed, not the IRS. In this case, the taxpayer owned and managed seven rentals and had a detailed log book with activities entered after the fact. While the evidence was inconsistent as to whether the log book was contemporaneously prepared, the tax court accepted the log book as it was detailed and there was no requirement that it be kept contemporaneously.

**c. *Incorrect.*** This is a case in which the taxpayer prevailed, not the IRS. In this case, the taxpayer was an airline pilot who had a side business chartering boats in the British Virgin Islands. The taxpayer prevailed based on the court's assessment of Test 3 with respect to material participation.

**d. *Correct.* This is a case in which the IRS prevailed. In this case, the taxpayer bought a sailboat while living in Dallas and his employer moved him to Connecticut. The taxpayer failed to substantiate material participation as hours were not well documented as after the fact estimates were primarily used.**

¶10,104

**5. a.** *Correct.* **This is an example of a case where a taxpayer prevailed. In this case, a sole practitioner attorney was involved in both horse racing and breeding on the side. Based on the evidence provided, the tax court concluded that the hours spent in various activities satisfied the material participation requirement.**

**b.** *Incorrect.* This is a case in which the IRS prevailed, not the taxpayer. In this case, the taxpayer bought a sailboat while living in Dallas and his employer moved him to Connecticut. The taxpayer failed to substantiate material participation as hours were not well documented as after the fact estimates were primarily used.

**c.** *Incorrect.* This is a case in which the IRS prevailed, not the taxpayer. In this case, a controlling shareholder of the Home Shopping Network was involved in various family-owned businesses, three of which were loss-generating businesses. Based on the narrative summary and no other records provided, the court ruled in favor of the IRS noting that the taxpayer's narrative summary was nothing but a post-event ballpark guesstimate.

**d.** *Incorrect.* This is a case in which the IRS prevailed, not the taxpayer. In this case, the president of a heating and A/C company did not adjust the time spend on his activities until 6 to 7 years later when preparing for trail. Although the taxpayer had four rental properties and claimed >750 hours, there was no proof because his records were after the fact ballpark guesstimates.

**6. a.** *Correct.* **Written evidence being more credible is one of the key lessons learned with respect to the cases presented. An additional lesson learned is that logs of activities without precise time allocations are not very helpful.**

**b.** *Incorrect.* One of the lessons learned is that a taxpayer is not required to keep contemporaneous time log of passive activity. However, it is noted that a contemporaneous record of time is a very good idea.

**c.** *Incorrect.* Typical taxpayers will re-create time and activity logs when the issue is raised instead of proactively keeping time and activity logs. However, there can be certain exceptions to the above when some other supporting evidence can be used to corroborate the after the fact time and activity records.

**d.** *Incorrect.* Having a full-time job actually makes it more difficult, not easier, to support the significant time in other activities. Additionally, it is a good idea to have the specific activities identified in addition to simply the time spent on those activities.

# ¶ 10,105 MODULE 1—CHAPTER 5

**1. a.** *Incorrect.* There are no FICA or FUTA taxes on payments to independent contractors.

**b.** *Incorrect.* Typically, a company does not pay for health coverage, retirement savings, or other fringe benefits for independent contractors.

**c.** *Correct.* **The hourly rate for an independent contractor typically runs higher than the rate for a comparable employee.**

**d.** *Incorrect.* Typically, independent contractors work from their homes.

**2. a.** *Correct.* **The amount of hours worked is not factored in the determination of worker classification.**

**b.** *Incorrect.* Behavioral control is vital in determining whether or not the worker is an employee.

**c.** *Incorrect.* Financial control, as evidenced by who pays for expenses, is vital in determining worker classification.

**d.** *Incorrect.* The relationship of the parties is important to deciding whether the worker is an employee or contractor; the belief of one party is indicative of worker classification.

**3. a.** *Incorrect.* There is no evidence to suggest that claiming a home office deduction will likely lead to an audit.

**b.** *Incorrect.* A home office can be a part of a room; no partition is needed.

**c.** *Correct.* **A home office is treated as a principal place of business as long as it is used for substantial administrative activities, such as bookkeeping, and the space is used regularly and exclusively for this purpose.**

**d.** *Incorrect.* No deduction can be claimed here because the room is not used exclusively for business.

**4. a.** *Incorrect.* It is true self-employment tax must be included with income tax and other taxes for estimated tax purposes.

**b.** *Correct.* **The deduction is claimed as an adjustment to gross income, not as a business expense.**

**c.** *Incorrect.* Because there is no wage base for the Medicare portion of self-employment tax, all net earnings are subject to this tax.

**d.** *Incorrect.* A worker with low net earnings can opt to use the optional method to pay self-employment tax that would otherwise not be owed; this creates Social Security benefits.

**5. a.** *Correct.* **According to the IRS this is not a substantial service provided for the benefit of tenants.**

**b.** *Incorrect.* Regular cleaning of the home, the unit, or the portion rented out is treated as a substantial service.

**c.** *Incorrect.* A substantial service provided for the benefit of tenants is changing the linens.

**d.** *Incorrect.* The IRS lists maid service as a substantial service.

**6. a.** *Incorrect.* Although it does not usually apply to rentals within the sharing economy, it could apply.

**b.** *Incorrect.* The PAL rules limit losses to the extent of passive activity income unless an exception applies.

**c.** *Incorrect.* This rule acts to limit rental expenses and dictates the order in which they are claimed.

**d.** *Correct.* **Although zoning rules may restrict whether a taxpayer can have short-term rentals, they has no bearing on deducting rental losses.**

# ¶ 10,106 MODULE 2—CHAPTER 6

**1. a.** *Correct.* Code Sec. 179 allows a taxpayer to elect to deduct the cost of certain types of property on its income taxes as an expense, rather than requiring the cost of the property to be capitalized and depreciated over its useful life. This property is generally limited to tangible, depreciable, personal property which is acquired by an accounting purchase for use in the active conduct of a trade or business.

**b.** *Incorrect.* Code Sec. 121 does not relate to the immediate expensing of purchases of qualifying equipment. Instead, Code Sec. 121 relates to the exclusion of gains from the sale of a taxpayer's principal residence.

**c.** *Incorrect.* Code Sec. 368 does not relate to the immediate expensing of purchases of qualifying equipment. Instead, Code Sec. 368 relates to definitions related to corporate reorganizations.

**d.** *Incorrect.* Code Sec. 1031 does not relate to the immediate expensing of purchases of qualifying equipment. Instead, Code Sec. 1031 relates to an exception and allows a taxpayer to postpone paying tax on the gain on a sale of property if the taxpayer reinvest the proceeds in similar property as part of a qualifying like-kind exchange.

**2. a.** *Incorrect.* Equipment purchased for business use does qualify for a Code Sec. 179 deduction. An example of property that does not qualify for a Code Sec. 179 deduction is any property that is not considered to be personal property.

**b.** *Incorrect.* Office furniture does qualify for a Code Sec. 179 deduction. An example of property that does not qualify for a Code Sec. 179 deduction is property purchased from related parties.

**c.** *Correct.* **Property used outside the United States does not qualify for a Code Sec. 179 deduction. An additional example of property that does not qualify for a Code Sec. 179 deduction is property acquired by gift or inheritance.**

**d.** *Incorrect.* Tangible personal property used in business does qualify for a Code Sec. 179 deduction. An additional example of property that does qualify for a Code Sec. 179 deduction is computers as well as computer off-the-shelf software.

**3. a.** *Incorrect.* The requirements prescribed by Code Sec. 168(k) related to bonus depreciation only apply to new tangible personal property. As a result, they do not apply to used property.

**b.** *Correct.* **The bonus depreciation outlined in Code Sec. 168(k) may be used in combination with Code Sec. 179. If using both, a taxpayer should use Code Sec. 179 first, then Code Sec. 168(k) will automatically apply to 50 percent of the remaining basis.**

**c.** *Incorrect.* There is not a $1,000,000 limitation on the amount of property placed in service. In fact, there is no limitation on the amount of property placed in service or the amount of the deduction.

**d.** *Incorrect.* A taxpayer is not required to elect bonus depreciation. It applies automatically unless a taxpayer elects out. This is different than Code Sec. 179, where a taxpayer is required to make this election.

**4. a.** *Correct.* **In this case, the taxpayer incurred significant legal and investment banking fees to fend off a hostile takeover attempt. The fees were large amounts and the taxpayer deducted them in the year incurred which was challenged by the IRS.**

**b.** *Incorrect.* The *AmeriSouth* case did not relate to the capitalization of certain large, one-time fees. Instead, this case related to a situation where the Tax Court limited the scope of certain deductions for new buildings. This was common in early 2000s because of big depreciation advantages given to tangible personal property over real estate.

**c.** *Incorrect.* The *Pecos Foods* case did not relate to the capitalization of certain large, one-time fees. Instead, this case related to a situation where the Tax Court limited the scope of certain deductions or new buildings. This was an example of a company that had aggressively claimed everything as tangible personal property rather than real property.

**d.** *Incorrect.* The *Zaninovich* case did not relate to the capitalization of certain large, one-time fees. Instead, this case related to the concept of "substantially" beyond and held that substantially beyond the taxable year means not more than 12 months beyond the taxable year. While not clear from the case, most commentators think this means 12 months beyond the end of the taxable year in which the expenditure is made.

**5. a.** *Incorrect.* The requirements of IRC Code Sec. 263A apply to tangible personal property produced by the taxpayer. In addition, these requirements also apply to real property produced by the taxpayer.

**b.** *Correct.* **Certain farm use property with various requirements is prescribed as an exception to the requirements of Code Sec. 263A. An additional exception to these requirements is producers of property with gross receipts of $10M or less during the last three years. However, this exception does not apply to resellers.**

**c.** *Incorrect.* The requirements of Code Sec. 263A apply to real property acquired by the taxpayer for resale. In addition, these requirements also apply to personal property acquired by the taxpayer for resale.

**d.** *Incorrect.* The requirements of Code Sec. 263A apply to producers of property with gross receipts of $20M or less during the last four years. However, they do not apply to producers of property with gross receipts of $10M or less during the last three years, with the exception of resellers.

**6. a.** *Correct.* **Expenditures that restore property to its operating state are classified as a deductible repair. Alternatively, expenditures that provide permanent improvement in life or value of the property are generally capitalized and recovered through depreciation over time.**

**b.** *Incorrect.* Direct raw material costs are not deductible in the current period, but are instead capitalized. Additional examples of types of costs that should be capitalized are purchasing and storage costs.

**c.** *Incorrect.* Engineering and design costs are not deductible in the current period, but are instead capitalized. Additional examples of types of costs that should be capitalized are wages, salaries, employee benefits, and payroll taxes.

**d.** *Incorrect.* Expenditures that provide permanent improvement in value of property are generally not deductible in the current period, but are instead capitalized. Additional examples of types of costs that should be capitalized are rent, utilities, insurance, taxes, and royalty payments.

# ¶ 10,107 MODULE 2—CHAPTER 7

**1. a.** *Incorrect.* The issuance of a new debt instrument should be reviewed to determine if it is actually debt or if it may be equity; and if it is equity, can it be classified as a second class of stock (which would affect the corporation's S eligibility).

**b.** *Incorrect.* Changes to the capital structure could potentially create a second class of stock, which would have a detrimental effect on the S status of the corporation.

**c.** *Incorrect.* S corporation shareholders have an equal right to distributions of the corporation. When distributions are disproportionate, the corporation could be considered to have a second class of stock and risk its S status.

**d.** *Correct.* **The concern with restricted stock is whether the shareholder made a Section 83(b) election, in which case the eligibility of the shareholder would need to be verified; but as long as the risk of forfeiture remains, the restricted stock is not considered when determining if the corporation potentially has more than one class of stock.**

**2. a.** *Incorrect.* Although it is true that if the shareholder has already reached the dollar-limitation he or she would not be able to use the S corporation's Section 179 expense election (the limitation does not allow for a deduction from other sources to increase the individual limitation), other factors affect the benefit to the shareholder.

**b.** *Incorrect.* It is correct that the Section 179 deduction is limited by the shareholder's taxable business income (if the taxable business income is zero, the shareholder would not be able to benefit from the S corporation's election to claim the deduction), but more factors affect the deduction for the shareholder.

**c.** *Incorrect.* In order to benefit from a Section 179 expense election, the shareholder must be actively involved (meaningfully participate) in the trade or business for which the S corporation is claiming the Section 179 deduction. Although this answer is correct, the benefit of the deduction is affected by other factors.

**d.** *Correct.* **A shareholder may not claim the Section 179 deduction passed through from the S corporation if the shareholder has already reached the Section 179 dollar-limitation or has no taxable business income, making the first two responses correct. Even if these restrictions did not apply, the shareholder has to have meaningfully participated in the trade or business for which the S corporation is claiming the Section 179 deduction to be able to claim the deduction as an individual, making the third response correct as well.**

**3. a.** *Incorrect.* The S corporation must attach a statement showing the income or loss for each passive activity. This reporting burden is greater if the activities are not aggregated.

**b.** *Correct.* **Shareholders can aggregate passive activities but they cannot disaggregate them. By not aggregating the activities, the S corporation allows the shareholders flexibility to aggregate in a way that is most beneficial to them individually.**

**c.** *Incorrect.* The net investment income tax applies to passive investment income and can be reduced if the S corporation does not aggregate passive activities, allowing the shareholders to aggregate the activities in a way that mitigates their individual passive income; however, allowing the shareholders to aggregate the activities does not eliminate the application of the net investment income tax altogether.

**d.** *Incorrect.* S corporations are not subject to the passive activity loss rules; these rules apply at the shareholder level.

**4. a.** *Incorrect.* The AAA allows a tax-free distribution of shareholder basis in the S corporation during the post-termination transition period (PTTP) after an S corporation transitions to a C corporation. Through the AAA, the shareholders prove distributions of basis are from the earnings of the former S corporation and not from the earnings of the C corporation, which makes it necessary for the S corporation to have an AAA in this scenario.

**b.** *Correct.* **The effect of tax-exempt income and expenses on the shareholder's basis is reflected through an 'other adjustments' account, not an AAA. Therefore, it is not necessary for an S corporation to have an AAA in this scenario, although is it recommended to maintain an AAA in case the S corporation acquires future earnings and profits.**

**c.** *Incorrect.* When making a QSub election, the S corporation acquires the C corporation's earnings and profits. Having an AAA allows the S corporation to determine how to tax distributions after the acquisition. If the distribution is from the AAA, it is taxed under S corporation rules, if the distribution is earnings and profits, it is taxed under the C corporation rules. It is necessary to have an AAA in this scenario so the shareholders can receive a tax-free return of basis in the S corporation.

**d.** *Incorrect.* If an S corporation has earnings and profits, an AAA must exist to determine the tax effect of distributions to the S corporation's shareholders. Any distributions from the AAA are tax-free to the extent of the shareholder's basis, with any amount in excess of basis being subject to capital gains tax; whereas distributions of the earnings and profits will have to follow the tax rules of the c-corporation.

**5. a.** *Incorrect.* When a partnership distributes property, the distribution is not treated as a sale and there is no tax effect to the partnership (the partnership does not recognize a gain); whereas when an S corporation distributes property, it is treated as a sale of the property at fair market value (FMV) to the shareholders, the gain is recognized on the S-corporation's tax return and passed through to the shareholders.

**b.** *Incorrect.* S corporations follow an entity-type of approach in regard to taxation whereas partnerships use an aggregate approach. S corporations, for the most part, follow the same tax rules as C corporations because they are respected as a separate entity while partnership taxation disregards the entity and looks to the underlying partners.

**c.** *Incorrect.* Cancellation of debt (COD) income and applicable exclusions are applied at the entity level for S corporations (any exclusion from COD income is not a taxable event to the shareholders); whereas a partnership does not realize Section 108 exclusions. The COD income is passed through to the partners and the individual partners determine whether or not they qualify for exclusion.

**d.** *Correct.* **S corporations and partnerships both use Schedule K to summarize the information that will be included on the Schedule K-1 for each shareholder or partner, respectively.**

**6. a.** *Correct.* **Making distributions from the S corporation's earnings and profits that are related to passive investments can reduce the S corporation's passive investment income to below the tax threshold (more than 25 percent of gross receipts).**

**b.** *Incorrect.* Stocks and securities are not considered passive investment income, but if sold for a gain, the gain is included in gross receipts; therefore, it would reduce the passive investment income to gross receipts ratio (and reduce the likelihood of paying passive investment income tax), if stocks and securities were sold that would generate a gain, not a loss.

**c.** *Incorrect.* Interest income is passive income and any increase to passive income results in a greater likelihood of paying the passive investment income tax.

**d.** *Incorrect.* Income generated from rental property that has significant (beyond normal) costs is not considered passive investment income; the income is included in gross receipts. Keeping the property would reduce the S corporation's PII to gross receipts ratio and reduce the likelihood of paying passive investment income tax. Divesting of the property would lower the S corporation's gross receipts and increase the likelihood of paying PII tax.

# ¶ 10,108 MODULE 2—CHAPTER 8

**1. a. *Correct.* Each of the three categories is required to be reported because they separately affect a partner's basis and at-risk basis.**

**b. *Incorrect.*** It is also necessary to distinguish the type of nonrecourse debt that will increase at-risk basis.

**c. *Incorrect.*** Debt issued by third-party lenders is reported on the Schedule K-1.

**d. *Incorrect.*** A debt guarantee may affect the classification of debt, but it is not the only type of debt that is reported.

**2. a. *Incorrect.*** The distinction between distributions and guaranteed payments is often difficult to distinguish.

**b. *Correct.* Guaranteed payments are those determined without regard to income and can be made for both capital and services.**

**c. *Incorrect.*** Preferences returns and guaranteed payments are not the same thing.

**d. *Incorrect.*** Distributions are reported in the capital account reconciliation but guaranteed payments are separately reported.

**3. a. *Incorrect.*** A partner loss would create a negative Code Sec. 734 adjustment.

**b. *Incorrect.*** If the basis to the partner is more than it was to the partnership, a negative adjustment would result.

**c. *Incorrect.*** No adjustment is made if the basis is exactly equal to a carryover from the partnership.

**d. *Correct.* Gain recognition by the partner is one of two situations that lead to a positive Code Sec. 734 adjustment.**

**4. a. *Correct.* The source of deductions determines their status as recourse or nonrecourse, and nonrecourse deductions are sourced to nonrecourse debt.**

**b. *Incorrect.*** Allocations of nonrecourse deductions cannot have economic effect.

**c. *Incorrect.*** Nonrecourse deductions may be allocated by agreement if certain conditions are satisfied.

**d. *Incorrect.*** The allocations of nonrecourse deductions may differ from the allocations of recourse deductions.

**5. a. *Incorrect.*** A hypothetical sale is not made at tax basis.

**b. *Correct.* Target allocations are based on a hypothetical sale of assets at book value followed by a hypothetical liquidation of the partnership.**

**c. *Incorrect.*** There is no assumption that tax basis relates to the value of assets in any way.

**d. *Incorrect.*** These assumptions are used to determine debt shares, not target allocations.

6. a. *Incorrect.* Partnerships do not recognize gain or loss from a distribution.

b. *Correct.* **Based on the tax result to the partner, there are four situations that can lead to a Code Sec. 734 adjustment to the partnership.**

c. *Incorrect.* Partners may recognize gain or loss from specific distribution situations.

d. *Incorrect.* Property usually takes a carryover basis from the partnership but not in all situations.

# ¶ 10,109 MODULE 3—CHAPTER 9

1. a. *Correct.* **The foreign tax credit is limited by the amount of precredit U.S. tax on foreign-source income; therefore, the U.S. person will need adequate income from foreign sources to be able to credit any foreign taxes paid.**

b. *Incorrect.* The sourcing rules do prevent U.S. income from being taxed by a foreign country, making the foreign country's tax rate irrelevant to the importance of sourcing income.

c. *Incorrect.* Foreign countries are not required to comply with U.S. sourcing rules; therefore, income allocated to U.S. sources can still be taxed by a foreign country.

d. *Incorrect.* There is a limitation to the foreign tax credit for the purpose of not allowing foreign tax paid to offset U.S.-source income. Even though Congress has ceded primary taxing jurisdiction to the foreign country, the limitation was imposed to prevent ceding more jurisdiction that would allow foreign tax to offset U.S. tax on U.S. source income.

2. a. *Correct.* **The foreign tax credit has a limitation of pre-credit foreign-source income multiplied by the U.S. tax rate. If the allocation of expenses eliminates the foreign-source income, the taxpayer cannot take the foreign tax credit for any foreign tax paid and would still need to pay U.S. tax on the foreign-source income, resulting in double taxation.**

b. *Incorrect.* The taxpayer will be able to claim the foreign tax credit for any foreign taxes paid up to the foreign tax credit limitation; which is the amount of foreign-source income, less any allocated expenses, multiplied by the U.S. tax rate. If the taxpayer does not have expenses to offset the foreign-source income, the result will be a higher foreign tax credit limitation, which allows the taxpayer to reduce U.S. tax by the amount of foreign taxes paid and alleviate, if not eliminate, double taxation.

c. *Incorrect.* If the foreign income tax rate exceeds the U.S. tax rate, as long as there is a sufficient foreign tax credit limitation, the taxpayer will not have to pay U.S. tax on the foreign-source income.

d. *Incorrect.* The taxpayer will still be liable for U.S. tax on the foreign-source income, but will not be taxed an amount over the U.S. tax rate.

3. a. *Correct.* **Dividend income is considered fixed, determinable, annual, or periodic income (FDAP) income, which is required to have U.S. tax withheld at a rate of 30 percent.**

b. *Incorrect.* If the activity constitutes a trade or business in the U.S., the income generated from the activity is effectively connected to a U.S. trade or business and taxed at a graduated rate, not a flat 30%

c. *Incorrect.* Rental income is sourced where the rental property is located and will not be subject to U.S. tax if the property is located in a foreign country.

d. *Incorrect.* Service income is exempt from U.S. tax if the foreign person is in the U.S. for less than 90 days, earned less than $3,000, and worked for a foreign person.

**4. a. *Incorrect.*** Interest income generally takes the location of the debtor into consideration. This exception applies to dividend income rather than interest income.

**b. *Incorrect.*** Interest paid by the branch of a U.S. bank located in a foreign country is foreign source income, even though the branch is owned by a bank located in the United States.

**c. *Correct.* In this case, the U.S. branch is treated like a subsidiary of the foreign corporation, and the U.S. branch, not the foreign corporation, is considered the debtor.**

**d. *Incorrect.*** Interest is sourced by the residence of the debtor. This scenario is an illustration of the U.S. sourcing rules for interest income, not an exception.

**5. a. *Correct.* Income from the sale of purchased inventory is considered foreign source income if title passes in the foreign country, regardless of where the inventory is purchased or the contract signed.**

**b. *Incorrect.*** Income from the sale of purchased inventory is sourced where title passes, which would be the U.S. in this scenario; there is no reportable foreign-source income.

**c. *Incorrect.*** Under the 50/50 rule, half of the income from the sale of manufactured inventory is sourced to where the manufacturing assets are located and half is sourced where title passes. For this scenario, half of the income will be U.S. source and half will be foreign source.

**d. *Incorrect.*** The inventory sourcing rules allocate at least half of the income from the sale of manufactured inventory to where the manufacturing assets are located. The manufacturing assets of a U.S. manufacturer are located in the U.S.; therefore, at least half of the income in this scenario will be U.S. source income.

**6. a. *Correct.* The portion of the gain on the disposition of depreciable personal property attributable to a prior depreciation deduction is treated as having the same source as the related deduction. Because there was no gain in excess of the amount of recaptured depreciation deduction, all income attributable to the sale is U.S. source regardless of the residence of the seller.**

**b. *Incorrect.*** Although the sale of an intangible asset is generally sourced by the residence of the seller, if the sales amount is contingent on productivity, the sale is sourced like a royalty; which is where the intangible asset is used.

**c. *Incorrect.*** The sale of foreign subsidiary stock in this scenario meets all of the requirements necessary to allocate the gain as foreign-source income:

- The U.S. company owns 80 percent or more of the shares of the foreign subsidiary
- The sale occurs in the foreign country in which the foreign subsidiary is engaged in the act of conduct of a trade or business
- The foreign subsidiary earns more than 50 percent of its gross income during the prior 3 years in the act of conduct of a trade or business

**d. *Incorrect.*** Scholarship income where services are not required to be performed are sourced where the payor is located. In this situation, because the scholarship is from a foreign country, the income is foreign-source.

# ¶ 10,110 MODULE 3—CHAPTER 10

**1. a. *Correct.*** This is an incorrect statement. A foreign entity is a partnership if it has two or more members and (not or) at least one member does not have limited liability if it does not elect.

**b. *Incorrect.*** This is a correct statement. Unless a foreign entity elects, it is a partnership if it has two or more members and at least one member does not have limited liability. Additionally, there are also grandfather provisions for certain eligible entities.

**c. *Incorrect.*** This is a correct statement. Unless a foreign entity elects, it is an association if all members have limited liability. It's also important to note that there are grandfather provisions for eligible entities existing on May 8, 1996.

**d. *Incorrect.*** This is a correct statement. Unless a foreign entity elects, it is disregarded as an entity separate from its owner if it has a single owner that does not have limited liability. Additionally, there are grandfather provisions for eligible entities existing on May 8, 1996, and no person treats the entity as a corporation.

**2. a. *Incorrect.*** This is not the first general requirement when making a late election through Rev. Proc. 2009-41. Instead, this is a component of the second requirement when making a late election.

**b. *Correct.* This is the first general requirement when making a late election through Rev. Proc. 2009-41. With respect to the second requirement, the entity must show that it has not filed a return for the first year in which the election was intended because the due date has not passed for that year's return or that it timely filed all required returns consistent with its requested classification for all the years it intended the requested election to be effective and no inconsistent returns have been filed by or with respect to it during any of the taxable years.**

**c. *Incorrect.*** This is not the first general requirement when making a late election through Rev. Proc. 2009-41. Instead, this is a component of the second requirement when making a late election. In addition to this requirement, there is another component of the second requirement along with a third requirement that must be satisfied.

**d. *Incorrect.*** This is not the first general requirement when making a late election through Rev. Proc. 2009-41. Instead, this is the third and final requirement when making a late election.

**3. a. *Incorrect.*** When an entity taxed as a corporation elects to be treated as a partnership, shareholders are deemed to contribute those assets to a newly formed partnership, not a corporation.

**b. *Incorrect.*** When elections are to be made for a series of tiered eligible entities effective on the same date, the order of the elections (and therefore, the order of the deemed liquidations) may be specified by the electing entities.

**c. *Correct.* When an entity taxed as a corporation elects to be treated as a partnership, the C Corporation is deemed to distribute all of its assets and liabilities to its shareholders in liquidation of the corporation and shareholders are then deemed to contribute those assets to a newly formed partnership.**

**d. *Incorrect.*** When an entity taxed as a corporation elects to be treated as a partnership, the C Corporation is deemed to distribute all of its assets and liabilities to its shareholders in liquidation of the corporation, not just its assets.

**4. a.** *Correct.* No U.S. tax on the foreign corporation is a characteristic of a Code Sec. 331 liquidation of a foreign corporation. Additionally, this type of transaction also results in a gain to the U.S. shareholders.

**b.** *Incorrect.* This is not a characteristic of a Code Sec. 331 liquidation of a foreign corporation. Instead, this is a characteristic of a Code Sec. 332 liquidation of a foreign subsidiary.

**c.** *Incorrect.* This is not a characteristic of a Code Sec. 331 liquidation of a foreign corporation, but is a characteristic of a Code Sec. 332 liquidation of a foreign subsidiary. A Section 331 liquidation results in a gain to the U.S. shareholders.

**d.** *Incorrect.* This is not a characteristic of a Code Sec. 331 liquidation of a foreign corporation. Instead, this is a characteristic of a Code Sec. 332 liquidation of a foreign subsidiary. The decision to "check the box" involves weighing deferral versus the overall effective tax rate.

**5. a.** *Correct.* A foreign tax credit is only available to C corporations. As a result, it is not available to S corporations, LLCs, partnerships, or their owners.

**b.** *Incorrect.* A foreign tax credit is not available to S corporations. An S corporation, for U.S. federal income tax purposes, is a closely held corporation (or, in some cases, a limited liability company or a partnership) that makes a valid election to be taxed under Subchapter S of Chapter 1 of the Internal Revenue Code.

**c.** *Incorrect.* A foreign tax credit is not available to LLCs. An LLC is a corporate structure whereby the members of the company cannot be held personally liable for the company's debts or liabilities

**d.** *Incorrect.* A foreign tax credit is not available to partnerships. However, by checking the box for the foreign corporation, an individual U.S. owner may take a foreign tax credit, as the earnings of the foreign entity pass-through and are taxed at the owner level.

**6. a.** *Incorrect.* Form 8832 is a form used by an entity to elect how it will be classified for federal tax purposes. It includes the options of a corporation, a partnership, or an entity disregarded as separate from its owner.

**b.** *Incorrect.* Form 1065 relates to the U.S. return of partnership income. Partnerships file an information return to report their income, gains, losses, deductions, credits, etc. A partnership does not pay tax on its income but "passes through" any profits or losses to its partners. Partners must include partnership items on their tax or information returns.

**c.** *Incorrect.* Form 1042 relates to annual withholding tax return for U.S. source income of foreign persons. This form, among other things, is used to report tax withheld under chapter 3 on certain income of foreign persons, including nonresident aliens, foreign partnerships, foreign corporations, foreign estates, and foreign trusts.

**d.** *Correct.* Form 8865, *Return of U.S. Persons with Respect to Certain Foreign Partnerships,* is used for transfer pricing audits and includes four filing categories. A person uses this form to report the information required under Section 6038 as well as other sections.

# Index

*References are to paragraph (¶) numbers.*

# ¶ 10,200 Glossary

**Accumulated adjustment account**—an account of the S corporation that reflects adjustments to shareholder basis and is used to determine the tax effect of distributions to shareholders. Distributions from AAAs are tax free to the extent of basis and taxed as capital gains once basis is exceeded.

**Bonus depreciation**—an additional amount of deductible "depreciation" that is awarded above and beyond what would normally be available based on current tax code regulations.

**Built-in gains tax**—a tax that may be imposed if the S corporation has a net recognized built-in gain within five years from when the S corporation acquired the assets of a C corporation in a tax-free transaction.

**Closely held corporation**—any company that has only a limited number of shareholders and its stock is publicly traded on occasion but not on a regular basis.

**Check-the-box election**—an election whereby an entity chooses its classification for federal income tax purposes by filing Form 8832, *Entity Classification Election*.

**Code Sec. 179**—the Internal Revenue Code Section that allows businesses to "deduct" the full purchase price of qualifying equipment and/or software purchased or financed during the tax year.

**Complex trust**—a trust for which the trustee is given discretion to either pay income or accumulate income so the trust is not required to pay income currently to beneficiaries; the trust may include charitable beneficiaries.

**Contemporaneous**—existing or occurring in the same period of time.

**Controlled foreign corporation (CFC)**—a foreign corporation that has more than 50 percent of its vote or value owned by U.S. persons.

**Depreciation**—an accounting method of allocating the cost of a tangible asset systematically over its useful life.

**Disclaimer**—an act by a beneficiary whereby the beneficiary declines, refuses, and renounces an interest in property otherwise bequeathed to the beneficiary.

**Distributable net income (DNI)**—taxable income plus tax-exempt interest, reduced by allocable expenses for a trust or estate.

**Dwelling unit**—a house, apartment, condominium, mobile home, boat, or similar property and all structures or other property appurtenant to such dwelling unit. Dwelling units do not include portions of units used exclusively as hotels, inns, or similar establishments.

**Effectively connected income**—income connected with the conduct of a trade or business. An individual must generally be engaged in the trade or business (e.g., perform personal services for the business) to be considered to have effectively connected income.

**Eligible entity**—for purposes of Treas. Reg. § 301.7701-3(a), any business entity that is not classified as a corporation.

**Estate**—everything composing the net worth of an individual, including all land, possessions, and other assets.

**Fixed, determinable, annual, or periodic (FDAP) income withholding**—dividends, interest, rents, royalties, and compensation earned by a foreign person that requires U.S. withholding at a 30 percent flat rate.

**Foreign person (for U.S. tax purposes)**—a nonresident alien; foreign corporation, partnership, trust, and estate; any person that is not a U.S. person.

**Foreign tax credit**—a U.S. tax credit designed to alleviate double taxation for U.S. persons with income subject to both U.S. and foreign taxes. The U.S. person must have net foreign-source income to be able to claim the foreign tax credit.

**Gig economy**—a system in which workers are engaged for short-term projects.

**Grantor trust**—a trust in which the grantor has retained certain rights; within terms of Code Secs. 671–679, the grantor remains taxable on the trust income.

**_INDOPCO_ case**—a U.S. Supreme Court case (**_INDOPCO v. Commissioner,_** 503 U.S. 79) in which the court held that expenditures incurred by a target corporation in the course of a friendly takeover are nondeductible capital expenditures.

**_Inter vivos_ trust**—a trust created by a living trustor.

**Material participation test**—a test to determine whether business income received by a taxpayer is active or passive.

**Net earnings from self-employment**—profit earned by a self-employed individual.

**Net investment income tax**—a 3.8 percent income tax on the lesser of the amount of the taxpayer's net investment income or the amount that the taxpayer's modified adjusted gross income exceeds $200,000 ($250,000 if married filing jointly or a qualified widow(er); $125,000 if married filing separately).

**Passive activity**—a trade or business activity in which the taxpayer does not materially participate.

**Passive activity loss**—a loss arising from activity that is concluded to be passive in nature, such as rental real estate, equipment leasing, interest and dividends, sale of undeveloped land or other investment property, etc.

**Period of nonqualified use**—any time after 2008 when a home was not used as the seller's principal residence or that of his or her spouse or former spouse with certain exceptions, as for temporary absences or time of qualified official extended duty.

**Personal property**—In general, any property other than real estate.

**Portability election**—an election in which if one spouse dies and does not make full use of his or her $5,000,000 federal estate tax exemption, and the surviving spouse picks up the unused exemption and adds it to the surviving spouse's own exemption.

**Post termination transition period (PTTP)**—the time period beginning the day after a corporation loses its S status due to reorganization. During the post termination transition period, the former S corporation's shareholders can receive cash distributions of the former S corporation's earnings. The distributions result in a reduction of the shareholders' basis.

**Principal residence**—a dwelling that includes a bathroom, plus eating and sleeping facilities that a person uses the majority of the time. In addition to a freestanding house, a principal residence may be a houseboat, house trailer, townhouse, shed, or condo.

**Qualified domestic trust**—a trust used to allow a non-U.S. citizen who is the spouse of a U.S. citizen to qualify for the unlimited marital deduction to keep the estate from being subject to federal taxes upon the first spouse's death.

**Qualified revocable trust (QRT)**—a trust treated as owned directly by the grantor-decedent under the grantor trust rules of Code Sec. 676.

**Qualified S corporation subsidiary (QSub) election**—the election made by an S corporation to treat the acquisition of C corporation stock as a deemed liquidation, where the C corporation becomes a subsidiary of the S corporation. Following the deemed liquidation, the S corporation has ownership and control of the subsidiary's assets; liabilities; and income, deduction, and credit items.

**Qualified Subchapter S trust**—one of several types of trusts that are eligible to hold stock in an S corporation. Its two primary requirements are (1) there can be only one beneficiary of the trust and (2) all income must be distributed at least annually (Sec. 1361(d)(3)(B)).

**Real estate professional**—a taxpayer who spends the majority of his or her time in real property businesses, meeting the 50 percent personal services and 750-hour tests of material participation.

**Real property**—any property attached directly to land as well as the land itself. It is any subset of land that has been improved through legal human actions.

**Regulatory election**—an election whose deadline is prescribed by a regulation published in the *Federal Register*; includes check-the-box elections but not certain other elections, such as Section 83(b) elections.

**Rental activity**—an activity from which an individual receives income mainly for the use of tangible property, rather than for services.

**Reverse QTIP election**—an election made to allow the first spouse to die to use a portion of the GST exemption that otherwise might not be used. A reverse QTIP election is only necessary when the amount of the GST exemption exceeds the applicable exclusion amount.

**S corporation**—a domestic corporation that is respected as a separate entity for tax purposes and allows corporate income, losses, deductions, and credits to flow through to its shareholders. S corporations can only have one class of stock and are subject to other restrictions that partnerships and other passthrough entities are not.

**Section 1031 exchange**—a transaction that allows the taxpayer to defer the gain from the sale of property if the proceeds are reinvested in similar property as part of a qualifying like-kind exchange.

**Self-employment tax**—the employer and employee shares of FICA plus a 2.9 percent Medicare tax for a total rate of 15.3 percent.

**Sharing economy**—any activity in which money is earned by sharing property that's owned, such as a home or business equipment.

**Simple trust**—a trust required to distribute all of its income currently; generally, it cannot accumulate income, distribute out of corpus, or pay money for charitable purposes.

**Social Security wage base**—the maximum amount of annual income subject to Social Security tax. For 2017 the wage base is $127,200.

***Taxpayer Relief Act of 1997*** (P.L. 105-34)—the law that developed the current capital gain exclusion rules for sales of principal residences.

**Trust**—a fiduciary relationship in which one party, known as a trustor, gives another party, the trustee, the right to hold title to property or assets for the benefit of a third party, the beneficiary.

**Unforeseen circumstances**—an event that a taxpayer could not reasonably have anticipated before he or she purchased and occupied a principal residence and that triggers application of a safe harbor for excluding up to the maximum allowance capital gains exclusion upon sale of the residence. Examples include an earthquake, divorce or legal separation, and multiple births from one pregnancy.

**U.S. person (for U.S. tax purposes)**—a citizen or resident of the United States; domestic partnerships and corporations formed in the United States under U.S. law; certain trusts; any estate that is not a foreign estate; and any person that is not a foreign person.

**U.S. real property holding corporation**—any U.S corporation that has over 50 percent of its net fair market value in U.S real estate over the past 5 years.

# ¶ 10,300 Final Exam Instructions

Completing your Final Exam online at **cchcpelink.com/printcpe** is the fastest way to earn CPE Credit with immediate results and no additional charge or Express Grading Fee. **Note, the processing fee will increase by $20.00 per module if you choose to mail or email your Final Exam for manual grading by CCH staff.**

This Final Exam is divided into three Modules. There is a grading fee for each Final Exam submission.

**Online Processing Fee:**
$170.90 for Module 1
$113.95 for Module 2
$75.95 for Module 3
$360.80 for all Modules

**Recommended CPE:**
9 hours for Module 1
6 hours for Module 2
4 hours for Module 3
19 hours for all Modules

**Manual Processing Fee:**
$190.90 for Module 1
$133.95 for Module 2
$95.95 for Module 3
$420.80 for all Modules

**IRS Program Number:**
Module 1: 4VRWB-T-02757-17-S
Module 2: 4VRWB-T-02758-17-S
Module 3: 4VRWB-T-02759-17-S

**Federal Tax Law Hours:**
9 hours for Module 1
6 hours for Module 2
4 hours for Module 3
19 hours for all Modules

**CTEC Program Numbers:**
Module 1: 1075-CE-1007
Module 2: 1075-CE-1008
Module 3: 1075-CE-1009

Instructions for purchasing your CPE Tests and accessing them after purchase are provided on the **cchcpelink.com/printcpe** website.

Alternatively, for an additional $20.00 fee per module you may scan and submit your completed Final Exam Answer Sheets for each Module by emailing **CPESubmissions@wolterskluwer.com**. Each Final Exam Answer Sheet will be graded and a CPE Certificate of Completion awarded for achieving a grade of 70 percent or greater. The Final Exam Answer Sheets are located at the back of this book. To mail your Final Exam, send your completed Answer Sheets for each Final Exam Module to **Wolters Kluwer Continuing Education Department, 2700 Lake Cook Road, Riverwoods, IL 60015**,

**Express Grading:** Processing time for your emailed or mailed Answer Sheet is generally 8-12 business days. To use our Express Grading Service, at an additional $19 per Module, please check the "Express Grading" box on your Answer Sheet and provide your Wolters Kluwer account or credit card number **and your email address**. We will email your results and a Certificate of Completion (upon achieving a passing grade) to you by 5:00 p.m. the business day following our receipt of your Answer Sheet. **If you mail your Answer Sheet for Express Grading, please write "ATTN: CPE OVERNIGHT"** on the envelope. NOTE: We will not Federal Express Final Exam results under any circumstances.

---

Recommended CPE credit is based on a 50-minute hour. Because CPE requirements vary from state to state and among different licensing agencies, please contact your CPE governing body for information on your CPE requirements and the applicability of a particular course for your requirements.

**Date of Completion:** If you email or mail your Final Exam to us, the date of completion on your Certificate will be the date that you put on your Answer Sheet. However, you must submit your Answer Sheet for grading within two weeks of completing it.

**Expiration Date:** December 31, 2018

**Evaluation:** To help us provide you with the best possible products, please take a moment to fill out the course Evaluation located after your Final Exam. A copy is also provided at the back of this course if you choose to email or mail your Final Exam Answer Sheets.

 Wolters Kluwer, CCH is registered with the National Association of State Boards of Accountancy (NASBA) as a sponsor of continuing professional education on the National Registry of CPE Sponsors. State boards of accountancy have final authority on the acceptance of individual courses for CPE credit. Complaints regarding registered sponsors may be submitted to the National Registry of CPE Sponsors through its website: www.learningmarket.org.

One **complimentary copy** of this course is provided with certain copies of Wolters Kluwer publications. Additional copies of this course may be downloaded from **cchcpe-link.com/printcpe** or ordered by calling 1-800-344-3734 (ask for product 10024491-0005).

# ¶ 10,401 FINAL EXAM: MODULE 1

**1.** Which of the following statements is true?

   **a.** The current gain exclusion of Section 121 is the first time there has been a gain exclusion for sale of a principal residence.

   **b.** Prior to the current gain exclusion of Section 121, there was once-in-a-lifetime gain exclusion for individuals age 55 or older and a gain rollover provision at Section 1034.

   **c.** Today there is both a gain rollover and a gain exclusion rule.

   **d.** The current gain exclusion under Section 121 may only be used once.

**2.** Which of the following statements is true?

   **a.** A principal residence must be affixed to land.

   **b.** The home must be a principal residence at date of sale to qualify for the Section 121 gain exclusion.

   **c.** Vacant land can be a principal residence if the taxpayer intends to build a home on the property.

   **d.** A taxpayer may only have one principal residence at a time.

**3.** George uses one room in his home regularly and exclusively as a home office. When George sells his principal residence:

   **a.** He must allocate the basis and amount realized between the home office and the rest of the residence in applying Section 121.

   **b.** He does not need to allocate the basis and amount realized between the home office and the rest of the residence in applying Section 121.

   **c.** He does not need to allocate the basis and amount realized between the home office and the rest of the residence in applying Section 121, but any gain attributable to depreciation claimed cannot be excluded under Section 121.

   **d.** He will not be allowed to apply Section 121 to the home.

**4.** Jane, a single individual, purchased a home in 1997 for $300,000 and used it as her principal residence until she sold it in 2014 for $650,000. Jane must treat this transaction on her 2014 tax return as follows.

   **a.** $100,000 capital gain

   **b.** $150,000 capital gain

   **c.** $350,000 capital gain

   **d.** $100,000 ordinary income

   **e.** $150,000 ordinary income

**5.** Tom and Diane, unmarried taxpayers, jointly own and use a home as a principal residence. The home was purchased in January 1994 for $400,000. In January 2014, they sell the home for $960,000. Tom, a single taxpayer, should report taxable gain of:

   **a.** $0

   **b.** $30,000

   **c.** $280,000

   **d.** $560,000

**6.** Which of the following reasons does not qualify as a sale due to "change in place of employment, health, or, to the extent provided in regulations, unforeseen circumstances" related to a "qualified individual"?

    **a.** Desire to live in a more expensive neighborhood.

    **b.** Work relocation with same employer where new work location is 100 miles from old home; current home is five miles from current work location.

    **c.** Loss of employment makes the home too expensive to maintain.

    **d.** Owner's doctor recommends that the taxpayer move to a warmer climate due to an asthmatic condition.

**7.** Even though a taxpayer meets the two years of use in the prior five years requirement, he may be denied benefit of the Section 121 exclusion because:

    **a.** The property was rented during part of the last five years.

    **b.** The taxpayer already used the Section 121 exclusion in the past 24 months.

    **c.** The taxpayer is divorced.

    **d.** The taxpayer's adjusted gross income is too high to qualify.

**8.** The five-year period of Section 121 may be suspended due to:

    **a.** Military service.

    **b.** Employer relocation.

    **c.** Time living with a child or parent so the taxpayer can care for them.

    **d.** Time spent in a rehabilitation center.

**9.** The sale of a principal residence by widow or widower can still get benefit of the $500,000 exclusion amount if:

    **a.** The residence is sold no later than two years after the date of death and the deceased spouse met the ownership and use requirements immediately before the date of death.

    **b.** The taxpayer has not remarried, regardless of the time between the spouse's death and the sale of the residence.

    **c.** The couple lived in the house for at least ten years prior to death of the spouse.

    **d.** The taxpayer seeks permission from the IRS prior to filing the tax return for the year of sale.

**10.** The Section 121 exclusion does not apply to the gain allocated to any period of "nonqualified use." Which of the following scenarios is an example of a period of nonqualified use?

    **a.** A one-year rental period prior to the date of sale of the residence.

    **b.** Fourteen months spent outside of the home while on "qualified official extended duty."

    **c.** A rental period prior to 2009.

    **d.** A two-year rental period immediately preceding the taxpayer moving into the home in 2012.

**11.** For tax years except for 2010, the estate's basis in property acquired from a decedent is the _____ of the property on the decedent's date of death.

    **a.** Amortized cost

    **b.** Net book value

    **c.** Fair market value

    **d.** Carrying value

**12.** Which of the following trusts do not permit amounts to be paid, permanently set aside, or used for charitable purposes?

a. Complex trusts

b. Simple trusts

c. Grantor trusts

d. Revocable trusts

**13.** The distributable net income concept serves each of the following purposes, *except:*

a. Establishes the maximum amount of the entity's annual income taxable to the beneficiaries.

b. Determines the amount of net income which includes capital gains.

c. Determines the character of the items of income taxable to the beneficiaries.

d. Establishes the maximum income distribution deduction that may be claimed by a trust or an estate.

**14.** Qualified dividend income is taxed at what rate when taxable income exceeds $12,400 ($12,500 for 2017)?

a. 20 percent

b. 25 percent

c. 30 percent

d. 35 percent

**15.** Which of the following identifies the exemption amount for an estate?

a. $300

b. $600

c. $1,500

d. $2,900

**16.** Which of the following types of interest expenses are deductible?

a. Interest payments for federal tax deficiencies.

b. Personal interest.

c. Interest paid on a qualified residence.

d. Interest payments for state tax deficiencies.

**17.** The carryforward period for capital losses is:

a. 5 years

b. 10 years

c. 15 years

d. Unlimited

**18.** Which of the following identifies the AMT exclusion for 2017?

a. $23,900

b. $24,100

c. $25,600

d. $27,200

¶10,401

**19.** An estate is not required to make estimated tax payments if there was no tax liability for the preceding full twelve-month tax year or the balance of tax due is less than what amount?

    **a.** $1,000

    **b.** $5,000

    **c.** $7,400

    **d.** $10,000

**20.** Currently, net investment income tax of _____ will apply to undistributed income of trusts and estates when the entity has taxable income in excess of $12,500 for 2017.

    **a.** 2.5 percent

    **b.** 3.1 percent

    **c.** 3.8 percent

    **d.** 4.6 percent

**21.** The final income tax return is due on what date of the year following the year of death?

    **a.** April 15

    **b.** May 15

    **c.** June 15

    **d.** July 15

**22.** IRAs and other retirement plan distributions received after death should be included on which of the following forms?

    **a.** Form 995

    **b.** Form 706

    **c.** Form 1041

    **d.** Form 1040

**23.** Currently, after death there is a personal residence sales exclusion of what amount?

    **a.** $100,000

    **b.** $250,000

    **c.** $500,000

    **d.** $1 million

**24.** Which of the following statements with respect to items of income and deduction is correct?

    **a.** In most situations, death is regarded as a disposition of an installment obligation.

    **b.** After the death of a decedent, estimated tax payments are not required to be made to avoid underestimation penalties.

    **c.** Only medical expenses paid in the decedent's final tax year prior to death may be deducted on the decedent's final income tax return.

    **d.** Charitable contributions are allowed to be carried over to the estate of the decedent.

**25.** Estates and trusts may elect to treat all or part of distributions made to beneficiaries within the first _____ days of the taxable year as if they were paid on the last day of the preceding taxable year.

   **a.** 30

   **b.** 45

   **c.** 65

   **d.** 90

**26.** Which of the following Code Sections prescribes the requirements with respect to qualified disclaimers?

   **a.** Code Sec. 2518

   **b.** Code Sec. 4615

   **c.** Code Sec. 8465

   **d.** Code Sec. 7845

**27.** Which of the following identifies an act by a beneficiary whereby the beneficiary declines, refuses and renounces an interest in property otherwise bequeathed to the beneficiary?

   **a.** Disassociation

   **b.** Estate refusal

   **c.** Disclaimer

   **d.** Bequeathed avoidance

**28.** A marital deduction will apply, even if the spouse is not a U.S. citizen, where the property passes to which of the following?

   **a.** Qualified domestic trust.

   **b.** Irrevocable fiduciary trust.

   **c.** Qualified revocable trust.

   **d.** Permissible domestic trust.

**29.** An estate has the option to report the value of the decedent's assets as of the date of death or as of the date that is _____ months after the decedent's date of death?

   **a.** Three

   **b.** Six

   **c.** Seven

   **d.** Eight

**30.** The death of a partner results in the basis of the partner's interest in the partnership being adjusted to which of the following on the date of the partner's death, or the alternate valuation date if elected?

   **a.** Net realizable value.

   **b.** Carrying amount.

   **c.** Fair market value.

   **d.** Carrying amount adjusted for gains/losses.

**31.** By satisfying one of the tests for material participation, a loss activity can be active so that losses are not limited by

   **a.** Section 389

   **b.** Section 469

   **c.** Section 785

   **d.** Section 987

**32.** When a closely held C corporation (CHC) becomes a non-CHC, suspended losses cannot shelter portfolio income but may offset which of the following?

    **a.** Active income in non-CHC years.

    **b.** Passive income in future CHC years.

    **c.** Active income in CHC years.

    **d.** Passive income in future non-CHC years.

**33.** Which of the following general statements with respect to material participation is correct?

    **a.** It is based on hours of participation.

    **b.** It includes work customarily done by an owner.

    **c.** Spouse hours are aggregated for qualified real estate professional status.

    **d.** It includes hours as an investor.

**34.** Which of the following material participation tests are based on prior participation and are viewed as antiabuse rules?

    **a.** More than 500 hours.

    **b.** Substantially all participation.

    **c.** Material participation in any three preceding years.

    **d.** Regular, continuous, substantial involvement.

**35.** Which of the following types of expenses were required to be proved with contemporaneous written logs based on the requirements of DEFRA in 1984?

    **a.** Auto

    **b.** Utility

    **c.** Depreciation

    **d.** Maintenance

**36.** Based on the IRS Audit Guide, each of the following is noted as an indicator of no material participation, *except:*

    **a.** Residence hundreds of miles away from activity.

    **b.** Significant W-2 wages requiring more than 40 hours per week.

    **c.** Taxpayer compensated for services.

    **d.** Taxpayer is elderly or has health issues.

**37.** Which of the following cases involved a taxpayer who claimed material participation, who bought a sailboat while living in Dallas but his employer subsequently moved him to Connecticut?

    **a.** *Goshorn,* TC Memo 1993-578

    **b.** *Speer,* TC Memo 1996-323

    **c.** *Carlstedt,* TC Memo 1997-323

    **d.** *Fowler,* TC Memo 2002-223

**38.** Which of the following cases involved a taxpayer who owned a trucking and waste removal business but subsequently developed an interest in in gold mining and treasure hunting?

    **a.** *Adeyemo,* TC Memo 2014-1

    **b.** *Harrison,* TC Memo 1996-509

    **c.** *Tolin,* TC Memo 2014-65

    **d.** *Kline,* TC Memo 2015-144

**39.** The material participation test is also used with respect to a qualified joint venture in accordance with which of the following sections?

   **a.** Section 761

   **b.** Section 785

   **c.** Section 798

   **d.** Section 801

**40.** For a person to qualify as a real estate professional, the person must devote more than how many hours to real estate activities?

   **a.** 250 hours

   **b.** 400 hours

   **c.** 575 hours

   **d.** 750 hours

**41.** Which statement about the gig economy is correct?

   **a.** Only unskilled workers are in the gig economy.

   **b.** The number of workers is growing.

   **c.** Only certain industries use gig workers.

   **d.** The gig economy benefits only workers and not businesses.

**42.** As a general rule, a worker in the gig economy can have:

   **a.** Withholding on earnings.

   **b.** Unemployment benefits.

   **c.** Work-life balance.

   **d.** Workers' compensation.

**43.** Which of the following is *not* a question asked about vehicle usage on Schedule C of Form 1040?

   **a.** The number of miles driven for business and other purposes.

   **b.** Whether the taxpayer has written evidence of business use.

   **c.** The cost of the vehicle

   **d.** Whether the taxpayer has another vehicle for personal use

**44.** The IRS suspects that a worker in the gig economy is underreporting income. Which of the following is the IRS least likely to rely on in examining a return?

   **a.** Forms 1099-MISC.

   **b.** Forms 1099-K.

   **c.** Bank statements.

   **d.** The tax return itself.

**45.** Which of the following costs related to working in the gig economy are treated as a business expense?

   **a.** Cellphone

   **b.** Health insurance

   **c.** Contributions to a SEP

   **d.** Contributions to a health savings account

**46.** Which of the following expenses of an Uber driver is *not* an adjustment to gross income?

    **a.** One-half of self-employment tax

    **b.** Contribution to a health savings account

    **c.** Personal use of a vehicle

    **d.** SEP contribution

**47.** Estimated taxes can be avoided in each of the following situations *except:*

    **a.** The gig worker has a job and withholding from wages covers gig income.

    **b.** The gig worker's spouse agrees to have his/her withholding from wages cover the gig worker's income.

    **c.** Projected estimated taxes are less than $1,000.

    **d.** Adjusted gross income is less than $150,000.

**48.** A homeowner wants to rent her home on Airbnb. Which statement is *not* correct?

    **a.** Rules in a homeowners association may bar or restrict this activity.

    **b.** Deductions related to rental income may be limited.

    **c.** Her homeowner's policy will cover liability and damages.

    **d.** Net rental income likely is reported on Schedule E of Form 1040.

**49.** If the 14-day/10 percent rule applies, which of the following is *not* a Step 1 deduction?

    **a.** Advertising

    **b.** Home mortgage interest

    **c.** Real estate taxes

    **d.** Depreciation

**50.** Which type activity is *not* taken into consideration for purposes of active participation under the PAL rules?

    **a.** Setting the rental rate.

    **b.** Performing 100 hours looking for new rental opportunities.

    **c.** Approving tenants.

    **d.** Hiring a plumber to fix a leak.

# ¶ 10,402 Final Exam: Module 2

**1.** Which of the following identifies the maximum Code Sec. 179 deduction amount for 2017?

    **a.** $500,000

    **b.** $750,000

    **c.** $1,000,000

    **d.** $2,000,000

**2.** If a taxpayer places $2,300,000 of qualifying Code Sec. 179 property in service in 2017, then the taxpayer may elect _____ as a Code Sec. 179 deduction.

    **a.** $0

    **b.** $200,000

    **c.** $300,000

    **d.** $500,000

**3.** Which of the following qualifies for a Code Sec. 179 deduction?

    **a.** Property used outside the United States

    **b.** Real property

    **c.** Property attached to a building that is not a structural component of the building

    **d.** Property purchased from related parties

**4.** The *Zaninovich* case held that the concept of "substantially beyond" the taxable year means not more than ___ months.

    **a.** 6

    **b.** 12

    **c.** 18

    **d.** 24

**5.** IRC Section 179 allows a taxpayer to elect to take an immediate expense deduction of certain ___ personal property placed in service during the taxable year.

    **a.** Intangible

    **b.** Real

    **c.** Tangible

    **d.** Material

**6.** Which of the following statements is correct with respect to expenses paid or incurred in defending or perfecting title to property, in recovering property, or in developing or improving property?

    **a.** They do not constitute part of the cost of the property and are not deductible expenses.

    **b.** They do not constitute part of the cost of the property and are deductible expenses

    **c.** They constitute part of the cost of the property and are not deductible expenses.

    **d.** They constitute part of the cost of the property and are deductible expenses.

**7.** In the *INDOPCO* case, the taxpayer incurred significant legal and investment banking fees related to which of the following?

    **a.** Initial public offering

    **b.** Hostile takeover attempt

    **c.** Corporate reorganization

    **d.** Disposal of significant assets

**8.** With the exception of resellers, the requirements of Code Sec. 263A do not apply to producers of property with gross receipts of which amount, during what period of time?

    **a.** $10M or less during the last three years

    **b.** $20M or less during the last three years

    **c.** $10M or less during the last five years

    **d.** $10M or less during the last five years

**9.** Which of the following identifies the *de minimis* safe harbor election amount per invoice or item under Code Sec. 263A if the taxpayer has applicable financial statements?

    **a.** $5,000

    **b.** $10,000

    **c.** $15,000

    **d.** $20,000

**10.** Based on the revised repair regulations issued in 2013, if a taxpayer has been treating items differently prior to these regulations, then the taxpayer is required to file _____.

    **a.** Form 3114

    **b.** Form 3115

    **c.** Form 5113

    **d.** Form 5114

**11.** If the answer to a question on Form 1120S is unknown, the tax preparer should refer to:

    **a.** AICPA SSTS No. 2.

    **b.** The 1120 S instructions.

    **c.** The client.

    **d.** The IRS.

**12.** Passive investment income tax will be imposed on an S corporation if:

    **a.** The S corporation has not established an AAA.

    **b.** Shareholders of the S corporation are engaged in passive activities.

    **c.** The S corporation has passive investment income, and earnings and profits (E&P) of the S corporation exceed $1 million.

    **d.** The S corporation's passive investment income from its earnings and profits (E&P) exceeds 25 percent of gross receipts.

**13.** A restricted option is considered a stock equivalent if:

    **a.** The owner of the option is also a shareholder.

    **b.** The owner of the option makes a Code Sec. 83(b) election.

    **c.** There is an economic certainty that the option will be exercised.

    **d.** The option must be exercised before the end of the corporation's tax year.

**14.** A C corporation that converts to an S corporation will be subject to the built-in gains tax if:

    **a.** The S corporation can prove the underlying asset was acquired after the conversion date.

    **b.** The S corporation recognizes a built-in gain within five years from the date of conversion.

    **c.** The S corporation recognizes built-in losses that meet or exceed the amount of recognized built-in gains.

    **d.** The S corporation waits until the recognition period is over before selling assets.

**15.** If an S corporation is liquidated, the due date of the corporation's final Form 1120S is:

    **a.** The same as that of a C corporation.

    **b.** Six months after the date of liquidation.

    **c.** March 15 of the year following the close of the S corporation's tax year.

    **d.** The 15th day of the third month following the close of the S corporation's tax year.

**16.** Earnings and profits of an S corporation are generated from:

    **a.** Acquisition of a C corporation.

    **b.** The S corporation's investments in passive activities.

    **c.** Shareholder contributions.

    **d.** All of the above.

**17.** Typically, an S corporation's distributions are initially distributed from:

    **a.** The S corporation's accumulated adjustments account.

    **b.** The S corporation's earnings and profits.

    **c.** The S corporation's other adjustments account.

    **d.** None of the above; distributions are proportionate across all accounts.

**18.** An S corporation will not lose S status if:

    **a.** The S corporation is required to pay the passive investment income tax for three consecutive years.

    **b.** The S corporation reclassifies distribution as compensation.

    **c.** Corrective action is not taken with regard to a disproportionate distribution.

    **d.** An existing debt instrument is reclassified as equity, which creates a second class of stock.

**19.** Which of the following is a shareholder-level account?

    **a.** Earnings and profits.

    **b.** Other adjustments.

    **c.** Basis.

    **d.** Accumulated adjustments.

**20.** How does a Schedule K-1 from an S corporation report items affecting basis?

    **a.** With codes.

    **b.** As a net amount on Line 1.

    **c.** As a separate statement sent with the K-1.

    **d.** As a notation at the bottom of the K-1.

**21.** With respect to a technical termination, the "old" partnership is terminated by which of the following?

    **a.** Sale of 60 percent of the interests in capital and profits.

    **b.** A redemption of 60 percent of the interests in the partnership.

    **c.** A sale of 100 percent of the membership interest in an LLC.

    **d.** An affirmative election to terminate the partnership.

**22.** A technical termination requires:

    **a.** A restart for amortization lives.

    **b.** A new EIN for the new partnership.

    **c.** The old partnership to file a final tax return with the final return due date measured by reference to termination.

    **d.** The new partnership to begin deprecation using a fair market value basis.

**23.** The treatment of guaranteed payments includes:

    **a.** Only payments subject to entrepreneurial risk.

    **b.** No deduction to the partnership.

    **c.** Fixed payments other than for capital.

    **d.** Reporting separately stated income to the partner.

**24.** A preference return is a priority that is:

    **a.** Intended to carry over and be cumulative.

    **b.** Intended to be matched with an allocation of income.

    **c.** A payment that is determined by reference to income.

    **d.** A payment that creates its own income and deduction.

**25.** Adjustments caused by Code Sec. 734 include all of the following *except:*

    **a.** A distribution creates gain to a partner.

    **b.** A partner purchases an interest from another member.

    **c.** A partner takes less than a carryover basis in distributed property.

    **d.** A partner takes more than a carryover basis where a distribution liquidates the partner's interest.

**26.** Partner K-1 reporting issues show all of the following *except:*

    **a.** Allocable share of profit and loss.

    **b.** Reconciliation of capital account.

    **c.** Separate reporting of allocations of nonrecourse deductions.

    **d.** Share of liabilities.

**27.** A Code Sec. 704(b) safe harbor compliant agreement may contain:

    **a.** A minimum gain chargeback.

    **b.** Liquidating distributions following tax basis capital.

    **c.** Operating distributions in proportion to capital.

    **d.** Preferred income chargebacks.

28. A target allocation agreement would generally include:
    a. A prescribed allocation percentage.
    b. Capital maintained using tax basis.
    c. A "hypothetical" sale of assets at book value.
    d. A "hypothetical" minimum gain chargeback.

29. The basic premise governing Code Sec. 704(c) allocations of pre-contribution gains and losses includes all of the following *except:*
    a. Allocations related to items of gain and loss that arise before the owners are in a partnership form.
    b. Gains and losses that arose before the owners became partners should be shared by all owners.
    c. Allocations related to a period before a new partner acquires an interest by contribution of money for an interest.
    d. Regulations that compare book and tax capital to measure Code Sec. 704(c) items.

30. When determining or using the partners' shares of liabilities:
    a. Increases and decreases in partners' "shares" of entity liabilities affect the basis of partners' interests.
    b. A "share" of liability is determined by the partnership agreement.
    c. Nonrecourse liabilities are not shared using economic-risk-of-loss principles.
    d. Recourse liabilities include only those that are guaranteed by a partner.

# ¶ 10,403 Final Exam: Module 3

**1.** The compensation component of a defined benefit plan is sourced where the _____.

    **a.** Services were performed.

    **b.** Plan administrator resides.

    **c.** Company resides.

    **d.** Taxpayer receiving the benefit resides.

**2.** International taxation of athletes is complex because _____.

    **a.** Most athletes own real estate in a foreign country.

    **b.** Many athletes are at least 10 percent owners of controlled foreign corporations (CFCs).

    **c.** Sponsorship income may not be taxed by the foreign country.

    **d.** Sponsorship income can be defined as service income or royalty income.

**3.** When an individual receives payment for services performed both within and outside the U.S., the income is typically apportioned based on _____.

    **a.** Hours worked.

    **b.** Number of days.

    **c.** Commuting distance.

    **d.** Type of services performed at each location.

**4.** What type of income is always sourced in the United States?

    **a.** Social Security benefits

    **b.** Income received from a flow-through entity located in the United States

    **c.** Scholarships and fellowships when services are not required to be performed

    **d.** Any gain on the sale of tangible equipment that is attributable to a prior amortization deduction

**5.** A U.S. taxpayer cannot claim the foreign tax credit for foreign taxes paid if the _____.

    **a.** Foreign tax rate is less than the U.S. tax rate.

    **b.** Taxpayer has no foreign-source income.

    **c.** Taxpayer is located in a foreign country at the time the tax return is prepared.

    **d.** Amount of the taxpayer's U.S. source income is less than the amount of foreign-source income received during that tax year.

**6.** It may be difficult to allocate lease income because _____.

    **a.** Lease payments are often paid in arrears.

    **b.** The leased property is typically depreciable property.

    **c.** It is sourced by where the underlying property is used.

    **d.** It is sourced by where the lessee conducts business.

**7.** Residency is established by the _____ when sourcing income from the sale of personal property.

    **a.** Green-card test

    **b.** Substantial presence test

    **c.** Buyer's tax home

    **d.** Seller's tax home

**8.** Payers required to withhold for FDAP income must _____.

    **a.** Withhold based on gross income.

    **b.** Withhold based on net income.

    **c.** Determine the veracity of the purported deductions related to the income.

    **d.** Periodically review the foreign person's green card status.

**9.** Foreign persons do not pay tax on ____.

    **a.** Dividends received from a U.S. corporation.

    **b.** Income that is effectively connected with a U.S. business.

    **c.** Interest income from deposits with a U.S. bank.

    **d.** Royalties received from a U.S. source.

**10.** Which of the following is the proper method to allocate deductions?

    **a.** Allocate deductions to a class of gross income then apportion the deductions by source.

    **b.** Apportion deductions between U.S. and foreign income and subtract from total U.S. and total foreign income, respectively.

    **c.** Allocate deductions to a class of gross income by using a reasonable method (such as units sold) and apportion the net deductions between foreign and U.S. income.

    **d.** Determine total deductions and apportion to total U.S. and foreign income on a pro-rata basis.

**11.** Which of the following is a matter of whether an organization is an entity separate from its owners?

    **a.** Federal tax law.

    **b.** Foreign tax law.

    **c.** State tax law.

    **d.** Local tax law.

**12.** As a default rule, unless a foreign entity elects, it is disregarded as an entity separate from its owner if it has a single owner that does *not* have:

    **a.** Sufficient equity.

    **b.** Uncollateralized debt.

    **c.** Limited liability.

    **d.** Positive cash flows.

**13.** Grandfather provisions for eligible entities are available for those existing on May 8 of what year?

    **a.** 1996

    **b.** 1997

    **c.** 1998

    **d.** 1999

**14.** An election effective on the first day of a taxable year is due no later than the:

    **a.** 15th day of the next taxable year.

    **b.** 16th day of the next taxable year.

    **c.** 76th day of that taxable year.

    **d.** 75th day of that taxable year.

**15.** Which of the following type of late election methods is an expensive procedure with a $10,000 IRS filing fee?

  **a.** Rev. Proc. 2010-32.

  **b.** Rev. Proc. 2009-41.

  **c.** Expedited election.

  **d.** Private letter ruling.

**16.** If a late election is to be effective for any period prior to the time that it is filed, each additional person who was an owner between the date the election is to be effective and the date the election is filed must also:

  **a.** Sign the election.

  **b.** Fill out a separate election form.

  **c.** Notarize the election.

  **d.** Request a private letter ruling.

**17.** Each of the following is a consideration for an S election for an LLC taxed as a partnership to minimize self-employment tax and new Medicare tax risk, *except:*

  **a.** Compensation must be reasonable.

  **b.** There is an inside basis step-up on death.

  **c.** Benefit is clearer for a service business, but reasonable compensation risk is higher.

  **d.** There is limited ability to remove assets without triggering gain and limited flexibility in allocating gains and losses.

**18.** In an S corporation acquisition, an entity should use which of the following?

  **a.** F Reorganization/LLC Conversion.

  **b.** G Reorganization/LLC Conversion.

  **c.** H Reorganization/LLC Conversion.

  **d.** J Reorganization/LLC Conversion.

**19.** The decision to "check the box" involves weighing deferral versus which of the following?

  **a.** Marginal tax rate.

  **b.** Enacted tax rate.

  **c.** Overall effective tax rate.

  **d.** Foreign tax credits.

**20.** When converting a Code Sec. 902 credit into a Code Sec. 901 credit and checking the box for the foreign corporation, an individual U.S. owner may take a foreign tax credit as the earnings of the foreign entity passthrough and are taxed at the _____ level.

  **a.** Entity

  **b.** Corporation

  **c.** Owner

  **d.** Stakeholder

# ¶ 10,500 Answer Sheets

## ¶ 10,501 Top Federal Tax Issues for 2018 CPE Course: MODULE 1

**(10047746-0001)**

Go to **cchcpelink.com/printcpe** to complete your Final Exam online for instant results and a reduced grading fee.

A $170.90 processing fee will be charged for each user submitting Module 1 to **cchcpelink.com/printcpe** for online grading. **The processing fee is $190.90 if you prefer to mail or email your Final Exam for manual grading by CCH staff.** To mail or email your exam, remove both pages of the Answer Sheet from this book and return them with your completed Evaluation Form to: Wolters Kluwer Continuing Education Department, 2700 Lake Cook Road, Riverwoods, IL 60015 or email your Answer Sheet to Wolters Kluwer at **CPESubmissions@wolterskluwer.com**. You must also select a method of payment below.

NAME _____

COMPANY NAME _____

STREET _____

CITY, STATE, & ZIP CODE _____

BUSINESS PHONE NUMBER _____

E-MAIL ADDRESS _____

DATE OF COMPLETION _____

PTIN ID (for Enrolled Agents or RTRPs only) _____

### METHOD OF PAYMENT:

☐ Check Enclosed    ☐ Visa      ☐ Master Card      ☐ AmEx

☐ Discover    ☐ Wolters Kluwer Account* _____

Card No. _____      Exp. Date _____

Signature _____

**EXPRESS GRADING:** Please email my Course results to me by 5:00 p.m. the business day following your receipt of this Answer Sheet. By checking this box I authorize Wolters Kluwer to charge $19.00 for this service.

☐ Express Grading $19.00      Email address: _____

* Must provide Wolters Kluwer account number for this payment option

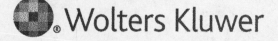 Wolters Kluwer

## Module 1: Answer Sheet

(10047746-0001)

Please answer the questions by indicating the appropriate letter next to the corresponding number.

| | | | | |
|---|---|---|---|---|
| 1. _____ | 11. _____ | 21. _____ | 31. _____ | 41. _____ |
| 2. _____ | 12. _____ | 22. _____ | 32. _____ | 42. _____ |
| 3. _____ | 13. _____ | 23. _____ | 33. _____ | 43. _____ |
| 4. _____ | 14. _____ | 24. _____ | 34. _____ | 44. _____ |
| 5. _____ | 15. _____ | 25. _____ | 35. _____ | 45. _____ |
| 6. _____ | 16. _____ | 26. _____ | 36. _____ | 46. _____ |
| 7. _____ | 17. _____ | 27. _____ | 37. _____ | 47. _____ |
| 8. _____ | 18. _____ | 28. _____ | 38. _____ | 48. _____ |
| 9. _____ | 19. _____ | 29. _____ | 39. _____ | 49. _____ |
| 10. _____ | 20. _____ | 30. _____ | 40. _____ | 50. _____ |

**Please complete the Evaluation Form (located after the Module 3 Answer Sheet) and return it with this Final Exam Answer Sheet to Wolters Kluwer at the address on the previous page. Thank you.**

# ¶ 10,502 Top Federal Tax Issues for 2018 CPE Course: MODULE 2

### (10047747-0001)

Go to **cchcpelink.com/printcpe** to complete your Final Exam online for instant results and a reduced grading fee.

A $113.95 processing fee will be charged for each user submitting Module 2 to **cchcpelink.com/printcpe** for online grading. **The processing fee is $133.95 if you prefer to mail or email your Final Exam for manual grading by CCH staff.** To mail or email your exam, remove both pages of the Answer Sheet from this book and return them with your completed Evaluation Form to: Wolters Kluwer Continuing Education Department, 2700 Lake Cook Road, Riverwoods, IL 60015 or email your Answer Sheet to Wolters Kluwer at CPESubmissions@wolterskluwer.com. You must also select a method of payment below.

NAME _____

COMPANY NAME _____

STREET _____

CITY, STATE, & ZIP CODE _____

BUSINESS PHONE NUMBER _____

E-MAIL ADDRESS _____

DATE OF COMPLETION _____

PTIN ID (for Enrolled Agents or RTRPs only) _____

## METHOD OF PAYMENT:

☐ Check Enclosed      ☐ Visa          ☐ Master Card      ☐ AmEx

☐ Discover      ☐ Wolters Kluwer Account* _____

Card No. _____      Exp. Date _____

Signature _____

**EXPRESS GRADING:** Please email my Course results to me by 5:00 p.m. the business day following your receipt of this Answer Sheet. By checking this box I authorize Wolters Kluwer to charge $19.00 for this service.

☐ Express Grading $19.00      Fax No. _____

\* Must provide Wolters Kluwer account number for this payment option

**Wolters Kluwer**

## Module 2: Answer Sheet

(10047747-0001)

Please answer the questions by indicating the appropriate letter next to the corresponding number.

| | | | |
|---|---|---|---|
| 1. ____ | 9. ____ | 17. ____ | 25. ____ |
| 2. ____ | 10. ____ | 18. ____ | 26. ____ |
| 3. ____ | 11. ____ | 19. ____ | 27. ____ |
| 4. ____ | 12. ____ | 20. ____ | 28. ____ |
| 5. ____ | 13. ____ | 21. ____ | 29. ____ |
| 6. ____ | 14. ____ | 22. ____ | 30. ____ |
| 7. ____ | 15. ____ | 23. ____ | |
| 8. ____ | 16. ____ | 24. ____ | |

**Please complete the Evaluation Form (located after the Module 3 Answer Sheet) and return it with this Final Exam Answer Sheet to Wolters Kluwer at the address on the previous page. Thank you.**

# ¶ 10,503 Top Federal Tax Issues for 2018 CPE Course: MODULE 3

## (10047748-0001)

Go to **cchcpelink.com/printcpe** to complete your Final Exam online for instant results and a reduced grading fee.

A $75.95 processing fee will be charged for each user submitting Module 3 to **cchcpe-link.com/printcpe** for online grading. **The processing fee is $95.95 if you prefer to mail or email your Final Exam for manual grading by CCH staff.** To mail or email your Final Exam, remove both pages of the Answer Sheet from this book and return them with your completed Evaluation Form to: Wolters Kluwer Continuing Education Department, 2700 Lake Cook Road, Riverwoods, IL 60015 or email your Answer Sheet to Wolters Kluwer at CPESubmissions@wolterskluwer.com. You must also select a method of payment below.

NAME _____

COMPANY NAME _____

STREET _____

CITY, STATE, & ZIP CODE _____

BUSINESS PHONE NUMBER _____

E-MAIL ADDRESS _____

DATE OF COMPLETION _____

PTIN ID (for Enrolled Agents or RTRPs only) _____

## METHOD OF PAYMENT:

☐ Check Enclosed ☐ Visa ☐ Master Card ☐ AmEx

☐ Discover ☐ Wolters Kluwer Account* _____

Card No. _____ Exp. Date _____

Signature _____

**EXPRESS GRADING:** Please email my Course results to me by 5:00 p.m. the business day following your receipt of this Answer Sheet. By checking this box I authorize Wolters Kluwer to charge $19.00 for this service.

☐ Express Grading $19.00 Fax No. _____

* Must provide Wolters Kluwer account number for this payment option

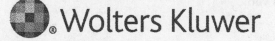 Wolters Kluwer

## Module 3: Answer Sheet

(10047748-0001)

Please answer the questions by indicating the appropriate letter next to the corresponding number.

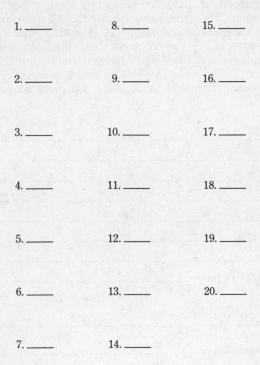

1. \_\_\_\_      8. \_\_\_\_      15. \_\_\_\_

2. \_\_\_\_      9. \_\_\_\_      16. \_\_\_\_

3. \_\_\_\_      10. \_\_\_\_      17. \_\_\_\_

4. \_\_\_\_      11. \_\_\_\_      18. \_\_\_\_

5. \_\_\_\_      12. \_\_\_\_      19. \_\_\_\_

6. \_\_\_\_      13. \_\_\_\_      20. \_\_\_\_

7. \_\_\_\_      14. \_\_\_\_

**Please complete the Evaluation Form (located after the Module 3 Answer Sheet) and return it with this Final Exam Answer Sheet to Wolters Kluwer at the address on the previous page. Thank you.**

# ¶ 10,600  Top Federal Tax Issues for 2018 CPE Course: Evaluation Form

(10024491-0005)

Please take a few moments to fill out and submit this evaluation to Wolters Kluwer so that we can better provide you with the type of self-study programs you want and need. Thank you.

## About This Program

1. Please circle the number that best reflects the extent of your agreement with the following statements:

|     |                                                                                              | Strongly Agree |   |   |   | Strongly Disagree |
|-----|----------------------------------------------------------------------------------------------|---|---|---|---|---|
| a.  | The Course objectives were met.                                                              | 5 | 4 | 3 | 2 | 1 |
| b.  | This Course was comprehensive and organized.                                                 | 5 | 4 | 3 | 2 | 1 |
| c.  | The content was current and technically accurate.                                            | 5 | 4 | 3 | 2 | 1 |
| d.  | This Course content was relevant and contributed to achievement of the learning objectives. | 5 | 4 | 3 | 2 | 1 |
| e.  | The prerequisite requirements were appropriate.                                              | 5 | 4 | 3 | 2 | 1 |
| f.  | This Course was a valuable learning experience.                                              | 5 | 4 | 3 | 2 | 1 |
| g.  | The Course completion time was appropriate.                                                  | 5 | 4 | 3 | 2 | 1 |

2. What do you consider to be the strong points of this Course?

3. What improvements can we make to this Course?

**THANK YOU FOR TAKING THE TIME TO COMPLETE THIS SURVEY!**